Studies in Contemporary and Historical Archaeology 3

'The Garden of the World'

An historical archaeology of sugar landscapes in the eastern Caribbean

I0096090

Dan Hicks

BAR International Series 1632

2007

Published in 2016 by
BAR Publishing, Oxford

BAR International Series 1632

Studies in Contemporary and Historical Archaeology 3
'The Garden of the World'

ISBN 978 1 4073 0046 7

BAR Publishing is the trading name of British Archaeological Reports (Oxford) Ltd.
British Archaeological Reports was first incorporated in 1974 to publish the BAR
Series, International and British. In 1992 Hadrian Books Ltd became part of the BAR
group. This volume was originally published by Archaeopress in conjunction with
British Archaeological Reports (Oxford) Ltd / Hadrian Books Ltd, the Series principal
publisher, in 2007. This present volume is published by BAR Publishing, 2016.

Printed in England

BAR
PUBLISHING

BAR titles are available from:

BAR Publishing
122 Banbury Rd, Oxford, OX2 7BP, UK
EMAIL   info@barpublishing.com
PHONE   +44 (0)1865 310431
FAX   +44 (0)1865 316916
www.barpublishing.com

STUDIES IN CONTEMPORARY AND HISTORICAL ARCHAEOLOGY

Studies in Contemporary and Historical Archaeology is a new series of edited and single-authored volumes intended to make available current work on the archaeology of the recent and contemporary past. The series brings together contributions from academic historical archaeologists, professional archaeologists and practitioners from cognate disciplines who are engaged with archaeological material and practices. The series includes work from traditions of historical and contemporary archaeology and material culture studies from Europe, North America, Australia and elsewhere around the world. It promotes innovative and creative approaches to later historical archaeology, showcasing this increasingly vibrant and global field, and celebrating its diversity, through extended and theoretically engaged case studies.

Proposals are invited from emerging and established scholars interested in publishing in or editing for the series. Further details are available from the series editors: email Dan.Hicks@bris.ac.uk or Joshua.Pollard@bris.ac.uk

In this, the third volume in the series, Dan Hicks presents a detailed long-term account of the changing landscapes of the islands of the eastern Caribbean between the early 17th century and the 19th century, with particular reference to the effects of sugar cultivation. Drawing upon the results of landscape survey conducted on the islands of St Kitts and St Lucia, the study presents an extended case study in the archaeology of British colonialism, and contributes to the growing field of Caribbean historical archaeology. Tracing a sequence of landscape change from 17th-century enclosures to early sugar landscapes and to 18th-century landscapes of 'improvement', the book considers how the perspectives of landscape archaeology can be used to contribute to the study of the histories, geographies and legacies of colonialism.

Joshua Pollard (Series Co-Editor)

Dedicated to Uta Lawaetz in St Lucia
and to Jackie Armony in St Kitts

TABLE OF CONTENTS

LIST OF FIGURES

LIST OF TABLES

ACKNOWLEDGEMENTS

Archaeology is an inherently collaborative bundle of methods and practices, and while the research presented in this study was originally submitted as a doctoral thesis undertaken at the University of Bristol between 1999 and 2002, it would have been impossible without the help and support of a wide range of people. I am indebted to Mark Horton, who acted as my doctoral supervisor, and to Nicholas Purcell and Chris Gosden who commented on an earlier draft of the text. Thanks are also due to Kate Clark, Mick Worthington and Nigel Jeffries – and again to Mark Horton – for their contributions to the fieldwork in St Kitts and St Lucia. Above all, thanks are due to Olivia, for her support and patience throughout my doctoral research and overseas fieldwork.

Caribbean fieldwork was undertaken in March-May 2000, December-February 2001, March-April 2001, July-August 2001, and December 2001-February 2002. Sincere thanks are due to the British, Canadian and American students with whom I have worked in the Caribbean, and without whom the research would not have been possible: Rachel Berry, Andrew Brown, Scott Cooper, Nick Corcos, Rebecca Craig, Iestyn Davies, Jim Dixon, Archie Drake, Ruth Fabiano, David Fallon, Katherine Forgacs, George Hambrecht, Margaret Harris, Gemma Jones, Janet Keck, Clementine Lovell, Noah Miller, Marc Montague, Vicky Oleksy, Jane Rahaim, Kim Ray, Kelly Reed, Natasha Robinson, Gabriella Rosal, Ian Rotsey, Ben Rowe, Helen Rule, Ella Searle, Jane Seiter, Alec Shaw, Kathy Smith, Elen Stokes, William Sumner, Daisy Thornton, Sadie Watson, Bonnie Wright and Ann Zilec.

I am indebted to those who supported my field research in St Kitts and St Lucia. In St Lucia, thanks are due to Robert Devaux, Giles Romulus at the St Lucia National Trust, Jim Sparks, Charmaine Nathaniel, Rosmunde Renard, Uta Lawaetz, Verena and Anitanja Lawaetz, Avery Trim, Binta Pinchez, Dwight Desir, and Margot Thomas at St Lucia National Archives. In St Kitts, thanks are due to Jackie Armony and all at the St Christopher Heritage Society, Vicky O'Flaherty at the National Archives of St Kitts and Nevis, Larry Armony, Toni Frederick, Richard Boon of the Timothy Beach Hotel, Nick Menon of TDC, Ras Benjie of the Department of Environment of the Government of St Kitts, Campbell Evelyn, Maurice Widdowson, and especially to Christine Walwyn for her kindness and hospitality. Special thanks also due to David Rollinson and Vincent Hubbard on Nevis, as well as David Small and Christine Eickelmann. Thanks also to Vincent Floquet, Herbert Seignoret and Jennifer Lutton for their companionship and encouragement. Grants towards the research and fieldwork were provided between 2000 and 2002 by the Arts and Humanities Research Board and Bristol University, to whom I am grateful.

Finally, thanks are due to Matthew Johnson, who acted as external examiner for this doctoral thesis, and whose book *An Archaeology of Capitalism* (Blackwell 1996) was the catalyst for me to begin the research presented here.

CHAPTER 1

INTRODUCTION

From the early 17th century, English colonial settlements developed in the eastern Caribbean, forming the basis of the sugar and slave societies of the 18th and early 19th centuries. By 1681, tropical Caribbean islands such as Barbados, across which during the previous half a century a new plantation landscape had spread, could be conceived by British writers as 'the garden of the world' (Houghton 1681, 2-3). Research into the history of these sugar plantations has traditionally been undertaken by economic and social historians, and historical archaeology in the region has begun to develop only since the 1970s.

Caribbean historical archaeology is an emerging and hybrid field, in which much of the best work has drawn upon historical geography. Pioneering work carried out over the past three decades includes Pulsipher's studies of Montserrat (1977, 1994), Handler and Lange's studies of slave cemeteries in Barbados (1978) and Armstrong's study of a sugar plantation in Jamaica (1990), and is increasingly built upon by new studies – as demonstrated by the recent collections of Jay Haviser (1999), Paul Farnsworth (2001) and Mark Hauser (forthcoming). But studies in Caribbean historical archaeology have rarely aimed to contribute to thinking in historical archaeology elsewhere in the world: as Michel-Rolph Trouillot has observed for cultural anthropology, so also in historical archaeology the Caribbean region remains an 'open frontier...where boundaries are notoriously fuzzy'; a diverse and 'undisciplined' field that has rarely been able to contribute to metropolitan perspectives 'lessons learned on the frontier' (1992: 19-20, 35).

This study uses the perspectives of which might be termed the 'empirical tradition' of British landscape archaeology that developed in the 1960s and 1970s, especially in industrial archaeology (cf. Johnson 2005), to explore the early modern history of these 'garden' landscapes formed by British colonialism in the eastern Caribbean, and their place in the world. It presents a detailed chronological sequence of the changing material conditions of these English-/British-owned plantation landscapes during the 17th, 18th and early 19th centuries, with particular reference to the origins, history and legacies of the sugar industry. The study draws together the results of archaeological fieldwork and documentary research to present a progressive account of the historical landscapes of the islands of St Kitts and St Lucia: sketching a chronological outline of landscape change. This approach to landscape is

characterised by the integration of archaeological field survey, standing buildings recording and documentary and cartographic sources, and focuses upon producing accounts of material change to landscapes and buildings (see Hicks 2003). By providing a long-term perspective on eastern Caribbean colonial history, from the nature of early, effectively prehistoric contact and interaction in the 16th century, through early permanent European settlements and into the developed sugar societies of the 18th and 19th centuries, the study sets out a temporal and thematic framework of landscape change that might inform the further development of historical archaeology in the island Caribbean region.

The broader aim of the study relates to exploring how archaeological techniques can be used to contribute a highly detailed, empirical case study to the interdisciplinary study of postcolonial landscapes and British colonialism. In order to achieve this goal, the study draws upon the techniques of what has been called the 'empirical tradition' of landscape archaeology. My point of departure here is that not only the western conceptions of 'landscape' but also many of the field methods employed in the British empirical tradition of landscape archaeology (on which see Aston 1985) are far from neutral scientific perspectives. They are historically situated, and are entangled with European colonial thought and practice. As sociologist Mimi Sheller has observed, the European representation of colonial landscapes in the Caribbean has shifted through a number of tropes: from 'productions of nature' to the 'scenic economy' of the aesthetic appreciation of landscape and the 'romantic imperialism' of the 19th and 20th centuries (Sheller 2003, 37-8). A reflexive awareness of these legacies – the contingency of the methods and practices of contemporary British archaeology upon European colonialism, and the contemporary challenges of negotiating colonial heritage in the postcolonial world – does not, however, mean that landscape archaeology cannot be used as part of the generation of postcolonial and politically-engaged archaeologies. By exposing the detail of landscape change, landscape archaeology tends to privilege the actions of the European colonial elite – the creation of plantation fields, houses, mills, etc by those with the ability to reshape landscapes through their power to mobilise unfree labour. But on the other hand, by documenting the material conditions in which the changing impulses to shape landscapes from contact to colonialism were worked out, archaeology is in a unique position to critique approaches to colonialism that overdetermine the ideological power of the coloniser (Rowlands 1998) – exposing contingency and complexity.

Fifteen years ago Jalil Sued-Badillo, addressing the Society for American Archaeology, suggested that 'archaeological research in the Caribbean, still dominated by a North American orientation and North American capital, has simply refused to address the subject of colonialism and underdevelopment in the region' (1992, 603). A contribution from British landscape archaeology is perhaps an unlikely solution to this problem, and the chosen methodology and focus will mean that the present study is limited in its contribution to African-Caribbean and Indigenous archaeology in the region. However, the 'empirical tradition' of landscape archaeology that is utilised here does provide a distinctive contribution to postcolonial studies in two respects: its material focus, and its contribution to the archaeological study of British colonialism.

Over the past two decades, one particularly dominant approach in postcolonial studies has been to examine 'colonial discourse' (especially since Said 1978). The risk with such a literary focus, interwoven with the work of cultural geographers on 'reading landscape' (especially since Daniels and Cosgrove 1988), is that it leads to a reduction of particular colonial landscapes to generic 'landscapes of colonialism' – in which the complex, and often contradictory, historically constituted materials of landscapes are invisible. In historical archaeology, discussions of European colonialism (e.g. Johnson 1996, 94, Deetz 1991, 4) have sometimes failed to capture of the complexities and contingencies of particular situations, or of historical change. The present study, then, attempts to contribute a highly detailed archaeological study as a counterpoint to textual models of colonialism and landscape, in which the complexities of material landscapes are acknowledged (Hauser and Hicks forthcoming). Inspired by similar impulses in historical geography (Jacobs 1996, 9), historical anthropology (Thomas 1991) and the historical archaeology of colonialism (Gosden 2004), this study aims to use the methods of material documentation provided by the empirical tradition of British landscape archaeology to explore the details and historical contingencies of colonialism as it was practised in these particular changing landscapes. In doing so, it also aims to bring a more detailed chronological resolution to historical archaeology in the region – highlighting how different the landscapes of the early 17th century were from those of the early 18th century, or the late 18th century, and the commonalities and differences between different islands.

Such an approach is unfashionable in British archaeology, where post-processual approaches, developed especially in British prehistory, have critiqued the empirical tradition of landscape archaeologies that 'describe the landscape as a history of things that have been done to the land... [merely] cataloguing...the material transformations wrought upon the land' rather than seeing the landscape as

inhabited (Barrett 1999, 26). But complementing the line of thought developed by post-processual archaeologists such as Julian Thomas (1993, 19-20) and most recently Matthew Johnson (2005), which has rightly critiqued purely descriptive accounts of landscape, this study is written in the belief that the archaeology of European colonialism requires a close attention to material detail – without which a generic 'landscape archaeology of colonialism' emerges, overdetermining the power of the colonisers' ideologies of landscape. By using landscape archaeology to provide a detailed chronological account of landscape change in the early modern eastern Caribbean, the study aims simultaneously to provide an extended case study in the material dimensions, and material consequences, of European colonialism.

As an archaeological study of British colonialism, this volume is informed by an awareness of how archaeology's contribution always occurs in the present. Archaeological fieldwork employs a bundle of contemporary methods and practices for working with the remains of the past in the contemporary world. The sites at which I conducted fieldwork – the ruined, crumbling and overgrown walls of slave plantations that still evoke their former roles as places of horror and violence – are overwhelming in their sheer quantities, and in their affective power. They continue to shape the contemporary landscapes of the Caribbean – some abandoned in the bush, some demolished, and some converted into hotels and guest houses. Here, an archaeological perspective inevitably involves political engagement. By suggesting that these sites form part of, but cannot be reduced to, 'British archaeology', this study aims to start a process of rethinking the material geographies of archaeologies of European colonialism that will be continued in a second, more wide-ranging volume that explores archaeological conceptions of the early modern Atlantic (Hicks in preparation). It also aims to underline the importance of understanding the material dimensions of elite colonial ideologies (such as the idea of improvement, discussed in Chapter 4 below) in developing archaeologies of European colonialism in the Caribbean region.

European Colonialism in the Eastern Caribbean

The Lesser Antilles form an arc of volcanic islands in the eastern Caribbean, between modern Venezuela and Guyana to the south, and Puerto Rico to the west (**Figure 1**). They consist of the Leeward Islands (comprising the Virgin Islands, Saba, Montserrat, St Kitts, Nevis, St Eustatius, St Martin/St Maarten, St Bartélemy, Anguilla, Guadeloupe, Antigua and Barbuda), the Windward Islands (comprising Grenada, St Vincent, the Grenadines, St Lucia, Dominica, Martinique and Barbados), as well as Curaçao, Aruba, Bonaire, and Trinidad and Tobago which lie much closer to the South American mainland. These volcanic islands are limited in area, and most are dominated by a central volcanic mountain such as Nevis Peak, or mountain ranges, with well-watered lowlands around the coastline (Martin-Kaye 1959, 1969; Earle 1922). In contrast, some

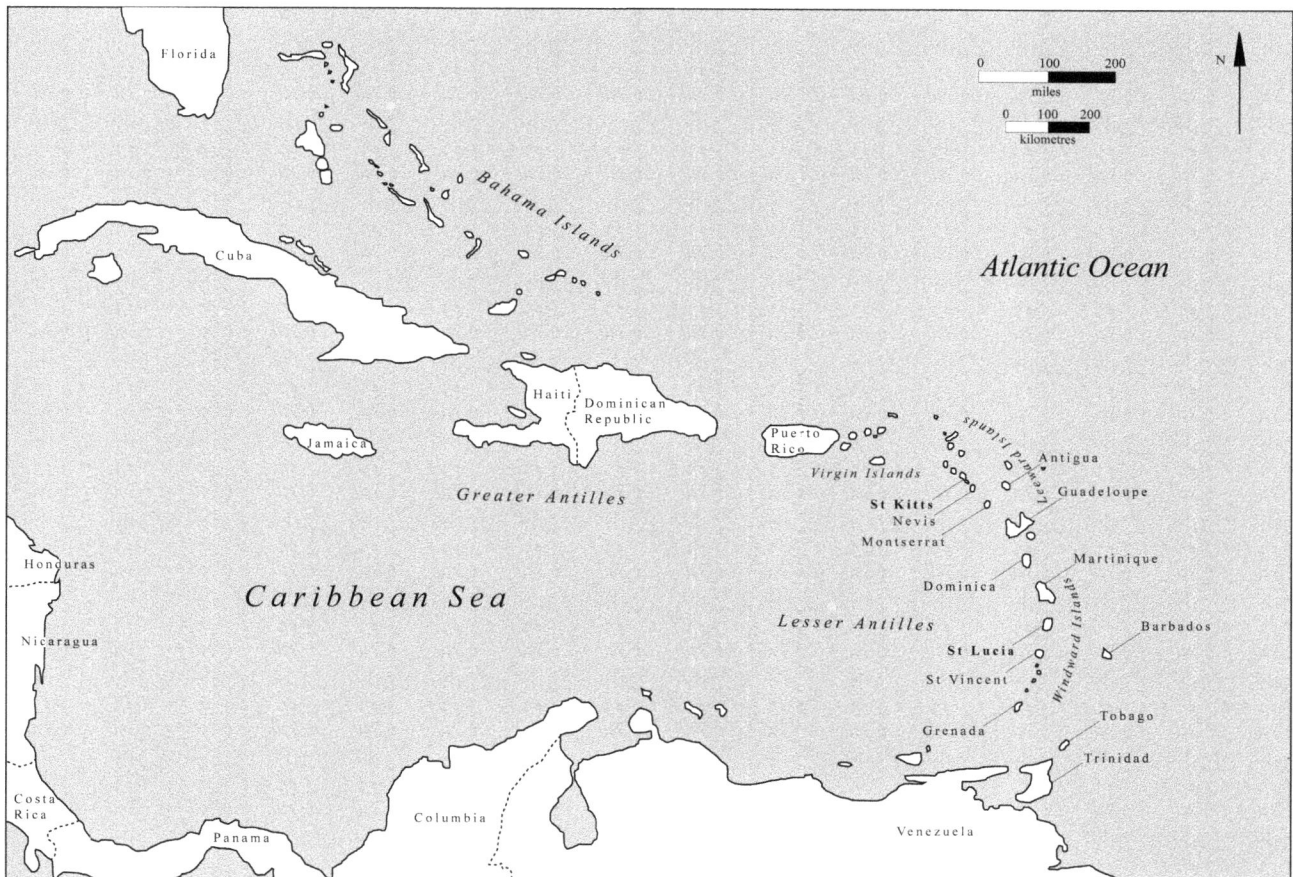

FIGURE 1. THE GREATER AND LESSER ANTILLES, SHOWING LOCATIONS OF ST KITTS, ST LUCIA AND OTHER ISLANDS DISCUSSED IN THE TEXT.

islands, such as Antigua and Barbados, are much flatter. This study will examine in detail primary archaeological data and documentary evidence for the islands of St Lucia and St Kitts (St Christopher) where I directed field projects between 2000 and 2002. Particular reference will be made to the sites of Wingfield Estate, St Kitts and Balenbouche Estate, St Lucia (**Figures 2 & 3**). St Kitts and St Lucia are around 168 and 616 square kilometres in area respectively. The leeward (western) sides of the islands are generally more sheltered, especially from hurricanes, than the windward sides.

General histories of the Caribbean conventionally describe the establishment of sugar plantations during the 17th century on the islands of Barbados, Montserrat, St Kitts, Nevis and Antigua. Similar English sugar plantations were established in Jamaica, 1000 miles to the west, after Cromwell's Western Design of 1655, but there built upon a plantation landscape previously established under Spanish rule. During the early 18th century, Jamaica and the islands of the eastern Caribbean saw the development of virtual sugar monoculture, in contrast with the settlements of the 1620s-1680s which cultivated a range of crops: cotton, sugar, indigo, ginger, and especially tobacco, as well as subsistence crops such as cassava, beans and plantains. The 18th century saw increasing concerns with the creation

of formal, artificial plantation landscapes: the new sugar estates were complex arrangements of planters' houses, mills and sugar processing structures, distilleries, ancillary buildings, cane fields, slave accommodation and gardens, and access to road and water transport (France 1984). Other tropical staples such as cocoa and coffee continued to be cultivated on other islands of the Lesser Antilles (Trouillot 1993), and a complex process of interrelated island-specific histories began, which were subject to the vagaries of international trade, frequent military conflicts and shifts in colonial control.

The second half of the 18th century is a complex period in the region, presented by some as one of decline, yet characterised also by the confident expansion of the British sugar economy into the Windward Islands. It is also the period of the Haitian revolution (1791-1804), and a period of temporary freedom for slaves in the French islands in the eastern Caribbean that formed a crucial part of the 'transnational issue networks' (Cooper 2005: 89) of the movements against slavery and the slave trade and that in a British Atlantic context led to abolition of the slave trade (1807) and emancipation (1834-1838), and in many ways laid the foundations for later transatlantic political networks such as the anticolonial movements of the 20th century (Cooper *ibid*).

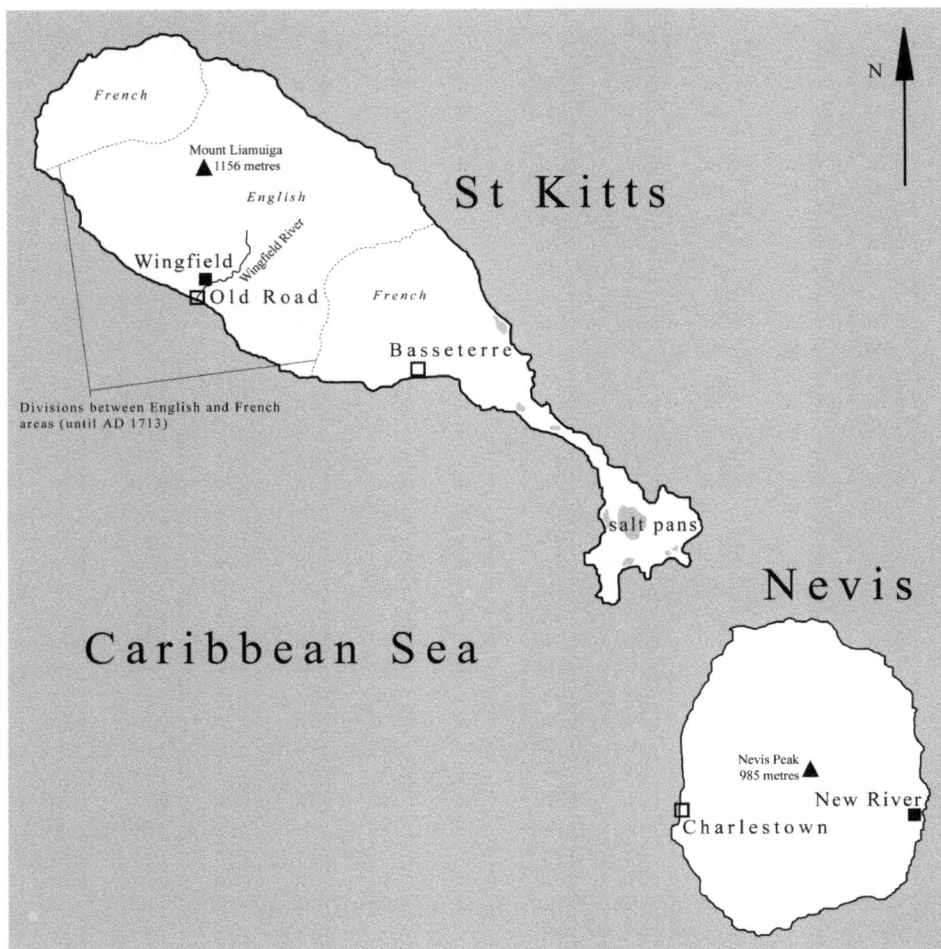

Figure 2. St Kitts and Nevis, showing location of Wingfield and principal towns

Figure 3. St Lucia, showing location of Balenbouche and principal towns.

4

Some historians have seen sugar plantations as, from the outset, strange, seemingly anachronistic phenomena (Scott 2004) – characterised by the combination in a single location of agriculture and industrial processing; the bringing together of skilled, unskilled, free, indentured and slave labour; and the work discipline and time consciousness necessitated by cane processing (Mintz 1985; C.M. Goodwin 1987). Certainly, sugar plantations appear not to fit neatly into conventional Anglo-American economic history:

> 'In the preindustrial world of the seventeenth century, the Caribbean sugar planter was a large-scale entrepreneur. He was a combination farmer-manufacturer.' (Dunn 1972, 189)

The new sugar plantations made use of European indentured servants (Emerson Smith 1947; Beckles 1990; Galenson 1981a, 1981b) and some enslaved Indigenous people (see Chapter 2 below), but by 1700 the plantations had developed a distinctive and almost exclusive use of African slave labour (Blackburn 1997, 270). Slavery continued until the abolition of the British slave trade in 1807, and the effecting of emancipation of slaves in British islands in 1838. Elsewhere in the New World slavery persisted until 1848 in French possessions, 1865 in the United States, 1886 in Cuba and 1888 in Brazil. The sugar industries continued into the 20th century, and the decision in Autumn 2001 by the St Kitts government to move out of sugar production, and the implementation of that decision in 2005, marked a watershed in the West Indian landscape history, as the last major sugar landscape of the eastern Caribbean began to disappear.

Previous Research in Caribbean Historical Archaeology

Before proceeding with the rest of the study, a bibliographic survey sketching previous published work in historical archaeology in the eastern Caribbean is first helpful – especially because such work has not previously been drawn together in a single survey. While the following paragraphs are very closely referenced, making them difficult to read through, the disparate fragmented nature of Caribbean historical archaeology (falling as it does across so many different countries) means that such a summary, while not comprehensive, will form a useful point of departure for the rest of the study: capturing some of the character of previous work, explaining the research context of the present study, and perhaps acting as a reference point for further research.

A significant corpus of archaeological literature, mainly in the form of conference papers, interim reports, and journal articles on the historical period in the Caribbean has been generated in the past 35 years. The results of many other archaeological studies, the majority of which are focused upon prehistoric archaeology, are compiled in the Proceedings of the International Congresses for Caribbean Archaeology, of which since 1964 19 volumes have so far

been published (see index to proceedings at http://muse um.archanth.cam.ac.uk/IACA.WWW/procindx.htm). The main focus of such work has been upon excavated material culture, rather than upon landscape contexts, and has been almost exclusively conducted in Americanist traditions of field practice – often as field schools run from Anthropology Departments of universities based in the United States (but see Wright and Wright 1991), or as Masters or doctoral theses, or as unpublished manuscripts on file at American universities or Caribbean heritage societies or similar organisations. In some cases, such as the range of work on St Eustatius supervised by Norman Barka at the College of William and Mary during the 1970s, 1980s and 1990s, substantial collections of unpublished manuscripts have been developed.

General Surveys

While the published and unpublished literature is fragmented, a number of useful general surveys of the archaeology of individual islands, including formal cultural resource management documents commissioned by governmental agencies, have been produced. These include Antigua (Dawud 1971; Pulsipher and Goodwin 1988), Barbados (Bullen 1966b; Drewitt and Harris 1991; Drewitt, Harris and Cartwright 1987; Loftfield 1994), Guadeloupe (Barbotin 1970; Delpuech 2001), Jamaica (Aarons 1983; Agorsah 1991a, 1991b, 1992; Howard 1965), the British and Netherlands Antilles in general (Watters 2001, Barka 1990b; Haviser 2001a), Nevis (Slayman 1996), St Eustatius (Attema 1976; Barka 1985, 1991a, 1996a, 2001; Dethlefsen 1982; Dethlefsen et al. 1979; Dethlefsen et al. 1982; Eastman 1996), St Kitts (Allaire 1974; Matthews 1971; Tyson and Tyson 1974; Manchester 1971; Tyson et al. 1993), St Lucia (Anon 1965; Devaux 1975; Hudson et al. 1992), Sint Maarten (Haviser 1988; van der Hoeven 1994), Tobago (Bullbrook 1960; Clement 1994) and the Virgin Islands (Vescelius 1977a, 1977b).

Biological Archaeology

Some of the earliest historical archaeological fieldwork carried out in the Caribbean focused on skeletal remains of slaves (Buxton et al. 1938; Stewart 1939). Since then, archaeological reports on the excavation of slave cemeteries and the physical anthropological analysis of burials have been dominated by work on Barbados (Corruccini and Handler 1980; Corruccini et al. 1982; Corruccini et al. 1985; Corruccini et al. 1987; Handler 1995, 1996, 1997; Handler and Corruccini 1983, 1986; Handler et al. 1979; Handler et al. 1986; Handler et al. 1989. Cf. Handler 1994). However, similar work has also been carried out on Guadeloupe (Barbotin 1978; Courtaud et al. 1999), Montserrat (Mann et al. 1987; Watters 1987, 1994; Watters and Petersen 1991), Jamaica (Fleischman and Armstrong 1990; Fremmer 1973) and in Suriname (Khudabux 1999). In the 1990s, practitioners such as Jerome Handler began to try to use burial evidence to explore the social identities of the individuals buried (Handler 1996, 1997).

Architectural Studies

Studies of colonial architecture also form an important part of previous archaeological research in the Caribbean. Notable are the studies of Codrington Castle and Highland House in Barbuda (Watters 1997; Watters and Nicholson 1982), as well as studies of early buildings on Barbados (Waterman 1949), Jamaica (Cotter 1970; Kelly and Armstrong 1991; Smith *et al*. 1982; Priddy 1975; Mayes 1970, 1972; Marx 1967, 1968a, 1968b, 1969a), St Eustatius (Barka 1986, 1988b, 1988c, 1989, 1990a; Nagelkerken 1985; Triplett 1995; Sanders 1988) and Sint Maarten (Barka 1993; Barka and Sanders 1990). Archaeological studies of churches and churchyards have been carried out on Jamaica (Osborne 1974) and St Eustatius (Paonessa 1990), and Jewish synagogues have been studied on St Eustatius (Barka 1988a) and Nevis (Terrell 2004; cf. Stern 1971), as well as a Jewish *mikve* on St Eustatius (Barka 1987). Military sites have been studied on Nevis (Morris *et al*. 1999; Smith 1987, 1989), on St Kitts at Brimstone Hill Fortress (Smith 1992, 1994, 1995) and Charles Fort (Schroedl 2000c, 2000d, 2000e) and St Eustatius (Barka 1991c; Howard 1991); as well as shipwrecks off Jamaica (Marx 1968c) and St Eustatius (Bequette 1991).

Landscape Archaeology & Industrial Archaeology

The archaeological investigation of sugar plantations has been undertaken in the Bahamas (Farnsworth 1993, 1994, 1996, 1999, 97-118; Gerace 1982, 1987; Turner 1993; Wilkie 1999, 2000 268-9, 2001; Wilkie and Farnsworth 1996, 1997), Barbados (Dash 1985; Handler 1972; Handler and Lange 1978, 1979; Loftfield 1991), Montserrat (Goodwin 1982; Pulsipher and Goodwin 1982, 1999, 2001), Jamaica (Armstrong 1982, 1983a, 1983b, 1985, 1990a, 1990b, 1991a, 1991a, 1991b, 1992, 1999; Armstrong and Fleischman 1993; Craton 1978; Craton and Walvin 1970; Farnsworth 1982; Higman 1974, 1975, 1976; Riordan 1973), Nevis (Chiarelli 1998; Wright and Wright 1991), St Eustatius (Barka 1987, 1991b), Tobago (Eubanks 1992; Clement 1995), and Sint Maarten/St Martin (Barka 1993; Haviser 1991; Dijkshoorn 1986). In addition, there have been studies of the windmill at Betty's Hope, Antigua (Goodwin 1994); and slave accommodation on Curaçao (Haviser and Simmons-Brito 1995) and Jamaica (Armstrong 1992). Further studies of sugar plantations include work at New Montpelier, Jamaica (Higman and Aarons 1978) and Galways plantation (Pulsipher 1991, 1994).

Other Caribbean industrial landscapes have also been investigated archaeologically. Delle (1996, 1998) has investigated coffee plantations in Jamaica. Candice Goucher (1990; 1999, 150-1) has examined a late 18th-century iron and brass foundry at Morant Bay, Jamaica, where over 250 free and slave metalworkers worked. An early 19th-century blacksmith's shop has also been excavated at Fort King George, Tobago (Goucher 1999, 153-4). Overall, the quantity and sophistication archaeological research into Caribbean plantation archaeology is growing, especially with the addition of Laurie Wilkie and Paul Farnsworth's

(2005) book-length multiscalar analysis of the Clifton plantation in the Bahamas (cf. Wilkie and Farnsworth 1999).

Historical landscapes have been examined by archaeologists across the Caribbean: in Jamaica (Armstrong and Kelly 2000, Delle 1994, 1998; Kelly 1989), Martinique (Mousnier and Caille 1990, Kelly 2004), Montserrat (Pulsipher 1977; Pulsipher and Goodwin 1999), St Eustatius (Barka 2001; Delle 1989, 1994, 1998; Righter 1990), Tobago (Clement 1995, 1997) and St John (Virgin Islands) (Armstrong 2001, 2003). In particular, Delle (1994), Mousnier and Caille (1990) and Clement (1995) have traced the development of the sugar economy on Jamaica, Martinique and Tobago respectively: identifying the sites of plantations through field survey and the use of documentary and cartographic sources.

Historical Geography

A number of historical geographers have also studied Caribbean landscapes: including detailed studies on Jamaica (Clarke 1975; Clarke and Hodgkiss 1974) and St Kitts and Nevis (Merrill 1958). David Watts (1987) provided a seminal study of West Indian environmental change from 1492, based upon his previous work on Barbados (Watts 1963, 1966). A similar study has been undertaken by Bonham Richardson (1992), and historical geographer Barry Higman (1986, 1987, 1988) has carried out detailed analysis of historic Jamaican estate plans. In a sophisticated study, Casid (2005) has recently built on this work, considering the relationship between landscape and colonisation in the 18th-century West Indies.

Material Culture Studies

The Americanist influence upon the development of Caribbean historical archaeology has led to a range of detailed studies of excavated material culture, and sometimes to the application of debates in colonial period archaeology in the eastern United States to material in this region. The material cultural focus of much Caribbean historical archaeology has made a number of significant contributions, most notably in the study of locally-manufactured unglazed earthenware ceramics – including late prehistoric pottery and 'colonowares' (also termed 'folk pottery', 'Afro-Caribbean wares', or named according to their probable island of provenance, such as 'Afro-Jamaican wares', 'Afro-Montserratian wares', etc). These ceramics bear marked similarities with the unglazed, clamp-fired, hand-thrown 'colonoware' ceramics found in the Chesapeake from the mid 17th century. Archaeological analysis of the manufacture of unglazed earthenwares in the early modern eastern Caribbean includes Barbara Heath's typologies of Colonoware on St Eustatius (Heath 1988, 1991a, 1991b), and Jerome Handler's studies of Colonoware pipes from Barbados (Handler 1982, 1983). A number of studies of particular ceramic traditions on individual eastern Caribbean islands have been conducted (Petersen *et al*. 1999): on Antigua (Handler 1964, Nicholson 1994),

Barbados (Handler 1963a, 1963b), St Croix (Gartley 1979), the Virgin Islands (Nicholson 1979); Montserrat (Petersen and Watters 1988) and in the Bahamas (Wilkie 1998). A midden deposit possibly related to African-Caribbean slave accommodation has been identified and investigated at Brimstone Hill Fortress, St Kitts by Gerald Schroedl (Klippel and Schroedl 1999; for other studies at Brimstone Hill see Ahlman 1997; Ahlman and Schroedl 1997; Ahlman et al. 1997; Schroedl and Ahlman 1998; Klippel 1997, 1998, 2000; McKeown 1997, 1998, 1999; Patterson and Klippel 1999; Savage and Schroedl 1999; Schroedl 1997, 1998, 1999a, 1999b, 2000a, 2000b, 2000f; Schroedl et al. 2000).

Studies of European artefacts have been carried out in the Caribbean in general (Goggin 1968), as well as on Antigua (Nicholson 1995), Barbados (Lange and Carlson 1985; Loftman 1991), Montserrat (Watters 1981), Jamaica (Aarons 1989; Marx 1968d, 1969b; Noël Hume 1968, 1973), and in the Spanish Caribbean (Deagan 1987; Ewen 2001). In the eastern United States, a long-running debate has been held over the relative African or Indigenous influences on colonoware (Barker and Majewski 2006: 208). The continued influence of ethnohistorical perspectives upon the study of 17th-century Chesapeake (Axtell 1978) and upon African American archaeology (Singleton 1985) forms an important context for this debate. However, while in the Chesapeake colonoware has been identified as an important syncretic artefact type, through which interaction between European, African and Indigenous populations may be traced (Ferguson 1992), in the Caribbean the study of African influences upon Caribbean historical material culture have often been emphasised in isolation from broader processes of migration and interaction, and especially in isolation from Indigenous influences (Haviser 1999). This trend is also visible in studies of settlement patterns. While studies such as Agorsah's (1999) comparison of settlement patterns of Maroon villages in Jamaica with settlement patterns in Ghana (cf. Agorsah 1993, 1999), Farnsworth's (1999) examination of the connections between the plantation landscapes of slavery and the present day, through documentary research and statistical analysis of European ceramic assemblages, or Goucher's (1999) study of similarities between 18th-century material culture in Benin and Tobago all provide important counterpoints to accounts of European influences upon landscape, no study has considered the influence of precolonial and Indigenous landscapes upon later colonial settlement. Goucher's work underlines the limitations of such analyses. Discussing the identification of a Tobago-made Edo-style mask, he writes this is 'suggestive of an African presence' (1999, 155). As Perry and Paynter have observed, the identification of African populations in the 18th-century New World, or even of occasional artefacts of African provenance, seems 'a bit beside the point' (Perry and Paynter 1999: 301). Similar criticism could be levelled at Handler's account of a Ghanaian pipe from Barbados (1982).

The emergence of studies in New World historical archaeology that start to acknowledge the historical and geographical contingencies and complexities of contact, colonialism and ethnogenesis are most welcome (DeCorse 1999; Epperson 1999). Of particular importance is research that emphasises the historical processes of the formation of African diaspora in the Atlantic world, developed especially by those influenced by Merrick Posnansky (Posnansky 1984; DeCorse 1991, 1992; Orser 1998), and increasingly by African-based archaeologists (Agorsah 1996) as part of politically-engaged archaeologies in Africa (see Shepherd 2002). The study of creolisation, an interpretive concept borrowed from anthropologically-informed historical studies (Brathwaite 1971; Mintz and Price 1976; Gundaker 1998), has been central to such studies (cf. Ferguson 1992; Mouer 1993; Deagan 1996; Delle 2000; cf. Hicks 2000). Mark Hauser and Christopher DeCorse's (2003) discussion of the potential of the comparative study of low-fired earthenwares to inform archaeologies of the African diaspora captures some of the potential of this new work.

At the same time, in the archaeology of African slave populations important work has highlighted the potential of identifying 'African' designs, such as West African-inspired cosmograms carved onto Colonowares, that may represent resistance to slavery. However, until recently such perspectives have glossed over the important observation that slave populations obtained and used a broad range of artefacts, including European artefacts, and have failed to highlight the diverse range of African backgrounds of Caribbean slaves. In her work on early 19th-century deposits in the Bahamas, Laurie Wilkie has suggested that

> The vast majority of the materials recovered from enslaved peoples' houses in the Caribbean were made in England or other parts of Europe. While many of the European-manufactured materials recovered from plantation sites may have been made available to enslaved people by their owners, another portion of the materials is likely to have been procured by slaves through internal marketing systems (Wilkie 1999, 265).

Wilkie's identification of slaves as consumers, her acknowledgement of slave use of European goods, and her discussion of apparent differences in slaves' choice of hand-painted and banded creamwares, highlight the complexities of using material culture to explore identity. Although difficult in the current absence of stratigraphic excavations, unpicking from excavated assemblages the pre-emancipation inter-island commodity chains of Caribbean and European artefacts would be an important next step: work which Hauser and Armstrong (1999) have begun in their examination of the exchange networks of Colonoware in the Virgin Islands by provenance studies of ceramics from sites on St John's.

Studying Plantation Landscapes

Previous studies of New World plantations have been dominated by historians' and archaeologists' 'theories of the plantation' as a category of comparison. In the 15th century in the Portuguese and Spanish Atlantic possessions – the Azores, the Canaries and São Tomé in the Gulf of Guinea – sugar plantations which made use of enslaved African labour were developed. Similar plantations had existed on the Iberian mainland during the 14th century: and still earlier, the 8th and 9th centuries AD had seen the use of enslaved east Africans on sugar plantations in the Tigris/Euphrates basin, Sicily, Cyprus, Rhodes, Malta, Morocco and the south coast of Spain (Mintz 1985, 25; Solow 1987).

Some scholars have connected these situations, observing a particular and deeply embedded relationship between sugar and slavery (Mintz 1985; Williams 1970, 17). For example, Galloway (1977, 190) suggests that 'the link between sugar cultivation and slavery...became firmly forged in Crete, Cyprus and Morocco', and Solow observes that 'from the Muslim era, sugar and [African] slavery were associated' (Solow 1987, 52). David Brion Davis has most explicitly argued for an Old World pedigree for the sugar plantations of the West Indies – from north and east Africa, through the western Mediterranean and across the Atlantic. Some studies even present a development from Roman to Caribbean slavery (Davis 1966, Phillips 1984): genealogies have sometimes been accepted too easily by historical archaeologists (Eubanks 1992, 10-13; Goodwin 1987, 19-21). While there are clearly echoes running through Europe's relationship with sugar and slavery – the 18th-century refining of sugar in Bristol bears similarities with the sugar refining centre at Antwerp in the 13th century AD – the development of sugar plantations in the eastern Caribbean was a complex historical and geographical process – mixing from the outset free and unfree labour, as had those in the Canaries. The 17th century did not see the simple imposition of an Old World model of sugar and slavery upon the New World.

'Plantation archaeology' forms a significant part of contemporary historical and African American archaeology in North America and the Caribbean (Singleton 1985, 1999), but the field has generally been focused upon excavation and artefact analysis rather than the landscapes of estates. Some work has been informed especially by the emerging interest in 'landscape archaeology' in the United States (Delle 1998; Kelso and Most 1990; Miller and Gleason 1994; Upton 1985; Yamin and Metheny 1996), but in the Caribbean it has often conducted the interpretation of historical cartographic data in isolation from material remains such as earthwork features, standing buildings or other documentary evidence. While the idea of landscape archaeology covers a very diverse range of theoretical and methodological approaches, which is to be celebrated (Hicks and McAtackney forthcoming), in a Caribbean and North American context the failure of plantation archaeology to move beyond structuralist perspectives has unnecessarily limited the potential of the field. Thus, the thoughtful studies of Jamaican sugar and coffee plantations by Jim Delle (1996, 1998) have nevertheless chosen to deploy Lefebvre's (1991) model of the 'production of space' to unpick 'spatialities' and the 'manipulation of space' – relying on the reading of maps in isolation from the results of field survey (Hauser and Hicks forthcoming). Like Susannah England's use of historic maps to apply of a von Thünen model of settlement patterning to slave accommodation areas (England 1986, 1991), such work does not place the engagements of archaeological fieldwork at the centre of its interpretive practices. Equally, in the structuralist interpretation of artefact patterning within Douglas Armstrong's book-length study of the Drax Hall plantation, Jamaica (Armstrong 1990) and to a lesser extent the structural-ethnohistorical approaches of Jerome Handler and Frederick Lange to mortuary evidence from the Newton Plantation, Barbados (Handler and Lange 1978), particular theoretical perspectives serve to obscure, rather than to clarify, high-quality and highly significant field data.

At its best, Americanist plantation and landscape archaeology has presented rich and sophisticated studies of the close relationships between people and things in colonial plantation contexts. For instance, Laurie Wilkie's (2001) study of Clifton plantation in the Bahamas has explored the importance of the consumption of European-made commodities to African-Bahamian identities. Where such approaches have been extended to landscape and architecture, most notably in Anne Yentsch's (1994) account of the household of Charles Calvert (an early 18th-century Governor of Maryland), surviving material culture has been woven together with documentary sources, producing richly textured historical ethnographies of changing households over time. Another significant body of work, developed especially by scholars associated with the Archaeology in Annapolis project in Maryland, has used Foucauldian perspectives to develop accounts of the effects of the built environment in relation to social power (e.g. Epperson 1999, Leone 1984; cf. Hicks 2004a, 2005). The significance of the landscape archaeologies that have emerged from Annapolis is that they challenge archaeologists to think through the relationships between the built environment and social power (Leone 2005, 12). Designed landscapes such as plantations serve as ideal locations at which to consider these issues: but these landscapes are never unchanging, never purely the products of intentional human agency, but are rather emergent from ongoing interactions – including archaeological practices (Ingold 1993).

Where the emphasis upon material agency has been generalised, usually through ideas of 'constraint', rather than grounded in material complexity, in plantation archaeology then designed landscapes have been presented as simply illustrative of and embedded in the ideologies of capitalism and slavery. For example, James Delle's (1998) Lefebvrian study of Jamaican coffee plantations, while building in novel ways upon studies of designed landscapes as evidence of 'spatial inequality', is disappointing in its aim to 'read' capitalist power relations in local 'spaces', (Delle *ibid*, 9; Paynter 1982). The problem is most clear in Charles Orser's (1988a) discussion of 'plantations and space', which offers a general definition of the plantation as 'a capitalist kind of agricultural organization in which a number of laborers produce a certain kind of crop under the direction of others':

> The size of [the planter's] house can be viewed as a physical manifestation of plantation power... A plantation's landscape is a bounded universe with clear limits...the spatial arrangement of plantation housing should reflect power relations to some degree. It can be expected, given the plantation's primary economic function, that plantation houses were located closest to the work places of their inhabitants. Thus the millwright... lived near the mill pond and the mill building...and the landlord's servant lived near the landlord. However, what may be more indicative of power relations are the relationships between individual buildings themselves. In other words, the relationships between the buildings should have carried a social meaning created to reflect, among other things, the power relations enacted within the dominant mode of production at the plantation (Orser 1988a, 321, 328, 329).

By seeking to 'read off' power relations from unchanging, two-dimensional spatial organisation, modelling 'the plantation' as a category of comparative analysis, this study obscures the complexities of local variation and historical process (cf. Mandle 1973, Benn 1974, Armstrong 1999, 182; Orser 1988b). The structuralist legacy within Americanist landscape archaeology means that there is an ever-present risk that the contingent details of landscape change are lost in excessively broad or purely ideational models. The present study does not offer any alternative 'theory of the plantation'. Rather, I aim to make reflexive use of another tradition of landscape archaeology – the British 'empirical tradition' of landscape archaeology (see Johnson 2005) – to build on the fine-grained studies of the complex genesis of specific estates (e.g. Craton and Walvin 1970), and landscapes (Higman 1986, 1987, 1988) over time, presenting an extended empirically-grounded case study in the changing colonial landscapes in the eastern Caribbean.

The rest of the Study

The rest of the study draws upon detailed work at Wingfield Estates, St Kitts and Balenbouche Estate, St Lucia, to present a chronological account of the changing landscapes of the eastern Caribbean. A series of tropes in created or designed landscapes are presented: from enclosed landscapes during the early-mid 17th century (Chapter 2) to sugar landscapes during the early 18th century (Chapter 3), improved landscapes during the late 18th century (Chapter 4), and the legacies of this sequence from emancipation (effected in 1838) to the present day (Chapter 5).

CHAPTER 2

ENCLOSED LANDSCAPES (FROM *c.* AD 1624)

From the outset, any discussion of the landscapes of colonial encounters and interactions in the eastern Caribbean during the first five decades of English settlement (*c.* AD 1624-1675) is framed by two factors: the postcolonial legacies of late Victorian and early 20th-century historiography for the study of the past in the Caribbean region, and the alternative conceptions of the influence of Indigenous populations in the processes of landscape change during the early stages of English settler colonialism. In this chapter, these two issues will be considered before a discussion of the later prehistory of the eastern Caribbean. This leads into an account, drawn from documentary and archaeological sources, of the early colonial landscapes of St Kitts and the south coast of St Lucia: two locations that contrast strongly in their visibility and depiction in conventional historical accounts. The chapter suggests that the perspectives of landscape archaeology can be used to identify enclosed (ditched or walled) landscapes as a settlement type common to both early European and Carib populations in the early colonial period, and one which saw the interaction of diverse populations. It is argued that these enclosed landscapes influenced the generation of later sugar landscapes: a thesis that has implications for the study of the history of contact and colonialism in the eastern Caribbean. In particular, such observations lead beyond conventional Anglo-American historiographies of 'exploration' and 'pioneer' settlements: which can, of course, 'in the context of New World history…be studied only as invasions and conquests' (Sued-Badillo 2003a, 275). Instead of nationalist historiographies, archaeology can document the changing landscapes and material exchanges of contact and colonialism.

Anglo-American Historiographies

Apart from occasional accounts of attempted settlements such as that at Roanoke Island in the Chesapeake (Noël Hume 1994, 33ff.), documentary evidence for English colonising ventures in the New World during the late 16th century is very limited. While there is occasional evidence for privateering activities, most famously Drake's 1585 raid on the Spanish at Santo Domingo, and while there has been some work on Spanish documentary sources (Wright 1929; Andrews 1978), there is very little evidence of English attempts to establish settlements in the New World before the reign of James I. Even after the establishment of permanent settlements, which are better documented, archaeology has been framed as an important empirical source of information for historians of early English

contact and colonialism. Indeed, the archaeological study of early 17th-century English colonial settlement formed a major part of the development of historical archaeology during the closing decades of the 20th century. Such work resulted in significant integrative accounts of the buildings and material culture of 'pioneer' settlements in Virginia: at Martin's Hundred and Flowerdew Hundred (Noël Hume 1979; Deetz 1993).

However, despite considerable debate over the relationship of historical archaeology and early colonial history, most famously expressed in Ivor Noël Hume's discussion of the field's serving as 'handmaiden to history' (Noël Hume 1964), the potential of historical archaeology to generate different kinds of historical narrative for early European contact and colonialism remains little explored. Rather, the uncritical use of the approaches and attitudes of Anglo-American colonial histories – the early 20th-century historiographic tropes of origins, English identity and the figure of the 'pioneer' in the American story nation-building – have often been used uncritically in archaeology. Such tropes have been worked out most visibly at Colonial Williamsburg in Virginia (Handler and Gable 1997, 116), but more generally have led to a tendency for historical archaeologists to understate the diversity and complexity of colonial encounters, histories and their legacies. Archaeologists have generally limited their engagement with historical studies to early 20th-century metropolitan accounts, or even to the earlier 'portmanteau descriptions of the colonies' (Higman 1999a), rather than the sophisticated traditions of historiography that have emerged from the Caribbean itself, or that have aimed 'de-centre' conventional accounts by acknowledging non-western perspectives (see Higman 1999b). In this context, this chapter explores how Caribbean historical archaeology can problematise archaeologist James Deetz's contention that 'there was a standard way of setting up and creating an English colonial outpost in the seventeenth century' (Deetz 1991, 4).

Previous historical accounts of the 'pioneer' 17th-century English settlement in the Caribbean have been based on detailed studies of surviving archive sources: particularly those in the National Archives at Kew (CO and CSPC series). Recent historiography has tended not to question these narrative, imperial histories developed in the late 19th and early 20th centuries (e.g. Dunn 1972, Bridenbaugh and Bridenbaugh 1972, Watts 1987): Anglocentric narratives that are punctuated by a series of dates of 'first settlements'. In such accounts, the Elizabethan background to colonisation – such as the late 16th-century colonies at Guiana (Lorimer 1977, 1993; Whitehead 1988) and Roanoke – is outlined, setting the scene for the new permanent settlements at Jamestown (1607), Bermuda (1612) and, from the 1620s, the new colonies of the eastern Caribbean. Here, St Kitts is distinguished by its identification as the 'mother colony' – the first permanent English settlement in the island Caribbean, established in 1624. The permanent English colonies established during the 1620s and 1630s in the Leeward Islands (on Antigua, Montserrat, St Kitts and Nevis) are in turn distinguished from the 'abortive' colonies in Windward Islands, where scattered references describe attempted settlements on Tobago, St Lucia, St Vincent and Dominica. Unsatisfied with the role of archaeology as illustrating these imperial historiographies, this chapter seeks to bring together documentary and archaeological material in order to consider the landscapes of the early 17th-century eastern Caribbean. I shall compare early settlement at Old Road, St Kitts – conventionally identified as the 'Mother Colony' of English permanent settlement in the island Caribbean – and the apparent backwater of the south of St Lucia. This will facilitate a critical re-examination of conventional Anglophone historiographies of the early landscapes of European settler colonialism in the eastern Caribbean.

Prehistoric Sequence and Indigenous Archaeology

Before exploring the Indigenous histories in the early period of European contact and colonialism, a brief outline of the conventional sequence of prehistoric settlement in the island Caribbean will provide some helpful context.

Traditional Caribbean prehistoric archaeology presents a series of normative cultures and their diffusion or migration – a situation influenced especially by the legacy of the ground-breaking work of Irving Rouse (1953, 1962, 1992) and the early influence of Julian Steward upon the archaeological study of the region (Steward 1948). The archaeological sequence in the Lesser Antilles is conventionally divided into four broad phases: the aceramic *Lithic* and *Archaic* periods, and later *Ceramic* and *Historical* periods. Evidence for prehistoric activity in the Lesser Antilles is almost exclusively coastal (or sometimes riverside in the Windward Islands), and several archaeologists have suggested that rises in sea levels have led to many prehistoric sites being submerged (Nicholson 1976).

The earliest, aceramic Lithic period (*c.* 4000 BC – 2000 BC) was characterised by hunting-fishing-gathering groups (Keegan 1994, 262), and is limited to discrete find-spots and shell middens. While the subsequent 'Archaic period' (*c.* 2000-500 BC) remained aceramic, shell and bone tools and grinding stones were now used alongside worked stone tools (Pantel 2003). A range of regional terms are used for these periods, including Casimiroid, Ortoiroid or Palaeo-Indian. In these aceramic phases, populations appear to have relied for subsistence upon fishing, supplemented by limited hunting and gathering. The evidence for Lithic

period prehistoric activity in the Lesser Antilles is briefly summarised by Guarch-Delmonte (2003, 108-118) and Pantel (2003, 120-1).

The earliest evidence of the use of ceramics in the island Caribbean dates from the last centuries of the first millennium BC (Allaire 2003, 199-216). The 'Saladoid expansion' in the Lesser Antilles (*c.* 200 BC-AD 350) witnessed the introduction of fine, coil-made ceramics (named after the site of Saladero in Venezuela, sometimes painted red-on-white or decorated with fine incised or cross-hatched patterns) as well as ceramic 'incense burners', nostril bowls for ingesting hallucinogens, anthropomorphic adornos (rim or handle ornaments) and ceramic griddles and other new forms of material culture including polished stones and woven materials (Cruxent and Rouse 1958-9, Righter 1997). This new ceramic horizon also appears to have witnessed the introduction of small-scale, relatively permanent, subsistence agriculture, based on manioc, sweet potato and cassava cultivation, into the region alongside fishing (Keegan 2000, Pinchon 1952), although some sites, such as Pearls on Grenada, demonstrate the continued importance of the exploitation of marine resources (Allaire 2003, 203).

The millennium from the end of the Saladoid horizon until the late Suazoid period (below) is generally considered as a period of gradual, but 'pervasive decline' (Allaire 2003, 219). From the middle of the 4th century AD (*c.* AD 350-650), new types of more elaborate polychrome 'Barrancoid' ceramics and modelled-incised decoration, are found alongside white-on-red decorated ceramics. The overall distribution of Barracoid sites is more extensive than in the Saladoid period, and this is usually interpreted as a period of dynamic population increase and geographical expansion in human activity in the Lesser Antilles. While rock art, especially in the forms of petroglyphs, developed during the first millennium AD, no evidence of the ceremonial ball courts (*bateys*) found on Puerto Rico, Hispaniola and Cuba has been found in the Lesser Antilles (Alegría 1983).

The period from around the middle of the 7th century AD is characterised by more 'insularity and regionalisation' in ceramic styles that developed from earlier periods (Allaire 2003, 208-211), and saw the emergence of 'Troumassoid' ceramics (especially on St Lucia). During the later 'Suazoid' period (*c.* AD 1200-1450), 'a stronger dichotomy between a fine or ceremonial decorated ware, and a crude plain utilitarian ware that now often constitutes 80 per cent of the remains' emerges (Allaire 2003, 211).[1] These clamp-fired, hand-made, unpainted utilitarian 'Cayo' or 'Suazy' vessels are generally recovered from shell midden deposits or from unstratified contexts. These vessels are often characterised by fingertip or nail impressions decorating the rim, and the most common form was the tripod, oval bowl, often

---

[1] This period also sees the emergence of the anomalous 'Cayo' ceramic assemblages from St Vincent (Allaire 2003, 216).

with anthropomorphic *adornos* (Drewitt 1990). Fishing appears to have been the main form of subsistence during the Suazoid period (Allaire 2003, 212).

The conventional divide between the study of prehistory and historical (post-AD 1500) archaeology in Americanist archaeology has strongly influenced the development of Caribbean archaeology. However, the utility of this divide has been increasingly questioned by historical archaeologists (Hicks and Beaudry 2006). In an important paper, Stephen Silliman (2005) has suggested that archaeologists' distinctions between 'contact' and 'colonialism' have been particularly unhelpful in this respect. More radically, Kent Lightfoot (1995, 202) has suggested that prehistoric and historical archaeology represent 'segregated ethnic domains' which serve to restrain impulses towards producing narratives that account for the interactions of Old World (European and African) and New World (Indigenous) populations. In a Caribbean context, one part of the challenge is to acknowledge the sheer scale of early 17th-century migration from the Old World to the New, which included forced migration from a range of different African situations, and also the migration of tens of thousands of indentured servants – to Bermuda, Providence, Henrietta, Newfoundland, across the Chesapeake, Virginia and New England, the Bahamas, and the Mosquito Coast, as well as across the Lesser Antilles (Games 1999; Newton 1914, 1933, cf. Bailyn 1986). But in the eastern Caribbean the potential role and complexity of Indigenous populations, and the potential for complex processes of ethnogenesis in this frontier zone during the 16th and early 17th centuries, must be considered. As Jalil Sued-Badillo has argued, the ethnic complexity of Indigenous populations in the Lesser Antilles during the early periods of contact and colonialism cannot be adequately expressed through names such as 'Taino', 'Arawak' or 'Carib' – which often become 'new distortions' that perpetuate older 'caricatures that have for so long attempted to portray them as docile, cannibalistic, or backward' (Sued Badillo 2003a, 259).

As Louis Allaire observed in 1980, understanding the place of Carib populations in the early contact period in the Lesser Antilles requires the 'reconciling of history and prehistory' (Allaire 1980, 243). The evidence for Indigenous populations in the eastern Caribbean at the time of the first European contact in the late 15th century, and in the decades that followed, is obscure. Historical geographer Watts (1987, 109) considers that since the region was the object of European slave raids during the early 16th century, it is possible that the majority of the islands of the Lesser Antilles were depopulated by AD 1520. From the archaeological evidence, it is quite probable that the Lesser Antilles were virtually unpopulated in AD 1492. A hiatus in the archaeological sequence occurs after the Suazoid period, during the 15th century, and is suggestive of 'a late prehistoric depopulation' (Allaire 2003, 217). This hiatus may possibly represent the early slave raiding that accompanied the development of Iberian settler

colonialism in the western Caribbean, or may represent other changes in human activity in the region that resulted from European contact during the 15th century. What is certain, however, is that by the early 17th century, 'Carib' populations are documented across the Lesser Antilles: some living alongside, but soon suffering at the hands of, Europeans in the Leeward Islands, and a minority surviving away from permanent European settlement in the Windward Islands.

Research into the history and archaeology of Island Carib populations, while continuing to rely upon the culture historical accounts of earlier prehistory, have increasingly emphasised ethnic complexity and the importance of trade and exchange (Allaire 1980, Davis and Goodwin 1990, Keegan 1996). Dominican archaeologist Lennox Honychurch (1997, 293) has argued that the use of historical documentary sources (including Columbus) by Caribbean historians and archaeologists has led to two alternative models of the Carib population of the Lesser Antilles: the 'Carib invasion model' and the 'Arawak continuity model'. These two models have produced in Caribbean archaeology something close to what Robert Berkhofer famously called the 'good Indian'/'bad Indian' dichotomy (Berkhofer 1978, 28, 119) – here between 'Arawaks' and 'Caribs'. The 'Carib invasion' thesis is based on the apparent transition from earlier fine ceramics to the Suazy and Cayo coarsewares. Historical accounts of the cannibalism and aggression of Caribs who resisted European occupation in the Windward Islands into the 18th century, have inspired a model of the invasion by 'warlike Caribs' from the South American mainland, killing (and perhaps eating) the peaceful agricultural Arawak or Taino populations of the Lesser Antilles (Wilson 1993; Honychurch 1997). In contrast, the 'Arawak continuity' model sees Carib/Taino differences as the result of 'divergent trajectories of cultural change' during the late first millennium AD. Such an interpretation is presented in Christopher Goodwin's analysis of prehistoric St Kitts who states that the Indigenous population of the colonial period

> developed from its Saladoid base more or less autochthonously on St Kitts. In short, the precolonial Kittitians heretofore described in the historical literature as Caribs were Arawaks (R.C. Goodwin 1979, 307).

While these conflicting models remain 'the most hotly contested issue in current Lesser Antillean archaeology' (Honychurch 1997, 293), a focus on interaction and exchange – the idea of the Caribbean region not just as a 'cultural mosaic' (Wilson 1993), but a changing region in which saw the emergence of new identities – holds the potential to redirect these arguments to some degree, especially in relation to the early contact period. The increased focus upon interaction relates closely to the long-running rejection in some traditions of Caribbean archaeology of the Americanist idea of the Caribbean as a 'Culture Area' (Mintz 1966; cf. Curet 2004), and the presentation of a 'very heterogeneous cultural picture'

(Mintz 1966, 914). The region is often viewed by scholars from outside the Caribbean as an interstice between North, South and Central America defined by an archipelago whose relationship with 'other' world areas is defined often as peripheral in which its inhabitants, both pre- and post-colony are migrants to the archipelago (Trouillot 1992).

In unpicking the history and archaeology of Indigenous-European interactions in the Lesser Antilles, a number of interpretive problems present themselves. First among these is the problem of terminology. The term 'Arawak' has, confusingly, been used to refer to the Indigenous populations present in the Greater Antilles in the early contact period (referred to as Taino above), and to the pre-Carib population present in the Lesser Antilles in the first centuries of the first millennium AD (referred to as Saladoid or Troumassoid above). Additionally, the term 'Ciboney' has been used to refer to hunting-fishing-gathering populations in parts of the Greater Antilles in the early contact period. A second, more severe, problem is that unlike the situation in the western Caribbean the prehistory of the Lesser Antilles suffers from a severe lack of high quality data. Previously, prehistoric archaeology in the region has largely consisted of the surface collection and the identification of 'sites' with high densities of prehistoric artefacts. These important surveys have identified such densities across St Lucia (Devaux 1975), St Kitts (Goodwin 1979) and Nevis (Wilson 1989). In addition, *in situ* remains such as petroglyphs and rock-cut basins have been identified on many islands, including St Lucia (Jesse 1952). However, there remains a need for sustained programmes of survey and stratigraphic excavations of prehistoric sites in the region.

A third problem relates to the interpretation of the distributions of Lesser Antillean prehistoric 'sites', which are restricted to coastal locations: apart from riverside petroglyphs and rock-cut basins which are common in St Lucia (Devaux 1975). While, as suggested above, this may reflect the coastal nature of settlement and other human activity in the prehistoric period, it may also be a product of methodology and taphonomy. Goodwin's (1979) and Wilson's (1989) surveys both appear to have been largely focused upon beach-walking, and sherds of prehistoric pottery are easier to identify on a sandy beach than in the cane fields of St Kitts or the thick secondary bush of Nevis. In St Lucia and Nevis, there appear to be more prehistoric sites on the windward than the leeward coastlines, especially in the aceramic period. This may be a result of coastal erosion and more intensive historical settlement on the leeward coast. Equally, however, the picture may be accurate. It appears that all the islands of the Lesser Antilles were covered with a thick rainforest until clearance by European populations in the 17th and 18th centuries. Prehistoric activity along the coast and rivers is therefore in keeping with this picture, presumably with certain areas of clearance for cultivation. This issue cannot be resolved without the characterisation of these sites through stratigraphic excavations, but unfortunately the vast majority of prehistoric excavations in the eastern Caribbean have been carried out by arbitrary

level and arbitrary grid: focused on the recovery of artefacts with little consideration of stratigraphic context. It may be that previous attempts to identify Indigenous sites through excavated material culture alone have missed significant landscape features and buried stratigraphy.

A fourth problem, and perhaps the most significant challenge, relates to conventional conceptions of ethnicity in contact-period archaeology in the Caribbean. European-Carib interactions continued in the Windwards into the 18th century, although further work is needed on the substantial and little studied literature of 16th-, 17th- and 18th-century English and French ethnographic descriptions of Carib society (See Boucher 1992; Hulme 1986; Hulme and Whitehead 1992; Taylor 1949; Wilson 1993, 50). The Carib population was forcibly removed from the Leewards during the 17th century, the French and English uniting in military action against the Caribs by a treaty of 1659 (Higham 1921, 122-3). A significant Carib population exists today in the Windward Islands, and a community has been based at a reservation on Dominica since 1903. And yet standard accounts of European-Carib relations as entirely conflict ridden have overlooked evidence of exchange and interaction across the Windward Islands after AD 1600, especially by the French *coureurs des îles* who hunted, fished and traded with Carib populations. The degree of interaction is underlined by the production of a French-Carib dictionary (Boucher 1992; Breton 1665): analysis of the vocabulary in the dictionary shows that many words for European items with French or Spanish roots (cf. Hulme and Whitehead 1992). The complexity of 'Carib' and 'European' populations in the 17th century remains little studied, however.

Archaeological material culture studies hold significant potential to explore these issues of ethnicity and ethnogenesis. In a significant contribution to Caribbean material culture studies, Chris Clement (2000) has pointed out that in addition to African influences, prehistoric and Indigenous influences on 18th-century unglazed earthenwares in the Windward Islands should be considered – treating the ceramics as syncretic products of contact and colonialism. As Clement argues, current knowledge of the regional sequence of unglazed earthenwares means that it is very difficult not only to identify the differences between historical-period colonowares and prehistoric or 'Carib' wares through typological analysis, but also to consider whether such firm distinctions are useful in the first place. This argument in relation to material culture can be expanded in broader terms. From both archaeological and historical ethnographic evidence, it can be argued that during the 16th and early 17th centuries both Indigenous and Old World populations in the Lesser Antilles were bound up in complex historical processes of ethnogenesis. Indeed, as Jalil Sued-Badillo (2003b, 2) has suggested, in this period Caribs may represent 'the first case of ethnogenesis in the colonial Americas' – emerging from complex Indigenous, African and European populations. The sense of interaction and exchange that emerges from such studies shapes much of the argument presented below.

13

How can an archaeological perspective, focused upon landscape change, contribute to the study of early colonial interactions in the Lesser Antilles? One of the distinctive aspects of archaeological landscape survey is its emphasis upon combining documentary and archaeological sources to record features from all periods of a landscape's historical sequence, examining contingency and change rather than focusing upon particular sites or periods. The landscape surveys at both Wingfield, St Kitts and at Balenbouche, St Lucia, identified significant evidence of pre-sugar landscapes. The next two sections summarise the results of this documentary research and field survey (**Figures 2 & 3**). Having explored the similarities between these two archaeological landscapes, in which enclosures were identified, I shall consider how such early landscapes can be interpreted.

Documentary and Archaeological Evidence for the pre-sugar landscape at Wingfield, St Kitts

On St Kitts, the clearest evidence for 17th-century activity on the site of Wingfield Estate is provided by cartographic evidence. The Buor map of *c.* 1680 (**Figure 4a**) shows a series of plantations established on inland locations in English and French St Kitts. Old Road appears to have developed swiftly from the 1620s into a major town with a

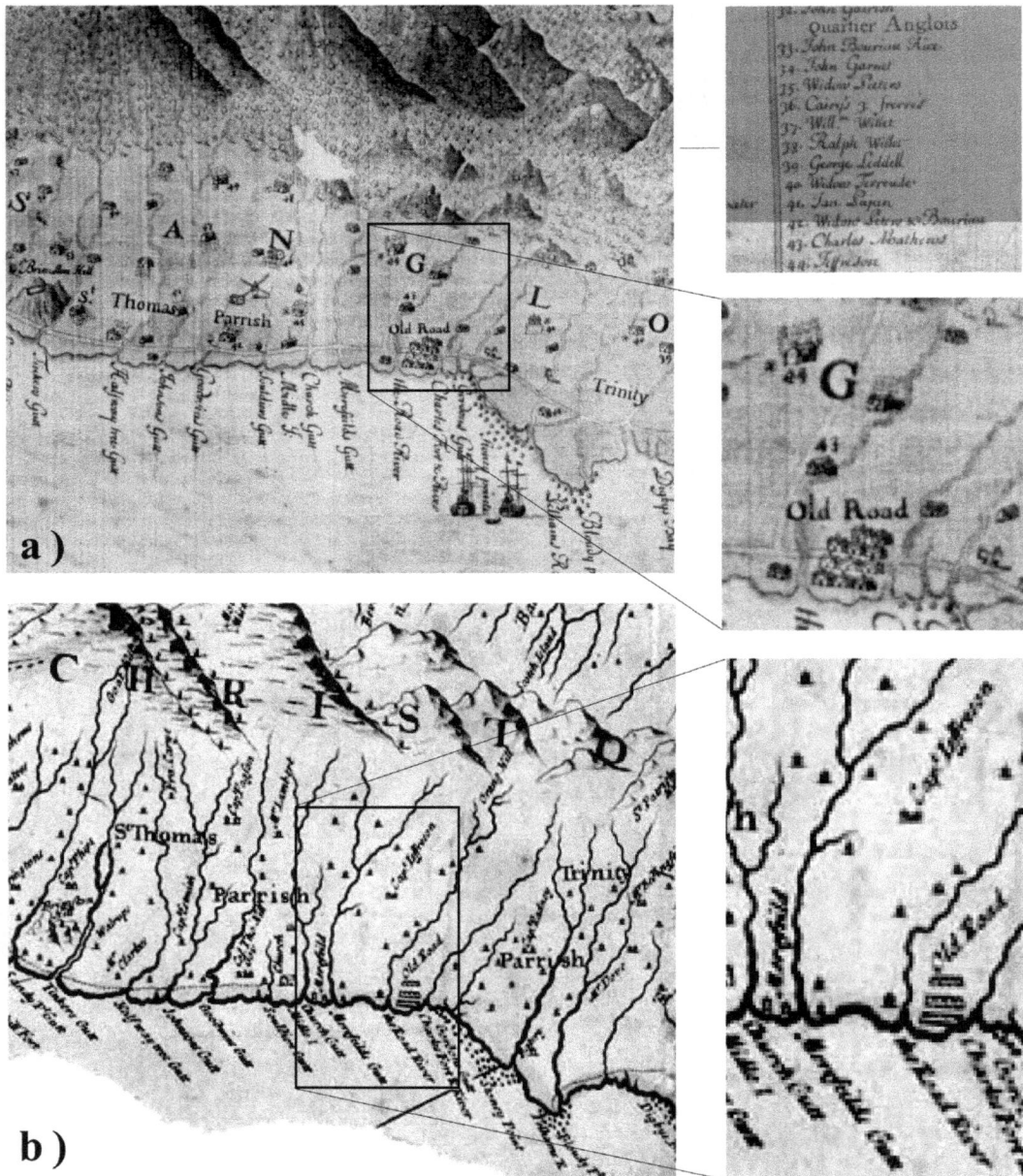

FIGURE 4. TWO LATE 17TH-CENTURY MAPS SHOWING OF OLD ROAD AND SURROUNDING AREA: A) BUOR MAP OF ST KITTS, *C.*1680, WITH DETAIL OF OLD ROAD AND WINGFIELD, AND DETAIL OF PLANTATION OWNERS' NAMES SHOWING CHARLES MATTHEWS (AT WINGFIELD) AND JEFFRESON (TO THE NORTH) (ST KITTS NATIONAL ARCHIVES); B) A NEW MAP OF THE ISLAND OF ST CHRISTOPHERS BY ANDREW NORWOOD (1698), WITH DETAIL OF OLD ROAD AND WINGFIELD RIVER AREA, SHOWING JEAFFRESON ESTATE TO THE NORTH (NATIONAL ARCHIVES CO 700 /ST CHRISTOPHER AND NEVIS 1).

fort (Charles Fort), and a port. The town continued as one of the major ports of the English West Indies throughout this period: even the famous voyage of Captain Woodes Rogers from Bristol (1708-11) landed in Old Road. Old Road is shown as a substantial town, with four rows of houses shown on the Buor map of around 1680 (**Figure 4a**). A town of similar size appears to have existed at Palmetto Point, to the east of Old Road, at this time. Three rows of houses are shown on the Norwood map of 1698 (**Figure 4b**, National Archives CO700/St Christopher and Nevis 1).

For the area of modern Wingfield, a house (43) is shown on the Buor map between Wingfield River and the road connecting the two English sides of St Kitts, as belonging to Charles Matthews, who was Governor of St Kitts at this time. The house of 'Jeffreson' (44) is shown even further inland, to the north-west. The Jeaffreson papers, held in the Beinecke Lesser Antilles Collection, Hamilton College, Clinton, New York, include the papers of Christopher Jeaffreson (1650-1725), who inherited his father's land at Wingfield Estate in 1660. Amongst the letters and accounts is a detailed survey of the Wingfield River and land of Charles Matthews drawn up in 1682, and traced for Christopher Jeaffreson IV in 1819 (**Figure 10** below). This is one of the earliest surviving plans of a West Indian estate, and shows a large Jacobean-style house, tobacco or indigo works, cattle mill, gardens and an area of accommodation for indentured labourers or slaves. A tobacco leaf is depicted

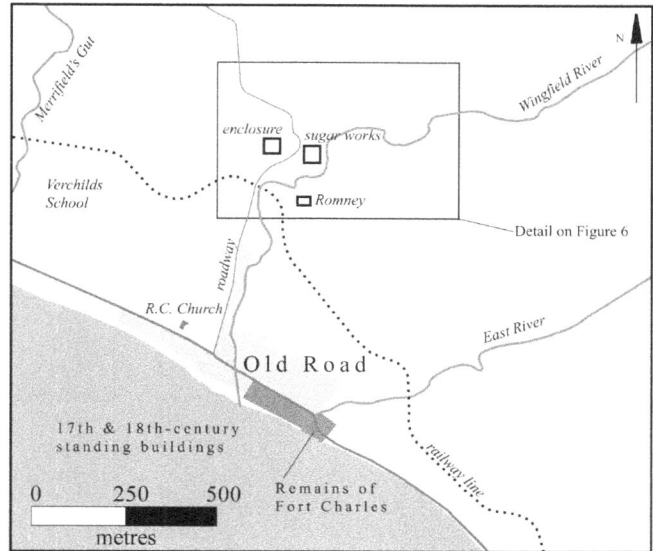

FIGURE 5. WINGFIELD ESTATE AND OLD ROAD, ST KITTS.

to the north-east of the residence, possibly suggesting that this was an area of tobacco cultivation.

During fieldwork at Wingfield, a range of historic building remains and landscape features which pre-dated the sugar works and estate houses recorded by the archaeological survey were identified (**Figures 5, 6 & 7**, Hicks and Horton 2001b). Standing buildings recording identified

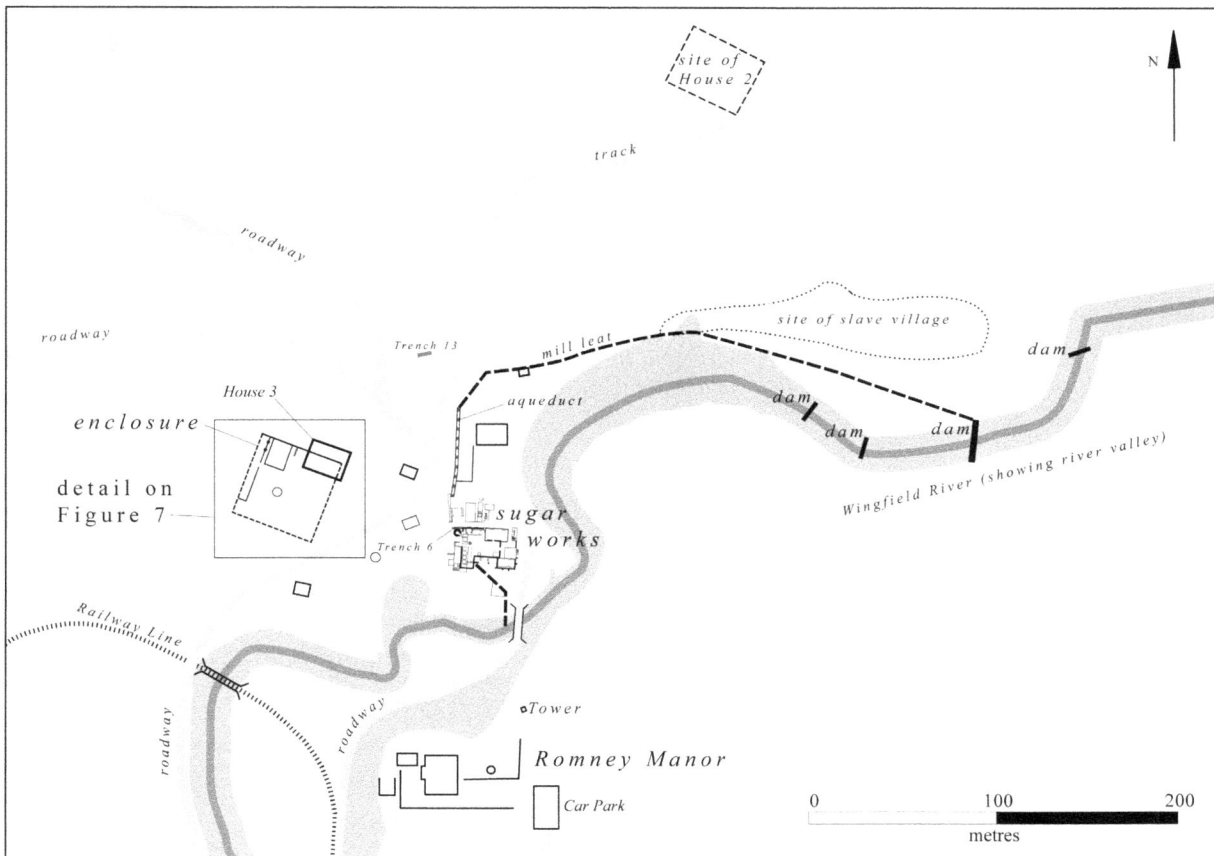

FIGURE 6. LANDSCAPE SURVEY OF AT WINGFIELD, ST KITTS (MULTI PERIOD)

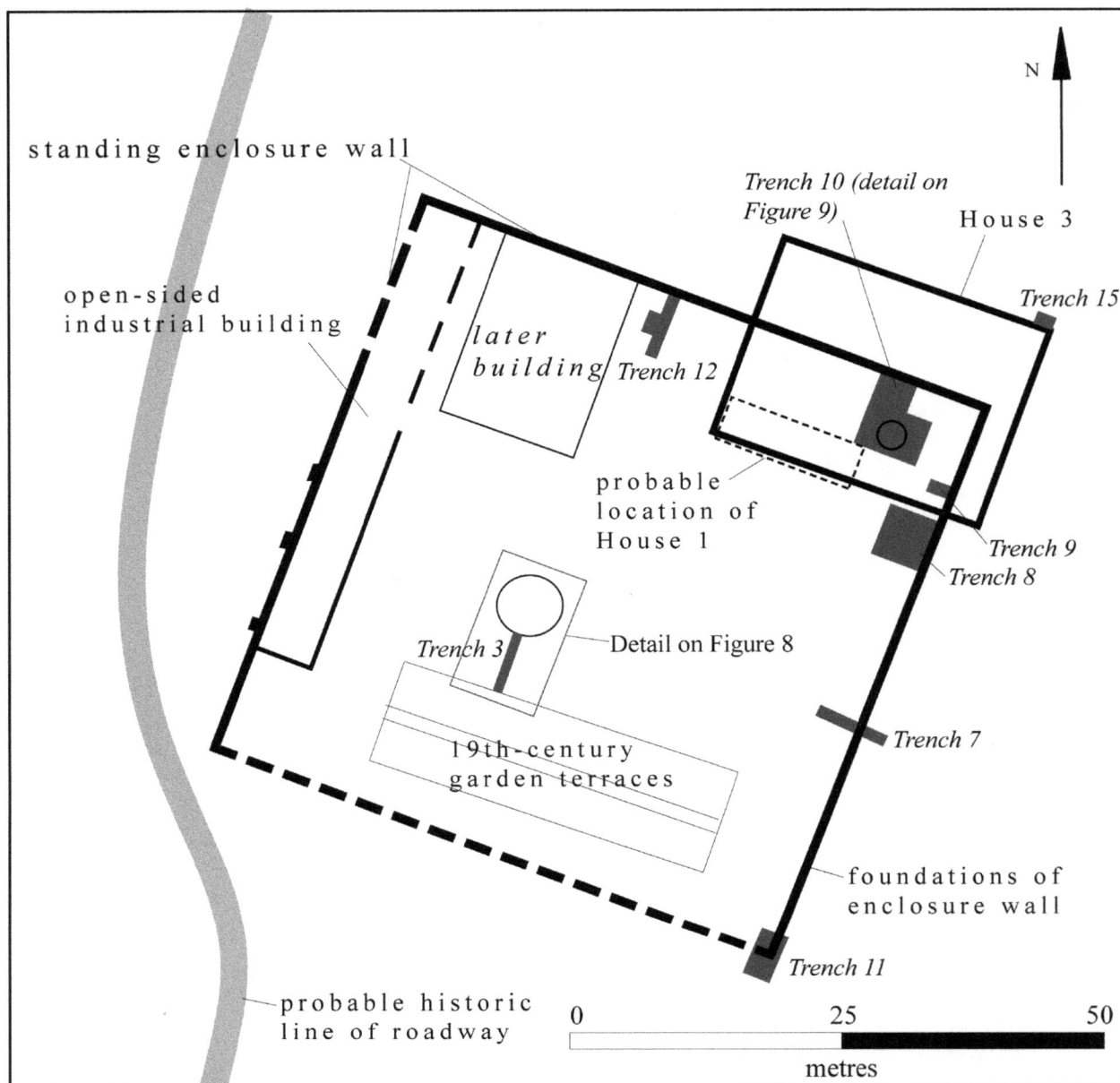

FIGURE 7. DETAIL OF LANDSCAPE SURVEY OF ENCLOSURE AT WINGFIELD, ST KITTS SHOWING 17TH-CENTURY ENCLOSURE, TRENCH LOCATIONS AND PROBABLE LOCATION OF HOUSE 1, WITH LATER FEATURES INCLUDING HOUSE 3 AND 19TH-CENTURY GARDEN TERRACES

a complex sequence of construction that pre-dated the early 19th-century estate house (the third estate house identified in the survey, hereafter termed House 3, see **Figure 7**). House 3 had used a very substantial earlier wall (referred to hereafter as Wall 1026), made of local volcanic stone with mortared and galletted construction, as part of its foundations. In Trench 15 it was shown that this wall was faced on both sides – having originally served as an above-ground wall before its conversion into a retaining wall during the construction of the later Estate House by the infilling of the area to the north with earth. The landscape survey identified that wall 1026 extended beyond the house to the west, and ran off at a right angle to the south. This north/south wall-line, was investigated

in four interventions (Trenches 7, 8, 9 and 11), and was shown to be a very substantial mortared foundation of local volcanic stone, with galletted faces on both sides. In Trench 9, it was confirmed that this north/south wall, like the east/west wall 1026, was earlier than House 3. To the west of House 3, a structure which had initially been interpreted as a 19th-century barn was revealed though building recording to be earlier in origin – forming a long, narrow structure 37 m in length and 5 m in width, with a series of openings opposite each other. The structure lay at the termination of east/west wall 1026. Such a long, open-sided building is suggestive of some kind of drying process (e.g. indigo or tobacco), or possibly industrial warehousing. The remains of the stone surfaces of a cattle

16

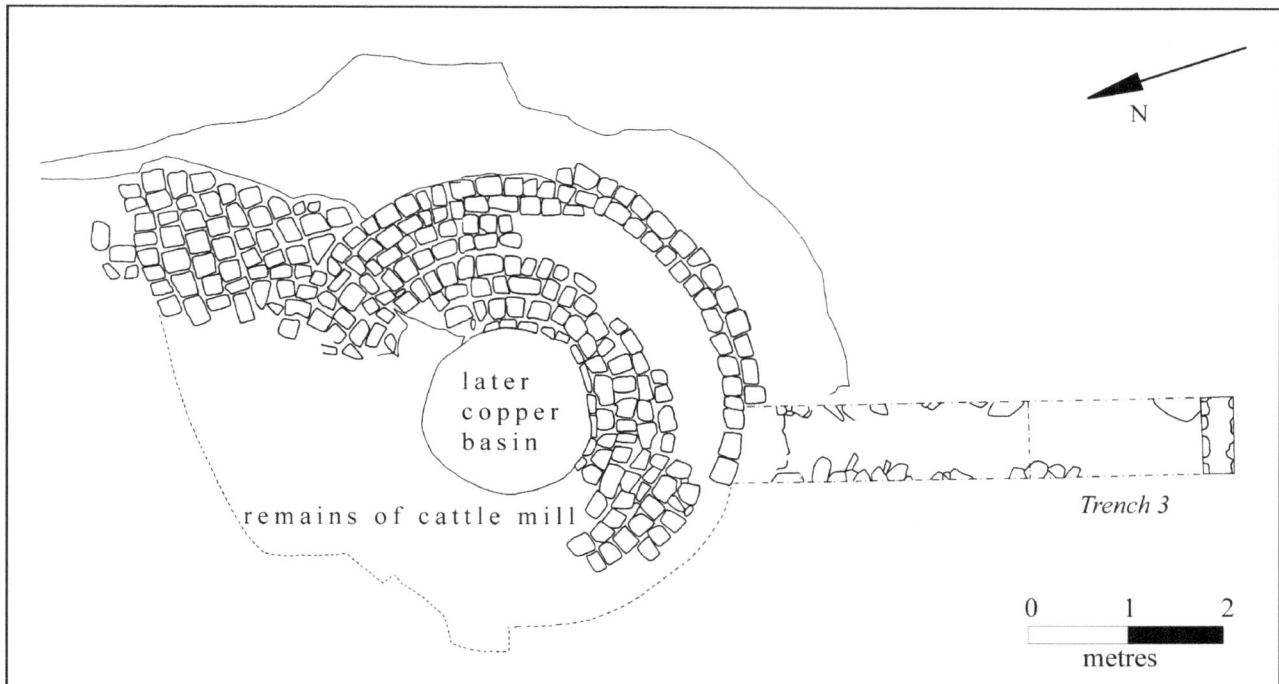

FIGURE 8. PLAN OF CATTLE MILL AND TRENCH 3, WINGFIELD, ST KITTS

mill were identified. Although the mill had been converted into a garden feature during the 19th century, excavation in Trench 3 identified a complex sequence of construction, wearing away and repair (**Figure 8**). Finally, below House 3 excavations in Trench 10 identified a very large post hole and several associated smaller associated post holes. These were sealed by a compact floor surface which in turn was cut by the construction of the northern enclosure wall. The most probable interpretation of these results is as evidence of the replacement of a timber palisaded enclosure with a similar structure using stone walls. Contemporary with the enclosure wall, the foundations of a circular tower also cut the floor surface (**Figure 9**). Further evaluative excavations within the enclosure (Trench 12) identified a deep pit or large post hole that was filled with very large quantities of unglazed earthenwares, red-slipped prehistoric wares and animal bone. No later material or European ceramics were recovered from the fill, and the range of unglazed earthenwares and prehistoric ceramics may be indicative of an early contact period date for this feature (Hicks and Horton 2001b).

As the results of the landscape survey were plotted (at a scale of 1:100) it became clear that the walls formed an enclosure in an almost perfect square – *c*. 45 m x 45 m (**Figure 7**). A comparison of the 1682 plan with the results

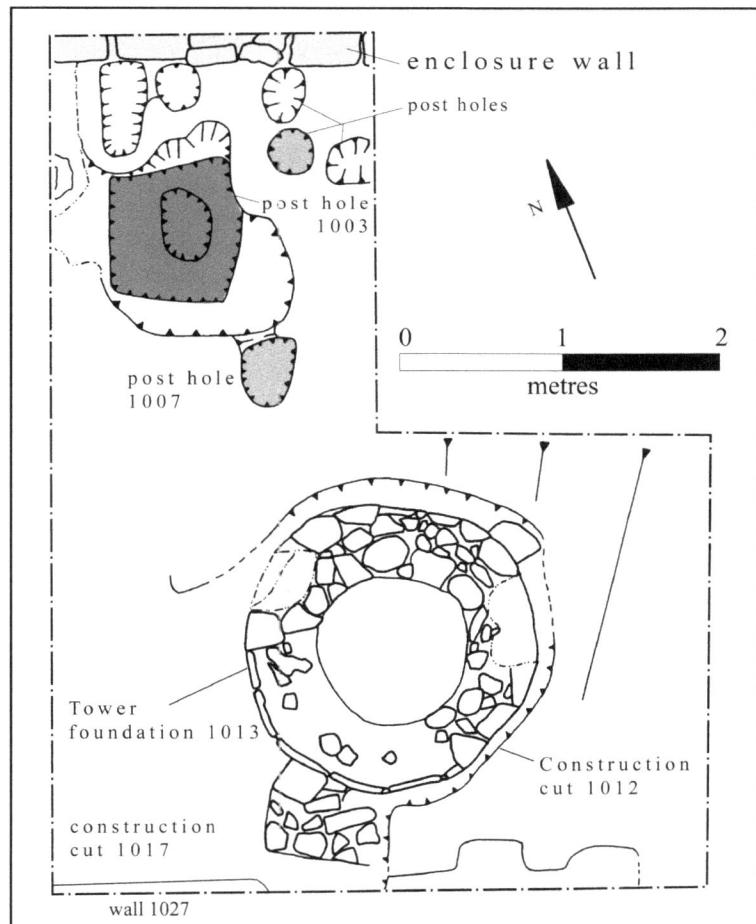

FIGURE 9. PLAN OF TRENCH 10, SHOWING FOUNDATIONS OF 17TH-CENTURY TOWER AT WINGFIELD

FIGURE 10. DETAIL FROM SURVEY OF WINGFIELD IN 1682, REDRAWN IN 1819 BY CHRISTOPHER JEAFFRESON (COURTESY OF THE BEINECKE LESSER ANTILLES COLLECTION, HAMILTON COLLEGE, CLINTON, NEW YORK)

of the survey is striking. The enclosure, cattle mill, industrial buildings in the western part of the enclosure, and tower in the north-east, are all located on both: and the angle at which the enclosure is orientated to the north is precisely the same on both (compare **Figures 7** and **10**). The industrial buildings shown in the north-west corner were in the same location as the long, open-sided building. The tower appears to have been a prospect tower of some kind. The probable location of House 1 was not investigated archaeologically (**Figure 7**).

As is detailed in Chapter 3 below, at the time of the 1682 survey, the new owner of the site, Christopher Jeaffreson, was concentrating on the development of a new water-powered sugar works. The enclosure clearly pre-dates the 1682 survey significantly, and the Jacobean double- or triple-gabled timber house is typical of southern England in the early 17th century. This walled enclosure, with its agricultural-industrial buildings that included a cattle mill and possible tobacco drying building, represented the earliest landscape remains identified during survey at Wingfield.

Archaeological Evidence for the pre-sugar landscape at Balenbouche, St Lucia

Such documentary sources do not survive for St Lucia during the 17th century. However, during fieldwork at Balenbouche the remains of a large subrectangular segmented ditched enclosure were identified, surviving as part of the leat system for the late 18th-century water mill (Hicks and Horton 2001a). The ditches enclosed

an area that measured c. 130 m east/west and c. 110 m north/south in size (**Figure 13**). Within this enclosure, evaluative excavation identified that the earliest archaeological horizon consisted of a midden deposit: a series of dumped layers containing prehistoric ceramics, tin glazed pottery and clay pipes, including one locally-made unglazed earthenware pipe. In the same contexts as these artefacts were other, hand-made, unglazed earthenware ceramics. The identification of a post hole within this sequence suggests that timber structures existed on the site: the details of which must await further open-area excavations. Cut into the primary layers of the midden deposit in the centre of the enclosure, the stone foundations of a narrow rectangular structure were identified. In the south-east corner of this structure, the circular stone foundation remains of a tower were identified (Hicks and Horton 2001a).

To the east of the ditched enclosure, the structural remains of a small coffee works were recorded. The coffee complex (**Figure 16**) comprised a simple water system serving two small water mills, a machine pit, a washing area and a drying area. The valley in which the works are located is formed by a seasonal tributary river to the Balenbouche: although now dry, a large earthen dam was provided, as well as two mill ponds which survive as earthwork features.

The production of coffee involves several processes between harvesting and shipping (Delle 1996, 127; Laborie 1798). The coffee works was provided with a pulping mill to remove the coffee beans from ripe berries; an area to wash beans out from the pulp (often involving the suspension of the pulp in water while separating the beans from the solution). Recorded accounts of washing out coffee beans involve the storing water in cisterns or vats (Delle 1996); drying platforms to dry the beans (known as 'barbecues' in Jamaica); and a second machine to remove parchment (thick skin). Structural remains representing all of these activities were identified. The buildings were terraced into the side of the hill, but in an area of fairly gentle slope, requiring limited earth-moving to establish a level foundation.

The main coffee processing building comprised three walled areas: interpreted (from west to east) as a wheel pit, machine pit, and washing area. The wheel pit was 1.2 m wide, and would have held a wooden wheel around 3.5 m in diameter. It would have been supplied by a short wooden launder from the mill ponds above. The machine pit measured 2.5 m north-south and 4.1 m east-west. The pit was completely filled with later hill-wash, but below this material, three mortar piers and a ledge (part of the eastern wall of the pit) were identified. They were all at the same height, and were interpreted as foundation piers to hold a pulping machine. To the west, the washing area measured 7.1 m east-west and 4.1 m north-south. A fine cobbled surface covered the whole area, although root disturbance had damaged this in the centre. Two slots ran from west to east across the area, and were interpreted as gutters to drain water from washing coffee beans out from the pulp. A break in the southern wall possibly represented an entrance. In addition, a short length of wall next to the wheel pit appeared to be part of the same structure extending to the north, but was not further investigated. A terraced structure built into the side of the hill to the north-west of the coffee works had been later partially re-built in concrete, but appeared to represent a 'barbecue' (drying platform), with a second small machine and wheel to remove parchment. It is possible that later construction of the sugar works buildings destroyed further buildings from this phase of activity, but this land was probably too steep for significant buildings prior to the terracing carried out to construct them.

The relationship between the ditched enclosure and the coffee works is unclear. However, the late 18th-century sugar works clearly post-dated the coffee works as its water system cut across the earlier arrangement, making it impossible for the coffee works to have remained in use, and the ditched enclosure clearly pre-dated the open sugar landscape constructed on the site in the late 18th century (Chapter 4 below). Together, these features are evidence of the character of the pre-sugar landscape at Balenbouche.

Enclosed Landscapes

A number of documentary sources indicate that enclosure – whether by stone wall, timber palisade or segmented ditch – may have been a more general feature of the landscapes of contact and colonialism between the 1620s and the 1670s in the eastern Caribbean. A number of documentary sources relating to 17th-century Old Road describe enclosures, some of which may be the enclosure identified at Wingfield. John Hilton's 1675 first-hand description of a West Country tobacco merchant arriving at Old Road in the 1620s:

> Soe we beate our dromms, gott our people togeather, & att their comeing ashore we did honourable entertaine them with a strong gard, & brought them *into ye fort to our governours house*, where we did feast them with wine & good victualls. (Hilton 1925 [1675], 9-10, my emphasis)

Similarly, Ligon, describing Barbados, stated that many planters had houses 'built in manner of Fortifications... in case there should be any uproar or commotion in the Island' (Ligon 1657, 29). The military discipline of some early colonies was certainly important: as Alison Games has suggested, 'colonies like Barbados, St Kitts, and Virginia, with their male majorities, resembled military encampments without the rigorous discipline and clear hierarchies of army life' (Games 1999, 95). Indeed, in a description in 1661 by Sir Thomas Modiford of Barbados describes how houses were 'like castles':

> In 1643 its buildings were mean with things, only of necessity; in 1645 the buildings were fair and beautiful,

and their houses like castles, their sugar houses and negroes' huts from the sea like so many small towns each enclosed by its castle. (CSPC 1661, 529)

However, enclosures were clearly more than simply defences. Earlier in his narrative, Hilton describes how the early English settlers, living alongside a Carib group led by 'King Tegreman', constructed an enclosure:

> with licence of King Tegreman, they did settle themselves between two rivers neare to ye Kings house, where he did live & begin to build theire houses, & alsoe a fort of pallesadoes with flanckers, & loopeholes for theire defence. The King viewing theire workes did aske what theire loopeholes and flanckers were for. And they told him it was made that they might looke after those fowles they had about theire houses; but how ye King understood it I knowe not, but within some time after ye King was minded to cutt them off (Hilton 1925 [1675], 1-2).

The reason given to Carib king Tegreman that the fences would keep in the 'fowles they had about their houses' suggests that the 'fort of pallesadoes' was not a conventional military structure.

A number of 17th-century accounts describe Carib enclosed gardens. In 1665, Breton described enclosed gardens on Montserrat – on high ground, inland (Breton 1958 [1665]). On St Lucia, Nicholl's account of 1605 describes similar gardens. Walking along a 'narrow path' through the bush,

> we had not travelled a Mile, but we entered down by a Thicket into a most pleasant Garden of Potatoes, which drove us into great admiration to behold the manner of it, for it was made round like a Bower, encompassed with a green Bank so equally, that made us think some Christians had made it for a strength to save them from the Indians: and upon the top thereof did grow a company of the most tallest trees that I ever beheld, which did naturally grow so near to one another, and so thick from the root to the top, that we could not perceive the sky through them. But following the path, we perceived it to pass through a narrow cut in the bank, where we travelled two or three miles further, passing mainly through many goodly Gardens, wherein was abundance of Cassada, Potatoes, Tobacco, Cotton-wool trees, and Guava trees... (Nicholl 1966 [1607], 53)

Here, Nicholl is describing a Carib garden enclosed by a large earthwork, planted with tall trees that limited access. Lydia Pulsipher identified the earthwork remains of a similar enclosed garden on Montserrat before the volcanic eruptions that began in 1995: this was identified as the 'high mountain place' described in early legal descriptions of estate boundaries as 'The Great Indian Garden', later used as a redoubt by English colonists, and today referred to as 'Gadinge', a name apparently derived from 'garden'

(Pulsipher (1977, 24; 1999, 12); cf. du Tertre 1667-71 IV, 203).

On Nevis, at New River in the south-east of the island, a suggestive place name, Indian Castle, survives to this day in this part of the island (**Figure 2**). Here, unpublished fieldwork and survey carried in Nevis out by the British TV series *Time Team* in 1998 identified a partially eroded large subcircular cactus enclosure (Mick Worthington *pers. comm.*). Inside this enclosure, a range of prehistoric pottery and a post hole were identified during excavations. Elsewhere on Nevis, a late 19th-century account described the 'extinguished...aboriginal Carib, whose sole mausoleum is to be seen at the extreme north of the island, where the remains of a rude castellated building still exist, through which they shot their arrows' (Iles 1871, 8). However, this is most probably a description of one of the numerous ruined 17th-century English redoubts or forts.

Such evidence, taken together with the results of field survey in St Lucia and St Kitts, suggests that enclosure may have been a characteristic of both Carib and English settlement in the eastern Caribbean from the 1620s and the 1670s. Perhaps partially defensive, such enclosed areas appear to have been places for the cultivation of tropical staples for trade and exchange, and for small-scale industrial processing, as well as for domestic accommodation. But how might the recognition of such landscape features inform historical accounts of early contact and colonialism in the eastern Caribbean? In this next sections, I want to consider alternative narratives of settlement, and how landscape approaches offer alternatives to Eurocentric accounts of 'pioneers' and permanency in settlement.

Alternative Narratives of Settlement

The establishment of the first permanent English settlement in the island Caribbean by Thomas Warner (*c.* AD 1575-1649) at Old Road (also called English Road, CSPC 1675-6, 618) in St Kitts, is relatively well documented (Anon 1638, CSPC 1661-8, 1368; Crouse 1940; Davies 1666; Labat 1722; Newton 1914; Smith 1908 [1629]). This event is often celebrated in the kind of British imperial historiography described above as a significant moment in West Indian history (Warner 1933). For economic historians, the early 17th century was a time of a new English engagement in European settler colonialism and Atlantic trade. Jacobean mercantilisation – a 'new preoccupation with trade' – developed, characterised by the chartering of the East India Company in 1600, or of Virginia tobacco planter Robert Rich's Company of Adventurers to 'Gynny and Bynny' (Guinea and Benin) by James I in 1618 (Shammas 1978, 166, 167).[2] English

settler colonies were established across the Atlantic New World. Indeed, conventional historiographies, the early development of New World plantations serves to illustrate such impulses. Thousands, including many English peers and Members of Parliament, invested in such overseas enterprises. However, in contrast with the joint stock companies of Virginia, Bermuda, Guiana and Old Providence, or the state enterprise in Jamaica in the 1650s, the new colonies of the eastern Caribbean were subject to proprietary patent, and colonising ventures were backed by merchants' investments.

One result of the use in conventional Atlantic world historiography of using colonial documents to illustrate broad, Eurocentric narratives of pioneers and exploration is that certain locations are left out of the picture. Thus, in contrast with St Kitts, St Lucia is peripheral to traditional historical accounts of the West Indies, especially before the late 18th century (but see the work of St Lucian-based historians Devaux 1975, Harmsen 1999 and Rennard nd). Where the island is mentioned, it is as the site of several abortive colonial settlements involving a few hundred men and swiftly ended by French or Carib hostilities. The island changed hands 14 times between English and French between the early 17th century and 1813, yet the motives for the island's apparent long-term importance to the English and French (as well as to Carib populations) have rarely been discussed. Instead, conventional histories of St Lucia begin in the mid-to-late 18th century with the establishment of permanent government in 1765, and widespread sugar monoculture.

An alternative approach is to examine how the new European impulses for trade and exchange were worked out in particular landscapes. In the case of St Kitts, Warner's venture was financed by London merchants Ralph Merrifield, and (from 1626) Maurice Thompson. Indeed, the island of St Kitts is referred to in some 1620s documents as 'Merwar's Hope' – an amalgam of the names of Warner and Merrifield (e.g. 30/8/1625; APC Col. 1613-1680, 90-91).[3] In 1627 St Kitts was divided by treaty between Warner and the French lords proprietors into three parts: a central English part from Sandy Point to west of Basseterre with a main town at Old Road, and a French area

---

[2] The chartering of the Company of Adventurers built upon an Elizabethan charter of 1588. Robert Rich was soon to be the Earl of Warwick. Rich's first cousin, Nathaniel Rich, was a major shareholder in the Bermuda Company, and his papers, now curated by Bermuda National Trust, are a key source for 17th-century colonial history (Ives 1984).

[3] The legal dimensions of the early colonial landscape of St Kitts are of some interest here, and the early settlement of the eastern Caribbean led to the production of a wealth of legal documents. Warner and Merrifield obtained a commission for the planting of four islands – 'St Christophers', 'Mevis', 'Moncerate' and 'Barbados' (perhaps Barbuda) – in 1625. After an approach from Warner and Merrifield, James Hay, First Earl of Carlisle, secured Letters Patent to the 'Caribbee Islands' – almost the whole of the Lesser Antilles – in 1627. The Earl of Marlborough was also involved, and 'behind Carlisle stood a group of London capitalists who had convinced themselves that the Lesser Antilles offered a lucrative investment' (Williamson 1926, 39). A rival proprietary patent for Barbados (previously included in the Carlisle patent) was obtained by the Earl of Pembroke on behalf of William Courteen in 1628. This was soon overturned by a second Carlisle patent in the same year (Williamson 1926, 47). In September 1629, during a visit to London, Warner was knighted at Hampton Court and appointed by Carlisle as Governor of St Christopher for life.

at the western and eastern ends, with a centre at Basseterre, and a town at Sandy Point. The salt pans on the island's south-east peninsula were held jointly (**Figure 2**). The 1625 French settlement was headed by Pierre d'Esnambuc, financed from 1626 through the newly formed *Compagnie de St Christophe*, organised by Cardinal Richelieu. This *Compagnie* was replaced by the *Compagnie des Iles de l'Amerique* in 1635, and Chevalier Lonvilliers de Poincy was appointed as Lieutenant General of all the 'Isles de l'Amerique' and Captain-General of St Kitts. De Poincy arrived in St Kitts in 1639, and the construction of his residence is discussed below. By 1651, this *Compagnie* was bankrupt, and its West Indian assets were sold, including St Christophe to the Knights of Malta.[4] The Carlisle patent for the 'Caribbee Islands' was leased to Francis, Lord Willoughby for 21 years in 1647 (Williamson 1926, 122-3). The proprietary patents were finally withdrawn in 1670, and soon afterwards in 1675 the Lords of Trade and the Plantations was formed (Williamson 1926). These changes led to the establishment of Crown rule in the colonies, and central to this process were the nascent legislatures: the Governors, elected Assemblies and nominated Councils of each British island. These bodies drew their authority from the original letters patent (such as the Carlisle patent) and whose organisation appears to have been formalised during the 1670s. These bodies appear to have sat together as a 'general assembly', modelled on the British Crown and Houses of Parliament (Burns 1954, 279-284). By focusing upon documentary sources relating to the legal basis of early settlement in the Leeward Islands and Barbados, it becomes clear that the first 50 years of settlement form a distinctive period for English settlement: one of proprietary patents and local rule before crown control was strongly exerted. Other primary sources can, however, highlight the complexities of early plantation landscapes.

The material conditions of establishing English plantations on St Kitts – clearing land and building houses – were vividly recorded by Sir Henry Colt, who arrived on the island in 1631, and established a plantation. Colt was dead by 1635. The location of his plantation is obscure, but it appears to have lain on the leeward coast of English St Kitts, close to Old Road: some commentators have stated it was at Palmetto Point, but there is no clear evidence from Colt's narrative for this. Colt described his establishment on St Kitts in letters to his son George Colt of 13 August and 20 August 1631:

> Butt now comes one of ye greatest labours & cares yt is for ye buildinge of a house. Although I have chosen a scituation between two riuers, for water is to be prised aboue anything els, yett was ye place wonderful discommodious. For timber we finde not any, palmito leaues for coueringe harder to be found; so yt all things

must be transported vppon ye shoulders of men, ye way from ye sea half a mile all vpp hill, ye grownd to cleer. Ye first thinge we employ is ye Axe an Instrament yt must sett all others to work. It is worthy of Consideration whatt a smale vnthought of want driue vs to wher we cannot borrow. We had forgott to bring a helue out of England, ye want of which keep vs Idle half a day. We must saw a helue, riue itt, cutt itt, plaine itt. Ye wood we must cut downe is ye pricklye tree hard & tough… (Colt 1925 [1631], 90-91)

Other contemporary sources highlight the importance of interaction between Carib and English populations during the early settlement of St Kitts. The account of John Hilton, recorded in 1675 when Hilton had lived on St Kitts and Nevis since the 1620s, of the settlement of Old Road is worth reproducing at length:

> One gentln of London one Capt Thomas Warner who was a good Souldier & a man of extraordinary agillety of bodie of a good witt & one who was truly honest & freindly to all men, who having made a trading voyage for ye Armasones, att his returne came by ye Careeby Islands, where he became acquainted with severall Indian Kings Inhabiting these Islands, amongst ye rest with one King Tegreman King of St Christophers. He well veiwing the Island thought it would be a very convenient place for ye planting of tobaccoes, which was a rich commodetie. Being arrived att London, [he] made some of his friends acquainted hearwith, who in hopes of great benefitt became part with him & did disburse theire monies towards ye Setting forth a Shipp & men for ye designe of tobaccoes, which was in ye yeare of our Lord 1623. (Hilton 1925 [1675], 2)

It is clear from Hilton's (1925 [1675]) and Du Tertre's (1654) descriptions that it was no accident that Warner's trip to the Roger North settlement in Guiana brought him into contact with the Carib population in St Kitts. Both locations were part of a single sphere of interaction, and the populations appear to have been connected. As seen above, in continuing with his description of the foundation of Thomas Warner's settlement at the site of modern Old Road, Hilton explains how this occurred 'with licence of King Tegreman,' and was sited 'neare to ye Kings house'. (Hilton 1925 [1675], 1-2), before the slaughter of the local Carib population by the English that occurred just a few years later (Hilton *ibid*).

Considering its general neglect in historical accounts of this period, turning to St Lucia the documentary evidence for close interactions between Carib and European people is surprisingly strong. A number of abortive European settlements are recorded in St Lucia during the 17th century, and appear to relate to four distinct events (cf. Jesse 1964, 16-23). The earliest of these accounts is that of the crew of the *Oliph Blossome* in 1605, discussed above (Nicholl 1966 [1607]). The ship was on its way to the Raleigh settlement in Guiana, but illness caused the crew to 'entreat the master to bring us to the nearest shore he could'. They arrived at

> an island...called Santa Lucia...inhabited only with a company of the most cruel Cannibals and man-eaters.

The ship's captain proceeded to purchase the 'five or seven houses planted by a pleasant fresh water River' for 'a Hatchet' from 'an Indian Captain called Anthony, who could speak a little Spanish, and he told us he had been a slave to the Spaniard in the Isle of Margareta'. The houses sold, the Indian 'captain...and all his company went to another town some three miles off' (*ibid*, 50). The settlement was abandoned in due course following arguments with the Carib population

The first recorded attempt at the English settlement of St Lucia came in 1638 or 1639 (Jesse 1969, 11-13). Various authorities describe the arrival of a party from St Kitts under one Captain Judlee, or under 'Indian' Thomas Warner, and from Bermuda under Governor Philip Bell. 'Indian' Warner was the son of the union between Thomas Warner (the founder of the St Kitts colony described above) and his Carib wife, and was later made Governor of Dominica in 1664. This account is given by Labat (1722) and Jesse (1964) and derives from Du Tertre (1654 Volume I, 434-438). Du Tertre states that after around 18 months, a failed attempt by an English party to kidnap a group of Caribs from Dominica led to an attack by Caribs from Martinique and St Vincent on the English settlement in St Lucia. Supposedly the Caribs smoked out the English by burning dried red pepper, and 'fell upon the English settlers, massacred many of them, and drove the rest away' – most going to Montserrat (Breen 1972 [1844], 46).

A French attempt was made in 1651 under Captain de Rousselan, who was married to a Carib woman (Du Tertre 1654; Labat 1722). Du Tertre describes the construction of a palisaded fort with a moat, within which the cultivation of tobacco, ginger and cotton took place (Jesse 1964, 18). The settlement, which included Carib and French population, thrived until de Rousselan's death in 1654, after which local French-Carib relations appear to have broken down and successive governors were killed, before an English attack put an end to the settlement around 1660.

Several accounts describe significant numbers (possibly around 7000 people, mainly of English or Irish extraction) moving from Barbados between 1661 and 1666 under Francis Willoughby, governor of Barbados (Higham 1921, 41, Watts 1987, 217, Du Tertre 1654, Volume III, 81-90). Between 500 and 1000 of these appear to have come to St Lucia. In particular, around 600 Caribs from Dominica, led by 'Indian' Thomas Warner, appear to have accompanied some 500-1000 Barbadians in 1664. 'Indian' Warner reportedly arranged the purchase of St Lucia from the Carib population in June 1664.

Higham (1921, 42) refers to an entry in the CSPC which discusses the fortification of the south coast of St Lucia by the English in the 1660s. St Lucia returned to French ownership after the Peace of Breda (1667), but the European occupation of the island remained minimal, and the general picture of 17th-century St Lucia is one of informal sharing of the island between the English and a French majority population. Another English settlement of St Lucia by one Nicholas Blake, a Barbados planter, was proposed in 1671, but appears to have come to nothing (Higham 1921, 128). An English population on St Lucia conducting a regular timber trade with Barbados was described in 1689.[5]

From Settlement to Landscape

There is a tendency in historical accounts of early colonial history in the eastern Caribbean (e.g. Bridenbaugh and Bridenbaugh 1972) to privilege the establishment of settlements – the study of colonial origins and pioneers, and a focus upon permanence rather than undocumented interactions – in a way that contrasts with the longer-term and material focus of landscape archaeology, which explores how natural and material conditions shape settlement histories. The point can be made at a number of scales.

Firstly, the broader maritime landscape contexts of the Lesser Antilles is an important dimension here. The Windwards were usually first landfall for ships crossing the Atlantic in the early modern world. Thus, a typical account as early as 1629 describes the fitting out of an English ship, the Faith,

> to take a voyage to the Island of St Christofers and thence to Newfoundland and the Straights (Littleton 1908 [1629]).

Famously Columbus, on his second voyage, first saw land at Dominica (Jane 1930, 22), before following the arc of the Lesser Antilles north-west towards the Greater Antilles. While the smaller islands of the Lesser Antilles were not settled by the Spanish, this journey must have been typical of 16th-century Spanish voyages to their possessions in the Greater Antilles. The route was also used for the early English Virginian plantations. An account of a journey in 1607 to Virginia makes the point: coming from the Canary Islands

> the first that wee could recover was the Ile of Saint Lucia...where we refreshed ourselves with wood and water (Stoneman 1906 [1607])

In another account, Anthony Hilton who settled Nevis in 1628 describes how he came to St Kitts when

---

[5] St Lucia would at this time have been a prime timber source for Barbados, whose landscape had been denuded by intensive cultivation by this time. Bridenbaugh and Bridenbaugh (1972) point out that Sloane (1707 Volume 1, 41) describes this population supplying wood as fuel and for ship timbers to Barbados.

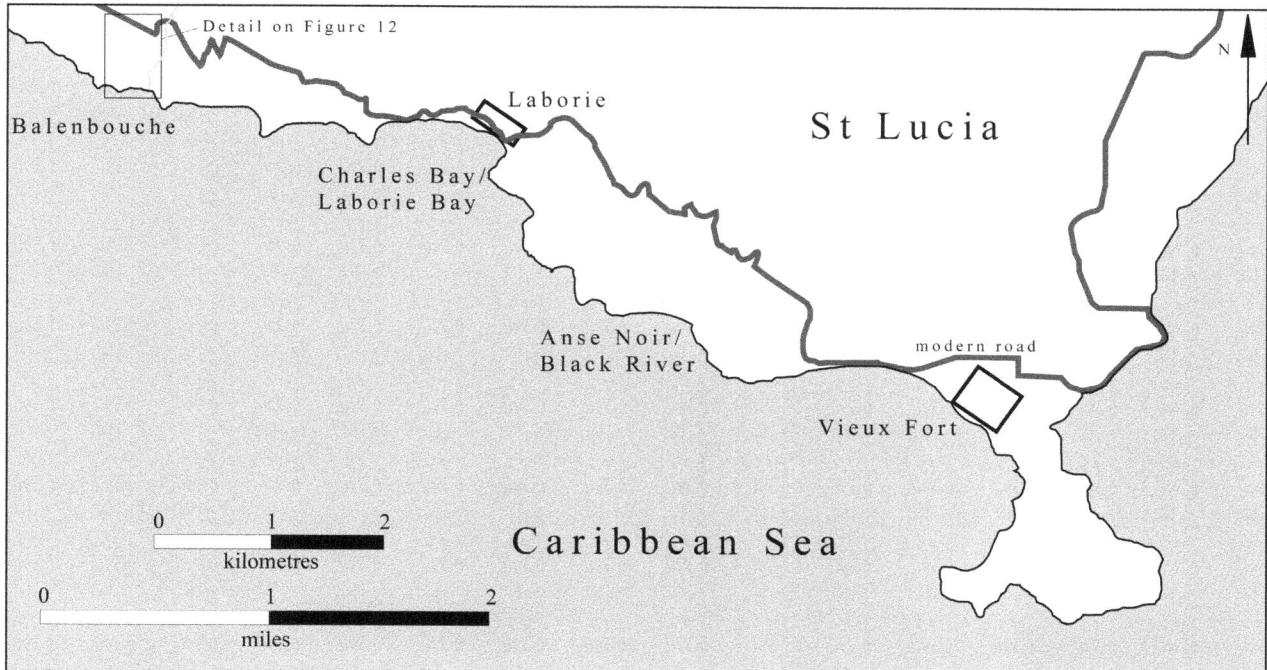

FIGURE 11. THE SOUTH COAST OF ST LUCIA, WITH SITES REFERRED TO IN THE TEXT

imployed by ye merchants of Barstable in ye west country for a voyage to Virginia, pass[ed] by St Christophers, as they knew no other way (Hilton 1925 [1675], Games 1999, 193).

Many contemporary accounts describe European sailors, after a long journey across the Atlantic, resting for several days at various locations in the Lesser Antilles: enjoying the good water supplies, and perhaps trading in salt from the ubiquitous salt pans. Captain John Smith stated in 1629 that

[i]n this little Ile of Mevis, more than twenty years agoe, I have remained a good time together, to wood and water and refresh my men (Smith 1908 [1629], 4).

In the early 17th century the Lesser Antilles were, then, within the busy circuit of European presence in the Caribbean that had been expanding for over a century. Some islands, such as St Kitts and Pigeon Island off the north-west coast of St Lucia, also appear to have been used as privateering bases during the 16th century (Watts 1987, 134, 142).

Secondly, the coastal landscapes of particular islands can be studied at a scale that is broader than particular sites or documented settlements. Locations such as Wingfield and Balenbouche were clearly attractive for their sheltered, leeward location and their proximity to good rivers for fresh water: as Henry Colt wrote of the settlement at Old Road in 1631, 'water is to be prised above any thinge els.'[6]

In the case of the south-east coast of St Lucia it is clear that physical geography of the area from Vieux Fort to Ance Noir, Laborie, and Balenbouche marks it out as a distinctive natural landscape (**Figure 11**). A broad, almost flat area slopes very gently away from a sheltered coastline of sandy beaches and good harbours. The ground breaks into steep hills to the north and west. Numerous large rivers run down from the higher ground. In this corner of the island, three main bays form natural harbours. The historic place name evidence for these harbours is informative. A map surveyed in 1775 (Jeffreys 1780) shows Ance de Vieux Fort, Ance Noir and Ance de Charles (modern Laborie).[7] The name 'Ance Charles' is suggestive of a reference to Charles I or II, place names which are common in the early English Atlantic world (e.g. Charles Fort at Old Road, St Kitts or Charlestown on Nevis).[8] Equally, the river at Ance Noir is labelled – in English – Black River: another common English colonial name of the 17th century, and the original name of the Wingfield River at Old Road, St Kitts. The town of Vieux Fort lies on a good river with a wide, sheltered bay. Two small hills rise up within the area of the modern town. Assuming these are natural features, these form dramatic positions within the harbour. In the mid-1960s, archaeologist Ripley Bullen (1966a) attempted to identify the location of the 1605 Oliph Blossome

---

[6] In the place name 'Old Road', 'Road' is clearly used in the sense of 'a sheltered piece of water near the shore where vessels may lie at anchor in safety; a roadstead' (Oxford English Dictionary).

[7] Thomas Jefferys 1829, St Lucia, done from surveys and observations made by the English whilst in their possession (National Archives CO700.St.Lucia.7).

[8] This is not to suggest that such names are necessarily contemporary with the reign of kings of the same name however. For instance, an indenture of September 1641 refers to the sale by William Warden to 'Simon Gordon, merchant' for 20000 lbs of tobacco of land 'near Prince Charles fort in the p. of St Thomas of 120 paces width' (Oliver 1908-17, Volume 3, 320).

settlement from Nicholl's description. He concluded that Vieux Fort was the most probable location. Purchas also provides a second contemporary account: that of William Turner, who wrote

> In this bay there are Halfe a dozen of Indian houses very pleasantly scituated upon the top of a hill, with a fresh water River at the foote of the same hill (Bullen 1966a, 30, quoting from Turner 1906 [1606]).

A plan of Vieux Fort bay from 1742 clearly shows the north-western of the two small hills to the east of the river in Vieux Fort as 'Hauteur ou les Anglais avoient construit un fort en 1663'. 'Anciens Retranchements que les Anglois avoient fait en 1663' are also shown to the south -west, with a 'Batterie' at the western extreme.[9] While the evidence remains inconclusive, it is very probably that the remains of 17th-century settlement survive at Vieux Fort. This evidence is in keeping with the letter from Willoughby recommending that the English settlement be established at 'Old Road' (= Vieux Fort, St Lucia).

The Lesser Antilles continued as a 'corridor' for ships entering the Caribbean, and complex landscapes of interaction developed at sheltered locations along this line of intersection between the European and Indigenous worlds. Similar settlements can be seen on other islands: at Plymouth, Kingsale and Stapletown on Montserrat (Pulsipher 1977 Figure 5) at Jamestown in Nevis, or at Old Road, Antigua. A glimpse of the haphazard complexities of landscape change is provided by a description of the settlement of Nevis written by John Smith in 1629. Describing an initial attempt to settle an island which is probably Barbuda rather than Barbados, Smith states that

> The last year, 1628, Master Littleton, with some others got a Pattent of the Earl of Carlisle, to plant the Ile called the Barbados, thirty miles northward of Saint Christophers; which...they called Dulcina, but when they came there, they found it such a barren rocke, they left it...At last...they came to Mevis, a little Ile by Saint Christophers; where they seated themselves, well furnished with all necessaries, being about the number of an hundred, and since increased to an hundred and fifty persons, whereof many were old planters of Saint Christophers, especially Master Anthony Hinton and Master Edward Thompson (Smith 1908 [1629], 4).

Rather than smoothing out such accounts to construct historical narratives of increasing permanence (and European dominance) at particular settlements, by looking at landscape at several scales of analysis, a more satisfactory archaeological account of early colonial encounters can be generated – highlighting interactions across the region. At smaller scales – those of enclosure – this benefit of such approaches is most clear, as the role of these places as locations for material exchange can be brought into focus.

Enclosure, Exchange and Ethnogenesis

Between the 1580s and 1620s, a general shift in English activities in the Caribbean took places, from privateering in the Greater Antilles to trading in the Lesser Antilles. This was a crucial part of the process which Carole Shammas has termed 'the commercializing of colonization' (Shammas 1978, 170, 173). There are numerous accounts of English ships travelling, especially in the Windward Islands, at this time actively seeking marketable products. By far the most important of these new commodities was tobacco (Shammas 1978; Keymis 1904 [1596], 478; Lorimer 1978). The significance of the Lesser Antilles in the development of English colonialism at this time was, however, more than a case of an area being subject to new impulses and desires from the metropole: the landscapes of enclosure and the complex social situations that they brought about were crucial elements in this process.

Very little is known about the historical anthropology of eastern Caribbean Indigenous exchange systems and how they changed during the period of European contact. One important source of evidence here is documentary sources. For St Lucia, two travellers' accounts dating from 1607 hold useful accounts for capturing some of the qualities of the exchanges of early European-Carib contact (Nicholl 1966 [1605], Stoneman 1903 [1607]; cf. Graecocke 1752 [1623]). Both Nicholl's and Stoneman's accounts are punctuated by descriptions of great quantities of material goods, especially on the arrival of the ships. Stoneman describes how

> certain of the Savages there, about fourtie or fiftie, came unto us at our Ship in one of the Cannoas, bringing us Tobacco, Potatos, Plantins and Cassava Bred (Stoneman 1906 [1607]).

In Nicholl's account, no sooner had they anchored, but

> the Carebyes came in their Periagoes or Boats aboard us with great store of Tobacco, Plantains, Potatoes, Pines, Sugar Canes, and other divers fruits, with Hens, Chickens, Turtles and Iguanas... (Nicholl 1966 [1607], 49).

Again,

> After the departure of our ship we remained in peaceable manner amongst the Indians, daily trading with them for all manner of victual as Plantains, Potatoes, Penas, Papains, Pumpkins, Callobashes, Pappes, Mammies, Guavas, with divers other fruits, and Tobacco abundance, all very pleasant to eat. Also they brought Turtles, Iguanas, Hens and Chickens, Wood-cocks and Snipes, with some Pelicans (Nicholl ibid, 51).

---

[9] *Plan de la Paye ou Rade du Vieux Fort des Anglois situé a la Bande sy Sud de l'Isle de Ste Lucie fait par Houel, Ingenieur en Chef aux Iles du Vent, le 1e Mars 1742.* Bibliotheque Nationale, Paris: Portefeuille 157, Division 11 M 1 (Reproduced in Bruneau-Latouche and Bruneau-Latouche 1989, 71).

And again,

> A little before our arrival, three Spanish ships were cast away, and much of the goods these Indians had saved with their Boats, and hid it in the Woods, they had so much Roan cloth, that all their Periagoes had sails thereof. They also had great store of stuff, Serge, and Spanish woollen cloth, cloaks and apparell: insomuch that if we had a barque of forty tons burthen, we could have laden her home with such commodities as would have made a saving voyage. All which we could have bought for hatchets, knives, beads, fish-hooks, and thimbles, with other trifles (Nicholl *ibid*, 52).

These descriptions are characterised not only by remarkable quantities of material goods, but by a mixture of European commodities and local produce – including domesticated animals as well as tropical staples and subsistence agricultural produce. An examination of local agricultural production is therefore an important part of understanding early colonial interaction in this period, and the character of Indigenous agriculture during the 16th and 17th centuries, and its relationship with the changing exchange systems of colonial contact, emerge as central issues.

The archaeological focus in this field has been upon subsistence agriculture. Carib agriculture has been considered by Lydia Pulsipher in relation to 17th-century Montserrat (1977, 23-27), where she discusses evidence for shifting and permanent agricultural practices. Highlighting Raymond Breton's description of the Leeward Islands, which describes swidden agricultural clearance, she argues that such slash-and-burn techniques were probably part of a system of shifting cultivation (Breton 1958 [1665], Pulsipher 1977, 24). However, there is considerable evidence that such subsistence agriculture was complemented by the production and trade of staples such as cotton or tobacco at an early date. A passage from Dr Chanca's descriptions of the Lesser Antilles from 1493, during Columbus' second voyage, throws into doubt the conventional model of prehistoric subsistence agriculture:

> They had much cotton, woven and ready to weave, and many cotton sheets, so well made as to lose nothing by comparison with those of our own country (Jane 1930, 30).

On St Kitts, in addition to the examples cited above, an indenture of land to John Jeaffreson and Edward Johnson dated 1628 describes their taking over of 'gardens late belonginge to the Indians the Savage Natives of that Island' (Jeaffreson Mss M3b (1628) Indenture of Land to John Jeaffreson and Edward Johnson). Contemporary documentary sources describe a substantial 'Carib' population and 'Indian gardens' on Saint Kitts when the English settlement was established in 1624 (Oldmixon 1969 [1741], 265-280), and 18th-century European accounts suggest that St Kitts was called *Liammuiga* – the fertile island – by Caribs. There are several accounts of the Carib population on St Kitts introducing British settlers in the 1630s to local methods of cassava and sweet potato cultivation (Watts 1987, 152). Moreover, in his description of his own plantation Henry Colt, who settled on St Kitts in 1631, suggests earlier Carib cultivation of sugar and 'Anotto' dyes alongside plantains on the site:

> We weer alsoe seated amongst plantaines & sugar canes yt growes like ye reeds or canes in ye ponds of England, very sweet in tast, but vnholsome. Alsoe planted ther was Anotto, a low tree wth a codd wch opens, & little smale redd berryes appeare wher wth ye Indians colour themselues. This was anciently a plantation of ye Indians, butt now all ouergrowne (Colt 1925 [1631], 90-91).

Scattered references such as these have been largely overlooked in previous accounts of Caribbean landscape change. Where they have been examined, the Carib population has been presented as an unchanging, prehistoric population: simply waiting for European contact (compare Wolf 1982). Rather than such populations being the last generation of long-term prehistoric occupation of the islands, an alternative perspective is to see Carib societies as dynamic, active and changing. For example, historical geographer David Watts' concern over references to sugar cane being already present on St Kitts, Martinique, Guadeloupe and St Vincent before permanent English or French settlement suggest to him the possibility that sugar was a 'pre-Columbian cultigen or wild plant in this region' (Watts 1987, 77). But while Watts makes it clear that it is far more probable that sugar was introduced by the Spanish in the last years of the 15th century, he does not consider the possibility that a Carib population could have planted such crops, having obtained sugar cane from the Spanish.

In western Europe, tobacco, sugar, indigo and spices such as ginger were increasingly available, albeit in small quantities, during the 16th century, and many of these were brought from the West Indies. Could some of these commodities have come from the eastern Caribbean? Lennox Honychurch has considered this question:

> Caribs appeared to be adding 'commercial' tobacco farming to subsistence farming. Alternatively they could have been redirecting their surplus from internal exchange networks to external ones. It is however questionable whether internal systems ever required such quantities. Whatever the source of supply, it appears that the Caribs had some significant influence on external tobacco trading (Honychurch 1997, 299).

Turning to the question of trade and exchange, the relationship between Indigenous exchange systems and emergent capitalism has been a significant theme in social anthropology in recent years (Thomas 1991). As Alfred Gell (1992) pointed out in his classic critique of traditional anthropological studies of gift exchange in Papua New Guinea, the exchange systems examined by anthropologists, far from representing 'primordial' situations, very often came about as a new form of exchange in response to colonial contact – through a 'hybridisation' of 'sharing' or 'generalised reciprocity' and 'swapping' or 'commodity exchange' which created a multivalent, ambiguous gesture:

'Neither fish nor fowl nor good red herring, the gift is admirably calculated to divert attention and conceal motives while certain crucial rearrangements of social relationships occur' (Gell 1992, 143).

Such engagement with the historical processes of colonial interaction offers ways of moving beyond the 'Carib invasion'/'Arawak continuity' debate – acknowledging the agency and complexity of 'Carib' populations. As Lennox Honychurch has argued,

Continuous interaction stimulated a heterogeneous Carib identity which resulted in a diversity of responses to contact and meant that interaction was a key part of Carib cultural logics which was given a new thrust with the meeting of Europeans. (Honychurch 1997, 294)

We may extend Honychurch's description of the continuing Carib population on Dominica to suggest that such 'stimulation' through 'interaction' played a role in the formation of Carib identities during the early colonial period. In this view the documentary accounts from the 17th and 18th century of the earlier appearance of 'warlike Caribs' in the eastern Caribbean would refer to the 16th and early 17th centuries rather than to the pre-contact period. Further evidence that Carib identity was influenced through historical processes of exchange during the early colonial period is provided by considering the limited archaeological and documentary evidence. Previous archaeological studies have found Caribs archaeologically elusive: but the identification here of 'enclosed gardens' as a distinctive settlement type allows access into the landscapes of early colonial encounters.

It is possible, then, that historically documented Caribs were significantly more complex and diverse populations, actively engaged in the formation of new landscapes of colonial encounters, than has been previously acknowledged. The impact of large permanent Spanish settlements in the Greater Antilles must have led to a fast-changing situation across the eastern Caribbean. There is some evidence that significant numbers of 'Tainos' migrated to the Lesser Antilles in flight from the Spanish, while tens of thousands of slaves were raided from across the Caribbean and the South American mainland to supply labour for Spanish plantations and gold mines. As suggested above, some islands in the Lesser Antilles may have been completely depopulated, although a Spanish attempt in 1526 to settle Guadeloupe was resisted (Wilson 1993, 48-9). It is suggested here, following the arguments of Jalil Sued-Badillo and others, that these displaced 'Tainos', along with free indentured servants, escaped slaves and many other assorted people made up an emerging 'Carib' population. Indeed, there are numerous descriptions of escaped slaves living among the Caribs (e.g. Higham 1921, 130). Carib ethnogenesis, then, may have been an ongoing process during early European contact and colonialism, including people of both European and African extraction from an early date (cf. Sued-Badillo 1986). Similar processes, in which ethnic boundaries were complex and sometime permeable, are visible in the documented life of 'Indian' Warner: the son of the 'pioneer' of St Kitts Sir Thomas Warner and an Indian woman, who went on to play a crucial role in European-Carib relations in the Windward Islands during the 1670s (Burns 1954, 201-2; See also Higham 1921, 131-4).

The shift from earlier fine wares to unglazed, clamp-fired, utilitarian ceramics is entirely in keeping with a new, displaced population. One other possibility, however, is that such crude ceramics are an indication of the low importance placed on locally-made ceramics. A new value system, fed by the constant arrival of exotic European goods and commodities, appears to have led to a new emphasis on the acquisition of such items (by growing and bartering 'cash crops') and their exchange.

The case of Old Road supports the model of new Carib identities emerging as part of the processes of colonialism and contact. Documentary sources suggest that the settlement at Old Road, St Kitts was set up at some point prior to 1622, when Thomas Warner visited the settlement from Roger North's settlement at Guiana. Several accounts of Sir Francis Drake's four-day stay in St Kitts in Christmas 1585, *en route* to Santo Domingo, report that there 'were not any people at all that we could heare of' (Keeler 1981). But this is in contrast with the recorded presence of Caribs there in the early 1620s, when the inhabitants appeared to be well known to the Guianan settlers. Clearly, the processes of human mobility, landscape enclosure, and material exchange were bound up closely across the eastern Caribbean during this period. Far from a narrative of firsts, pioneers and mother colonies, the picture from archaeology is one of a frontier zone in which new landscapes were being formed: landscapes which were to influence the later development of the region.

Conclusions

This chapter has suggested that practices of enclosure, documented in both 'Carib' and English situations, were closely bound up with processes of material exchange and agricultural production for trade, and with diversity and ethnogenesis during colonial encounters. Here, an alternative narrative of colonial interactions emerges: a regional model of material interactions, rather than biographical stories of permanency and pioneers, which are ultimately mortgaged to uncritical, early 20th-century historiographies of empire. The chapter has pointed to commonalities between the situations in St Kitts and southern St Lucia – places usually treated as the 'mother colony' of English colonialism in the Caribbean, and as an apparent backwater, respectively. Such commonalities relate to landscape processes, and are revealed through methods that operate across a number of geographical scales.

Enclosure took many forms: from stone walls and wooden palisades to segmented ditches. The idea of enclosing landscape was perhaps even visible in the actions of French Governor De Poincy, following his arrival in St Kitts in 1639: he created what a contemporary account described as a 'superbe chasteau': a castle and a palace, with large gardens and waterworks enclosed by walls of bricks imported from Europe, and a central three-storied building of brick and stone (du Tertre 1654, 26). Such landscapes contrast markedly with the later landscapes of sugar monoculture that will be described in Chapter 4 below.

The material presented in this chapter reveals the importance of acknowledging the active role of Indigenous populations in the shaping of colonial landscape. Enclosed 'gardens' provided commodities for trade and exchange during the early contact period, and were places for such exchange to take place. At the same time, alongside encounters and enclosure, colonial interactions and Carib ethnogenesis are important parts of this account. One parallel for the phenomena described here is provided by the archaeological studies of Palmares in north-eastern Brazil (Orser 1994; Funari 1999; Rowlands 1999). Part of this parallel relates to the form of the landscape: contemporary descriptions point to the provision of an enclosure around Palmares, and the only known image of Palmares shows a tall, narrow wooden tower (Orser 1996 Figure 2). Parallels also exist in broader terms: documentary sources suggest that this settlement developed at this coastal location during the 16th century, and thrived on the periphery of the Dutch sugar plantations at Pernambuco between *c.* 1612 and 1694. Some evidence points to the development of the population of Palmares as a 'runaway slave settlement' (Orser 1996, 41-3), but as Michael Rowlands has pointed out we must consider 'to what extent Palmares was multi-ethnic rather than a runaway slave settlement and to what extent it was anti-colonial', and investigate its role as a regional trade entrepôt (Orser 1996, 41-3; Rowlands 1999, 334).

The perspectives of landscape archaeology provide a material focus that can highlight the complexities of such situations. This is in contrast with a focus purely upon the ideologies or ideas of European colonialism: in many cases, the complex processes of interaction have been glossed over in the belief that 'the English settlers tended to perceive, if not actively construct, a *tabula rasa* whatever the reality', as Matthew Johnson (1996, 94), discussing Virginia and Ireland, has put it. In relation to the enclosures studied here, the recognition by some archaeologists of strong similarities between the palisaded enclosures or 'bawns' known from plantations in Munster and Ulster, Ireland and Virginia, USA requires discussion.

The enclosed landscapes described here are not unlike those landscapes, and in acknowledging global contexts, it is important to examine the contemporary attitudes to agricultural landscape in England. James Deetz (1993) argued that such enclosures are particularly characteristic of such early colonial situations, but parallels might also be drawn with late medieval processes of enclosure in England – which later culminated in parliamentary enclosure – that have been associated by Johnson (1996) with the commodification and the emergence of capitalism (cf. Johnson 1991). Indeed, archaeologists have discussed similarities between the plantation of Ireland and the plantation of Virginia since Ivor Noël Hume's (1979, 237) discussion of the early English plantation at Martin's Hundred, and such comparisons are now common-place in American historical archaeology. However, the Caribbean material presented here requires some qualification of the Noël Hume-Deetz model. The 17th-century Atlantic was not simply an arena for the extension of a number of uniform European cultures, and their interaction with normative Indigenous or African populations. Rather, it was a complex, varied, hybrid series of frontiers and exchanges, in which objects and landscapes were central. Landscape archaeology's material focus requires an acknowledgement of the many periods of landscape change, and the relationships between them: perspectives that require an engagement with the prehistory, as well as the historical archaeology, of the eastern Caribbean, and the period 'between impact and contact', from the early 16th century to the English settlement of St Kitts in 1624 (Deetz 1991, 5, cf. Games 1999, 212-4).

Overall, the foundations of English 'pioneer' colonialism in the eastern Caribbean were far more complex, and multicultural, than conventional Anglo-American historical accounts suggest. By adopting a long-term landscape perspective, archaeology is able to highlight the agency of undocumented populations – including the diverse Carib populations, which included Indigenous people, freed European indentured servants and escaped African slaves – in the emergence of the eastern Caribbean as a central location in the spread of European colonialism. In the distinctive settlement type of the enclosed landscape – used for agriculture and for exchange – the exchanges between European and non-European populations are visible. It is argued here that, *pace* James Deetz, any impulses towards standardisation in 'creating a colonial outpost' were radically modified by local material and human conditions, and by the shifting contexts of maritime trade and exchange.

The Carib and European enclosed settlements described here were part of a sphere of interaction which stretched along the arc of the Lesser Antilles. The importance of these observations will become clear in the next chapter, when continuities in landscape form in St Kitts will be explored. Arguably, the later landscapes of European colonialism in the eastern Caribbean were built upon an appropriation of

'Carib' livelihoods. But while the processes of commodity production and exchange outlined in this chapter, continued into the 18th century, such appropriations grew in violence during the 17th century, as increasingly English and French colonial populations 'seized the land on which to conduct the business of tobacco farming and export themselves' (Honychurch 1997, 299; see also Goodman 1993, 132). In the next chapter, the influence of the 'Carib' settlements of the frontier zone of the Lesser Antilles not just on the early development of 17th-century landscapes of settler colonialism, but on the early landscapes of sugar cultivation, will be explored further. Thus, landscape archaeology can offer a distinctive way of acknowledging the influence of 'prehistoric' situations on those of early colonial period, and the permeabilities between documented and undocumented situations.

CHAPTER 3

SUGAR LANDSCAPES

By the 1670s, sugar could be described by an English planter on St Kitts as 'the only thriving and valuable commodity' (Jeaffreson to Colonel George Gamiell, London. 12 May 1677. Jeaffreson 1878 Vol. 1, 210-212). This chapter explores the material dimensions of the beginning of this shift to sugar in the Leeward Islands and Barbados, with special reference to St Kitts, which would radically transform the landscapes of the eastern Caribbean in the coming decades. In doing so, the narrative focuses upon the actions and ideas of an elite group of white planters. This choice is made in order, as argued throughout this study, to reveal the material complexities of the emerging ideology of racial slavery, and to contribute to archaeologies of the modern world that seek to find new ways of studying the European colonialism.

The second half of the 17th century saw increasing crown control of the English colonies. A new state attitude to trade developed: a phenomenon generally termed 'mercantilism' (Smith 1776). The mercantile state promoted the accumulation of gold and silver, and sought to maintain a favourable balance of trade through discouraging imports and encouraging exports. Central to these efforts were the Navigation Acts (1651, 1660, 1670 and 1696) and the Tariff (1661) which were designed, in the face of Dutch competition, to maintain the balance of trade by tying English Caribbean sugar planters to English ships and the home market. Meanwhile, the Staple Act of 1663 required that European goods destined for the English colonies passed through an English port *en route*. While the impacts of these Acts have been widely discussed in economic history, legislation in the colonies, which was often based upon similar mercantile principles, also affected Atlantic trade: for example the 1670s, Barbados, Nevis, St Kitts, Antigua and Jamaica passed laws stipulating that planters provide a minimum number of indentured servants alongside slaves – thus creating an artificial demand which kept the trade in servants to the eastern Caribbean going into the early 18th century (Emerson Smith 1947, 31-2). In parallel with control of trade, this period saw increased state control of the colonies. 'Grants' of 4½ percent duties were enforced, and crown rule was imposed from 1675, with the setting up of the Lords Committee of Trade.

The proprietary patents, which had dominated the development of English-controlled landscapes in the eastern Caribbean, were almost entirely withdrawn in 1670, although with a few minor exceptions: such as the small non sugar-producing island of Barbuda, which continued after 1685 to be leased to the Codrington family until the 19th century.[10] As Williamson (1926, 103) describes, the loss of proprietary rights was a complex historical process that developed from the 1630s. For the first time, in the 1670s under James II, colonial governors without estates or other vested interests in the New World were increasingly chosen by the English government. The new freedoms in land ownership contributed to a radical shift in the nature of colonial projects in eastern Caribbean. In particular, agriculture saw a shift towards sugar monoculture in Barbados, Jamaica and increasingly in the Leeward Islands as well. The factors that contributed to this shift have, however, previously only been considered in broad-brush macro-economic terms: for instance Batie (1976) cites a decrease in the profitability of tobacco planting during the late 1630s, especially after a 'bumper Virginia harvest' in 1638 and 1639. While economic historians have restricted their studies to broad Atlantic contexts, social histories in the Caribbean have rarely considered the shift to sugar during the closing decades of the 17th century at all: preferring to discuss better-documented 18th-century situations. This has led to a lack of historiographic detail, in which studies of sugar and slaves have inappropriately transferred 18th-century situations back into the 17th century, seeing the first decades of colonial settlement as simply laying the foundations for the developed sugar and slave economies, in narratives very similar to the accounts of 'pioneer' origins critiqued in the previous chapter.

At the outset, it should be noted that far more documents relating to the 17th century survive from Barbados and Jamaica than from the other parts of the English Caribbean. This is mainly because both islands continued in British possession until independence in the 1980s, and so there was continuity in record-keeping which was not the same for the Leewards and Windwards, where warfare and sudden political changes led to the survival of far fewer documents. Accordingly, where the late 17th century has been studied by documentary historians, the experiences on the precocious sugar islands Barbados and Jamaica have been focused upon and regional processes and local variations within the Caribbean have been overlooked as researchers have written from their desks in Oxford or New York, Bridgetown or Kingston (e.g. Dunn 1972;

---

[10] For an annual rent of 'one fat sheep, if demanded' (Hall 1971, 59-95).

Bridenbaugh and Bridenbaugh 1972; Watts 1987).[11] By focusing upon the distinctive period of the shift to sugar from the late 17th century, and by developing an account from the perspective of St Kitts – rather than only Barbados or Jamaica – the perspectives of landscape archaeology (combining documents and material remains to build accounts of the shifting materialities of colonial situations, in fine-grained chronological detail) provides an important counterpoint to conventional historiographies.

Early Sugar Production

Portuguese sugar plantations had been established in the New World – in Brazil – as early as the 1530s, although their history and archaeology remains obscure (Blackburn 1997, 166-174; cf. Eubanks 1992, 35-6; Wolf 1982, 111-112, 150). However, the 1630s saw the large-scale production of sugar, similar to its earlier cultivation in the Mediterranean, established by the Dutch in Pernambuco and Bahia on the Brazilian coast (Boxer 1957, Flory and Smith 1978, Watts 1987, 178-182). Standard historical accounts of the transition to sugar in the English Caribbean (e.g. Dunn 1972, Sheridan 1973, Watts 1987) see the 'Pernambuco model of sugar production' *transferred* to Barbados, especially after the end of Dutch sugar production in Brazil after 1654. These accounts suggest that sugar manufacture and processing was then, in turn, transferred to other Caribbean locations from Barbados. This model is largely based on Richard Ligon's account of a Brazilian source for the first sugar cane in Barbados, which described how early planters there received

> new directions from Brazil, sometimes by strangers, and now and then by their own people, who...were content to make a voyage thither, to improve their knowledge in a thing they so much desired (Ligon 1657, 85).

Ligon also reports that in Barbados

> At the time we landed on this island, which was in the beginning of September 1647, we were informed that the great work of sugar making was but newly practised here (Ligon *ibid.*).

Another contemporary source describes Barbados as 'full of sugar' in 1646 (Massachusetts Historical Society 1947, 83-4). Indeed, it appears that sugar cultivation had been adopted on Barbados and on the French island of Martinique during the late 1630s or 1640s. In economic histories, the date of 1643 is often quoted for the date of the first significant exports of sugar from Barbados (e.g. Batie 1976, 1). At the same time, however, new Dutch sugar colonies were established in the late 1650s in Guyana and Surinam. This makes the 'transfer' model problematic: the

time-scales are such that it is more satisfactory to see the Dutch, French and English shifts to sugar as part of a more complex regional phenomenon: a new impulse towards permanency and investment in the agricultural production of a range of tropical staples.

The histories of pastoral and ranching activities, and of clearance for a frontier timber trade, have been little studied, but are likely to have been significant in the eastern Caribbean in the 17th century: there is, for example, no evidence that English settlers established tanneries, although several are documented in Spanish Jamaica (Dunn 1972, 151). Meanwhile, early sugar production took place alongside the continued cultivation of a range of tropical staples across the eastern Caribbean: including tobacco, coffee, ginger, indigo, pimento, and cocoa – as well, presumably, as Carib provisions such as cassava, manioc and sweet potatoes (Labat 1722, 351-63). A range of tropical staples were grown in St Kitts during this early phase of settlement – including indigo, tobacco cotton and sugar. Tobacco cultivation in St Kitts was prohibited by Governor Warner between 1639 and 1641, in an apparent attempt to force the English price up. The history of the cultivation and processing of these products in the 17th century is obscure, but to a large extent presumably continued at the enclosures described in Chapter 2. Different crops brought different material requirements for cultivation and processing. Tobacco, for example, simply needs to be grown, dried in an open-sided building, and rolled for shipment. Relatively complex processes are involved of indigo or cotton production, as well as tobacco production (Davies 1666, 189). The cultivation and ginning of cotton is a complex process, but simpler than indigo production, which requires great attention during cultivation due to its vulnerability to weeds. Indigo processing requires a series of (usually three) stone tanks arranged on descending levels, in which the leaves are steeped in order to induce residue precipitation in the lowest vat, the oxidisation of the precipitate, and fermentation (Bridges-Lee 1892). The remaining indigo is dried and cured. A drying shed and a good source of fresh water are also required. All of these products required relatively small areas for cultivation. Sugar production required larger areas of land to be cultivated, and a considerable increase in investment in the infrastructure of processing compared with previous crops.

The Shift to Sugar in St Kitts

In the Leewards, these impulses towards investment and permanency that were part of the shift to sugar took place during a turbulent and unpredictable period (*Table 1*) – especially for St Kitts, right up until the ceding of the lands of French St Kitts to the British in 1713. The catalogue of documented disasters suffered by the early settlers of St Kitts demonstrates the point. Thomas Warner's first tobacco crop was destroyed by a hurricane on the 19th September 1625, and numerous hurricanes struck the

---

[11] On the shifts in West Indian historiography, shifting from significant power bases in Oxford, London, to Cambridge and North America, and then to the new University of the West Indies in Barbados and Jamaica during the second half of the 20th century, see Higman 1999b, 89-121.

Dates	War	Concluding Treaty
1652-1654	First Anglo-Dutch War	-
1665-1667	Second Anglo-Dutch War	Treaty of Breda 1667
1672-1674-8	Third Anglo-Dutch War	Treaty of Westminster 1674
1688-1697	War of the Grand Alliance	Treaty of Ryswyck 1697
1702-1713	War of the Spanish Succession	Treaty of Utrecht 1713
1739-1748	War of Jenkins' Ear; War of the Austrian Succession	Treaty of Aix-la-Chapelle 1748
1756-1763	Seven Years' War	Treaty of Paris 1763
1776-1783	War of American Independence AND associated Caribbean action	Treaty of Versailles 1783
1791-1804	Revolution of St Domingue/Haiti	–
1793-1815	French Revolution and Napoleonic Wars	Treaty of Amiens 1802 Treaty of Paris 1814 Congress of Vienna 1815

Table 1. Major Wars and treaties affecting development in the West Indies during the 18th century (based upon Watts 1987, Table 6.3 and Merrill 1957, Table 4)

island, including three in one year in 1680 (Smith 1908 [1629], 188). Political instability was also a problem on occasions: in 1642, an unsuccessful rebellion against Governor Warner was led by one Phance Beecher (Bennett 1967). Warner was Governor until his death in 1649, whereupon he was succeeded by Roland Rich, a royalist (Higham 1921, 34). Military conflict led to great instability in the island: St Kitts changed hands between the English and the French seven times between 1666 and 1713. The crops and buildings of early planter settlements on St Kitts were destroyed by a Spanish fleet on 7th September 1629, and hostages were taken (Davies 1666, 163-8, 177).

St Kitts was also greatly affected by French attacks in April 1666, 1689 and February 1706. A sketch of the events of 1666 and 1706 will serve to underline their impact. The attacks of April 1666 began with a defeat at Sandy Point, during which Deputy Governor Watts was killed. The English retreated to Old Road and vented their frustration with the governor by pillaging his home. Terms of surrender were negotiated quickly after the English defeat at Sandy Point, and the French Governor Saint Laurent led his army to Old Road Town and took Fort Charles with no resistance. The Protestant church at Old Road was taken over by the French Catholic clergy, and renamed St Louis, Roi de France. The French quickly went about expelling the English population, and a contemporary (French) source claims that 8000 English inhabitants left St Kitts in 1666 for Virginia, Jamaica and Nevis. The French capture of St Kitts in 1666 is described at length by du Tertre (1654, IV, 1-52, cf. Du Tertre *ibid*, 62 and Higham 1921 45-47, 58-9; Crouse 1940, 49-50; April 1666 CSPC 1661-8, 1179.m). The restitution of St Kitts occurred with the Treaty of Breda in 1667, although the English did not re-occupy English St Kitts until July 1671, and even then the land was still largely held by 'French squatters' (Higham 1921, 81). Several accounts describe the pillaging of estates at the orders of Colbert by the French as they departed:

The peace was concluded ye 21-31 July 1667, a Coppy whereof did appeare ye French. And about ye last of October following heare did arrive ye Articles of ye peace made at Breda; att which time there came a Comand from ye french nacion [to] ye Inhabitants of this Island. Commanding all ye English Inhabitants then heare residing to keepe theire habitacions from Sunn Sett to Sunn riding upon perill of their lives. By which meanes and att which time from the latter end of October aforesaid to ye May following (then my Lord Willoughby appeared) they did transporte & carry away from ye English quarters all ye timber of our churches, & bells, ye Cannon belonging to ye forts, & demolished the said forts, & all ye timber of other housen & buildings Standing upon those plantacions called by the French ye Kings land because they were abandoned some by the proprietors, & of others that were Slaine in ye Combate, with many other housen & good buildings, & Coppers sold for a very small value, besides ye demolishing many good Indigeo & Sugar workes, the destruccion of all ye timber in ye woods & mountaines which hath made ye Inhabitants incapable of rebuilding; To ye utter ruine of us ye poore inhabits heare (29/4/1675, Harlow 1925, 22; cf. Higham 1921, 82-3).

However, further French invasions occurred in 1689 and 1706. The latter, on 11 February 1706, was a major attack by a French force of 2000 men commanded by Count de Chavagnac, and plantations, houses and cane fields burnt and pillaged across English St Kitts for seven days. Substantial claims for compensation for damage inflicted on English estates during the French occupation of English St Kitts of 1666-1671 and 1706 were made, and detailed claims survive in the National Archives at Kew. [12]

---

[12] CO 243/2 (1706) *An Account of the Losses sustained by the proprietors and inhabitants of the island because of the invasion of the French.* See also 13/8/1666, APC Col. 1613-1680, 686; 13/11/1667 CSPC 1661-8, 1629.

	Sugar (lb)	Tobacco (lb)
Nevis	39 064	27 516lb
St Kitts	2 444	89 368
Antigua	–	119 240
Montserrat	1 741	43 278
TOTAL	43 249	279 402

Table 2. Debts owed by Leeward Island planters to Dutch merchants in 1655 (after Dunn 1972)

The precise time-scales of the transition to sugar in the Leeward Islands are difficult to unpick. Many secondary histories list the numbers of windmills or cattle mills as indicators of this process, but this methodology cannot account for the taking in of other planters' sugar which, it has been argued here, characterised the early sugar landscape. A more promising point of entry into this process is Richard Dunn's tabulation of debts owed by Leeward Island planters to Dutch merchants in 1655 (*Table 2*). This shows a varied picture: and such inter-island variation underlines the limitations of many economic historians' attempts to characterise 'the sugar production of the Leeward Islands' at any particular date. The figures strongly suggest that Nevis was a major sugar producer by the mid 1650s, with the other English Leewards developing from the 1670s. This interpretation is also suggested by a description of 1652, which stated that Nevis

> is esteemed the best island for sugar: it makes little of any other commodities, only some tobacco to the windward. (Sheridan 1973, 162-3, quoting a 'Statement of an English man accompanying Prince Rupert on his West Indian voyage').

This early shift to sugar in Nevis appears to have been associated with the early role of Nevis' main town Charlestown as a trading centre. Just as nearby St Eustatius was established as a Dutch trading centre in the 1630s, Charlestown in Nevis developed as a major trading centre, especially as the first Leeward Islands' slave market for the Royal African Company (1671-1752) (Merrell 1957, 56; Higham 1921, 150). The presence of English-based companies such as the Royal African Company strongly influenced the adoption of sugar by planters in the Leewards. As economic historian Richard Sheridan put it,

> 'the transition to sugar was facilitated by the presence of a mercantile community which was large by comparison with that of neighbouring islands. Not only did the merchants and factors of Nevis supply goods and services to the planters, but they also used their trading profits and principals' effects to acquire plantations of their own' (Sheridan 1973, 163).

The relationships between trade and exchange and the shift to sugar in the Leewards will be explored further below, but first the material conditions of sugar production will be explored.

Producing sugar

Sugar itself brought particular requirements and constraints to the development of the agro-industrial landscapes of sugar production. It is the interaction between human agency, landscapes, the crop itself and a number of other heterogeneous components that is the focus of this section. The processes typical of 17th-century sugar manufacture in the eastern Caribbean are described in a number of documentary sources, most notably Richard Ligon's (1657) description of Barbados. This section will explore the natural and material details of the technology of sugar manufacture. Sugar cane is a large tropical or subtropical grass of the family *Gramineae*, originally of south-east Asian origin. It has a variable but long growing season (12-18 months). The Caribbean environment, with its lack of sharp changes in temperature during its growing season, and the autumn rainy season, was ideal for sugar. Sugar cane cultivation required relatively large fields, with seed cane cultivated along trenches or ridges. Planting appears to have usually taken place during the July-December rainy season (Barrett 1965; Goodwin 1987, 42).

After a 15-18 month growing season, harvesting involved the cutting of cane, and the removal of leaves. As Goodwin (1987, 44) observes, Ligon (1657) suggested a growing season of 15 months for Caribbean sugar, while Thomas (1690) suggests 18 months. Harvesting occurred in any season apart from the rainy season, because of the tendency of cut cane to rot when wet. After harvesting, cane fibres were chopped and crushed to extract cane juice, as swiftly as possible to avoid the cane drying out. The earliest crushing machines – *ingenios* – in the Caribbean consisted of three vertical rollers, between which the cane was passed. Deerr (1943, 3) suggests that the vertical three-roller crushing machine was present in Sicily in 1449. However, two-roller machines continued to be used in Brazil into the 17th century (Goodwin 1987, 22-3). These rollers may have been wooden, but from at least the 1660s, iron shells, usually manufactured in England, were supplied to encase wooden drums: for example, George Sitwell's iron works near Derby was producing iron sheaths for rollers for supply to the West Indies in 1663 (Sitwell 1888). The power for these rollers was derived from a mill – typically a cattle mill at the outset. However, as well as animal power, water- and wind-powered mills were common, according to local circumstances, from the 17th century. Water mills were not used until the 1670s, and later transitions to steam- and electric-powered mills, and other changes in sugar processing technology, are considered in Chapters 4 and 5 below.

After the juice was extracted, it was important to refine it before fermentation began. The boiling and curing processes produced two different products: hard granular sugar and dark liquid molasses. The boiling process was achieved through a series of liquid-solid transformations involving heating and cooling, including clarification and evaporation, were carried out in order to extract sucrose. These were carried out in a series of cauldrons or 'coppers', generally termed a 'copper wall', which was developed in a 'Jamaica train' arrangement from the 1680s (see Chapter 4 below). These were typically copper pieces manufactured in England for export to the West Indies, which were simply riveted together, although later coppers were single pieces. Four or five coppers were arranged above a series of furnaces fuelled by local wood, and the sugar cane juice was ladled between the coppers, into coppers of increasing heat and decreasing size. Impurities were skimmed off the top, and at the appropriate time, the juice was ladled into the next copper. The evaporation of the water in the juice brought about a refining process, until the liquid became supersaturated, and granules would begin to appear (a process often precipitated through the addition of lime). As the juice became increasingly refined, it thickened and darkened in colour. At the appropriate time, the sugar was removed from the final copper and cooled quickly ('struck'). Precise decisions had to be made regarding the temperatures and length of time for each boiling copper, and the timing of the movement of juice between coppers.

The sugar was next transferred to a curing house to dry the sugar and drain out the molasses. The sugar was packed into barrels or earthenware pots with plugged holes at the bottom. After standing for some time, the holes would be unplugged, and the molasses which had settled at the bottom of the containers would pour out. This process would be repeated for up to a month until only a dry block or 'loaf' of *muscovado* (semi-refined) sugar remained.

Some 17th-century Caribbean sugar producers took the process further, producing white 'clayed' sugar. This sugar, which still required further refining in Europe, was achieved by capping the sugar containers in the curing process with wet clay. As the water from the clay seeped through the sugar, it dissolved much of the molasses. This was a longer process, taking up to four months, which led to a smaller bulk of higher value to transport. Imports of white sugar were taxed very heavily in comparison with brown sugar by an Act of Parliament in 1685, and were also discouraged by Colbert around the same time.

Finally, while molasses was a valuable commodity in itself (a lively trade was developing to western Europe and North America), production of rum through distilling was a simple and common practice. Low-quality cane juice left over from the boiling process would be mixed with the impurities skimmed from the coppers and molasses in a large vat, in which it would ferment for around a week. The fermented liquid was then boiled, and the vapour condensed into rum (cf. Smith 2005).

Sugar Landscapes

Sugar cultivation also brought distinctive agro-industrial landscapes. The establishment of a sugar estate required the provision of a boiling house, curing house and possibly a still, and the use of a mill after harvesting. Other features of the new landscapes of sugar plantations included accommodation for planters, servants and slaves, and buildings for estate animals such as cattle and horses. Ligon (1657) also describes the provision of clay-lined dew ponds on Barbados sugar estates. The question of the relationship in these early years between sugar processing at these new sugar works and the cultivation of sugar cane requires careful consideration. Portuguese Brazil had seen sugar factories surrounded by small independent land holdings, 'attached to it in such a manner that they could not be alienated without the consent of the factory-owner' (Pares 1960, 24). In the eastern Caribbean, while the details of the early years of the sugar industry remain obscure, historians have assumed that – in contrast with Brazil – sugar was from the outset cultivated and processed by the same large land-owner, who invested in large amounts of land and labour: 'both functions...combined under single ownership and control' (Ward 1988, 10). However, as late as the mid 18th century, the papers of John Pinney, relating to the management of an 18th-century sugar estate on Nevis, contain several references to mill owners grinding another planter's canes for half the profit (Pares 1950, 16). It is very probable that it was commonplace in the early years of sugar production for mill owners to have milled cane that had been grown by their neighbours – who perhaps cultivated sugar elsewhere in the landscape, outside the enclosures described in Chapter 2 above. Thus, as late as 1672, Governor Charles Wheeler stated that St Kitts was different from other English islands, being mainly populated by former servants, and that small land holdings of 10 or 12 acres were run – presumably by tenants – with English servants (Emerson Smith 1947, 293, quoting CSPC 1669-1674, #977). As will be seen below, a sugar works at Wingfield destroyed by hurricane in the early 1680s was described as having been built 'to make my tenants' sugar canes' – and this almost feudal arrangement of planters and tenants will be an important part of the account of early sugar landscapes in the late 17th-century English Caribbean presented in this chapter. However, before exploring the landscape of Wingfield, it is important to underline that the study of sugar landscapes must be set in the context of other aspects of eastern Caribbean landscapes: human landscapes and population, urban landscapes, and land ownership.

Human Landscapes

Seventeenth-century landscape change in the eastern Caribbean is often presented as simply the clearance of the rain-forest and the development of plantations, especially in tobacco, indigo and sugar. A snapshot of a landscape of such nucleated plantations which made up these frontier societies is provided by the Buor map of St Kitts circa 1680 (**Figure 4**). The landscapes of St Kitts or Nevis were also dominated by coastlines of these islands were intensively fortified by closely-spaced forts and redoubts. Yet at the same time, while conventional secondary accounts do not characterise these societies as urban, contemporary maps show towns in surprisingly large numbers. The 17th-century towns of the English Caribbean were essentially maritime trading entrepôts, especially for European goods. The trade of salt (from the salt pans in the south-east of the island) at Old Road was recorded as early as 1631, and the safe harbours of such locations continued to attract traders. As the century developed, free populations began to offer their skills from these locations. There was also a significant Dutch presence in the towns of St Kitts: an account of a fire in 1663 describes the destruction of 60 Dutch store houses with foodstuffs to the value of two million livres at Basseterre (Higham 1921 quoting du Tertre 1654, Volume I, 586). The developing colonial landscapes of the Leeward Islands were, then, dominated by both plantations and towns.

These undocumented urban populations highlight how the development of settlement in the Leeward Islands brought about a complex population of planters, merchants, military, indentured servants and African slaves. While the harshness and horror of unfree labour increased with the shift to sugar, through serving an indenture, running away or even manumission servants and slaves sometimes moved between captivity and freedom – leading to the development of undocumented free black, Irish and other populations in towns. A range of religious and ethnic identities were brought together: Protestants, Catholics, Non-Conformists, Muslims and Sephardic Jews; African, Carib, Dutch, English, French, Irish, Scottish, Spanish and Swedish (Hicks 2000). From the outset, debt servants, criminals, political and religious non-conformists were imported from London as white indentured servants (engagés).

The attitude of the planter class in St Kitts to indentured servants, and the changing situation of the 1680s, are demonstrated by a description by one Christopher Jeaffreson, whose sugar works at Wingfield, St Kitts will be considered below, in 1681:

> Scotchmen and Welchmen we esteem the best servants; and the Irish the worst, many of them being good for nothing but mischief. I believe, if you will endeavour it, you may find Scotch and English, that would willingly change their clymate upon the afore-mentioned terms, and much more when they are directed to a certain place and person, of whose character they may be well informed. How many broken traders, miserable debtors, penniless spendthrifts, discontented persons, travelling heads and scatter-brains would joyfully embrace such offers:– the first, to shun their greedy creditors and loathesome goales; ...the third, to fill their bellies, through with the bread of affliction; the fourth to leave an unkinde mistress or dishonest wife, or something worse; the fifth to satisfy fond curiosity; the sixth, he knows not why,

unless to cross his friends and seek his fortune. They and the like humours first peopled the Indies, and made them a kinde of Bedlam for a short tyme. But from such brain-sick humours have come many solid and sober men, as these modern tymes testify (Jeaffreson to Poyntz 6 May 1681. Abridged in Jeaffreson 1878, the letter's text above is quoted by Higham 1921, 169-70).

The procurement of such servants quickly became a thriving, transatlantic business.[13] These labourers worked on fixed-period contracts, with the agreement that after the period of the contract they would be given a tract of land (Emerson Smith 1947; Pares 1960, 15). There was some experimentation with the enslavement of Caribs, but also the rapid development of the African slave trade to English plantations during this period. The slave trade to the New World had been dominated from the outset by the Dutch, who supplied the Portuguese colonies in Brazil throughout the second half of the 16th century. The Dutch West India Company was formed in 1621 (Blackburn 1997, 187-191) and Dutch colonial engagement reached a new phase in the 1630s when, at the same time as their plantations in Pernambuco were established, they established a trading post at St Eustatius, close to St Kitts (**Figure 1**). However, as will be seen below, the London-based Royal African Company was soon to establish a permanent foothold in the Leeward Islands (Davies 1957).

As well as increasing numbers of slaves and servants (both on plantations and port towns), smaller free populations developed. The constant stream of indentured servants into the Leewards led (after 4 years' service) to a continually developing free population, and the manumission of slaves – led to the development of a free black population. The question of whether small numbers of free Africans, as well as slaves, came to the West Indies during this period has not been studied. By 1655 St Kitts was the most populated island in the Leeward Islands, and was described in one account as 'almost worne out by reason of the multitudes that live upon it' (Dunn 1972, 121). Many of these 'multitudes' were clearly free and mobile populations, and new patterns of inter-island migration developed – for example from St Kitts to Jamaica soon after it was ceded to the English in 1655. Mobility is suggested by the dramatic difference between estimates of a population of around 20 000 in English St Kitts around 1650, with those from 1678, when the first census of St Kitts compiled for Governor Stapleton suggests a figure of around 3300 people (of whom 1436 were slaves). The dramatic difference between these population levels may not simply be a product of inaccurate sources of evidence or alternative criteria in accounting: the character of settlement in St Kitts appears to have changed radically during the 1660s-1670s, especially after the French occupation of 1666-7 and around the 1670s the onset of sugar monoculture and slave labour.

---

[13] see Higham 1921, 170-173 on Christopher Jeaffreson's procurement of prisoners for St Kitts in the 1680s.

Land ownership and divisions
Turning to the nature of land tenure, a glance at the review of early documents provided above demonstrates that the nature of land tenure during the first half-century of English settlement in the eastern Caribbean constituted an attempt to extend an English late medieval, feudal model. As historian Richard Pares has suggested,

> The lords proprietors were interested in land rather than trade: to be more exact, they wished to receive dues from the colonists, something like the manorial due which they were receiving at home (Pares 1960, 2).

Patents for very large areas of land were granted to a few influential men. For instance 10,000 acres on Barbados are shown as 'belonging to ye merchants of London' on a 1657 map (Ligon 1657). A similar deed dating from the 1620s from the Earl of Carlisle granted 1000 acres of land to John Jeaffreson (see below). At the same time, smaller and more numerous land divisions for leases appear to have resembled English-type enclosures. Very many grants appear to have been made, in a similar process to that of Barbados, where 67 389 acres were granted to 707 people (many of whom sub-let their leasehold further) between 1629 and 1638.

On St Kitts and Nevis, Richard Pares suggests that the early land divisions may be characterised as 'a series of long, narrow strips of land, leading up an indefinite distance into the mountain':

> In St Kitts, the layout of the land appears to have been designed to give everybody some access to the sea coast, since the canoe was the only means of transport until the trees were all down. This led to a series of long, narrow strips of land, leading up an indefinite distance into the mountain. Some of these strips might, by favour or by encroachment, enlarge themselves in the process; but, in order to turn them into workable plantations, it was usually necessary to buy them up in bundles (Pares 1960, 66. Note 32).

This model would be similar to the 1614 Norwood map of Bermuda, neatly divided by straight lines.[14] Pares suggests that both large and small holdings were common from the outset in the Leewards, but that many large estates were broken up into smaller leased plantations more appropriate for tobacco, etc. Then,

> after a date which varied from colony to colony (perhaps 1640 in Barbados, 1670 in Antigua, 1700 in St Domingue), the process was reversed, and small plantations began to be aggregated into great ones (Pares 1960, 19).

Moreover, an Act was passed in Barbados in 1671 to halt the creation of larger estates and thus reduce 'depopulation' (Pares *ibid*; Act of 14/7/1671; see CO 30/2, pp. 89-93). While the development of these processes will be considered further in Chapter 4, it is clear that the development of sugar production did not alter this fragmented and nucleated settlement landscape of many tenants in St Kitts overnight.

The Establishment of a Sugar works at Wingfield, St Kitts

In Chapter 2, the 17th-century landscape of Wingfield Estate was considered, and evidence of a 17th-century walled enclosure was identified. This section turns to the development of this landscape from the 1670s. Here again, archaeological evidence can be combined with detailed documentary evidence for the individual planters involved. Especially important here is an archive of letters, accounts and other papers relating to Christopher Jeaffreson and his ancestors that survives in the Beinecke Lesser Antilles Collection at Hamilton College, Clinton, New York. Further Jeaffreson papers were edited by an ancestor in the 1870s (Jeaffreson 1878), and some are held by the University of London. Jeaffreson's letters provide a unique window on the process of shifting to sugar production which was occurring across St Kitts, Nevis, Montserrat and Antigua at this time, and upon the thoughts and actions of early planters in the Leewards. The details of such documents are often both personal and evocative: for instance in his first letter from St Kitts Jeaffreson asks his cousin to send 'two gray hatts fir for my owne wearing (well wrought, or else the sunne will make them flap)' (Jeaffreson 1878, Vol. 1, 186). At the same time, they document the early development of landscapes that would witness the quotidian violence and horror of racial slavery.

Wingfield (**Figures 2** & **4**) lies just to the north of Old Road on well-watered land between Wingfield River (also known as Black River) and Merrifield's Gut – presumably named after Ralph Merrifield, one of the key backers of the Warner settlement of St Kitts of 1624 (see Chapter 2 above). John Jeaffreson (?-1660) and Samuel Jeaffreson were from Pettistree, Suffolk, near to Parham where Thomas Warner grew up. Both brothers were involved in Warner's St Kitts settlement, and John was Deputy Governor in the absence of Warner in the late 1620s. John Jeaffreson received a grant of 1000 acres of land – presumably in the area around modern Wingfield – at an early date. Upon returning to England, John Jeaffreson bought Dullingham Estate in Cambridgeshire from one Richard Reynolds, then aged 6, in 1656. The estate had been settled by Sir Anthony Wingfield in 1602, and the use of the name 'Wingfield' for the land in St Kitts appears to post-date this purchase.[15]

---

[14] Richard Norwood 1614. A Mapp of Description of the Summers Islans, sometimes called Bermvdas, lying in the West Indies. Copy (from 1739) (National Archives CO 700/Bermuda3).

[15] Anthony Wingfield was the son of Sir Robert Wingfield (d. 1596). It is probable that Edward Wingfield, president of the first council at Jamestown, Virginia (1607-) was a relation of Robert Wingfield. After Anthony Wingfield's death in 1602, Dullingham was owned by Sir Thomas Wingfield. After his death in 1610, his widow married Henry Reynolds. Her son was created a baronet in 1627, and died in 1638. The estate then passed to Anthony Reynolds, and then to the infant Richard Reynolds.

The purchase of the larger estate of Dullingham in 1656 may, perhaps, be seen as an early example of a returning rich West Indian planter buying into the circles of landed gentry in southern England. John Jeaffreson's son Christopher (1650-1725) inherited his father's estate on his death in 1660, and in 1675, after the death of his young bride, he travelled to St Kitts to see the estate he had inherited. After the return of his father, the estate had been rented out to a Mr Worley. Christopher Jeaffreson arrived on the island on 24th May 1676 at the age of 26 (Jeaffreson 1878, Volume 1, 68-72). He remained in St Kitts until July 1682, and continued to involve himself in the maintenance of his estate as an absentee until his death in 1725. The new 'landed' rhetoric of this planter is seen in the appearance from the mid 1670s of references to the land in St Kitts as 'Wingfield Manor'.

Christopher Jeaffreson proceeded to establish a sugar works, apparently replacing the production of tobacco and possibly indigo. In a letter written back to London just days after his arrival at St Kitts (5 June 1676), Jeaffreson noted that

> every body that is able [is] working upon sugar, which is a certaine gaine (Jeaffreson to George Gamiel, 5 June 1676; Jeaffreson 1878, Vol. 1, 189).

On 22 June 1676, Jeaffreson wrote to his cousin William Poyntz in London,

> I have noe more to request of you at present, but that you would if possible procure me a carpenter and a mason. They would bee verry usefull to mee, now that I am about to setle my plantation myselfe. For I intend to turne planter, and to set up a sugar worke, which will cost me some pence, but much lesse if I could have such servants (Jeaffreson to his cousin William Poyntz 22/6/1676, Jeaffreson 1878, 67).[16]

Again, on 11 November 1676, Jeaffreson wrote

> Now I must doe what I can, and I intend, God willing, to contynue some tyme here to settle my plantation, and build a sugar-worke; which will be a great charge, but I esteeme it only as soe much ventured, as the merchants doe at sea...I shall be forced to draw some moneys or goods over hither towards the settlement of my plantation, for which, when it is settled, I hope I may find an honest and able tenant, or may place such an one upon it, as may make more considerable retournes into England, than have been ever yet made (Jeaffreson to Poyntz 11 November 1676; Jeaffreson 1878, 198-9)

The investment necessary for establishing a sugar works was underlined in a latter dated 12 May 1677 to his Father-in-Law:

> I goe on expending money upon my plantation, in hopes it will repaye mee with interest; but I must have patience, for it will require tyme, as well as a large expense, before the sugar-worke can be perfected. It is now esteemed here a great folly for a man to expose his tyme or goods to the hazard of indigo or tobacco, sugar being the only thriveing and valuable commodity. (Jeaffreson to Colonel George Gamiell, London. 12 May 1677. Jeaffreson 1878 Vol. 1, 210-212).

Yet by July 1677, Jeaffreson was shipping 7712 lb of sugar to one Mr Helmes at Nevis, for shipment back to England (Jeaffreson to Helmes 21 July 1677, Jeaffreson 1878, 220). The location of this sugar works is not clear from Jeaffreson's letters. However, as detailed above the Buor map of c. 1680 (**Figure 4a**) shows the area of the walled enclosure as owned by Matthews (43), while 'Jefferson' (44) is marked further inland, to the north-west. This site is more accurately located on the 1756 Baker map (**Figure 14**), where a small works with a cattle mill – still owned by the Jeaffresons – is shown. This location on high ground appears to have been where Christopher Jeaffreson established his house and works – probably a relatively simple arrangement of cattle mill, boiling house and curing house. The indigo or tobacco works within the walled enclosure appears to have been run as a separate operation by Charles Matthews until 1681.

Jeaffreson appears to have built a new sugar works during 1679 or 1680. This is suggested by his vivid first-hand description of the double-hurricane which hit St Kitts on 27 and 28 August 1681 (reproduced as *Appendix 1*). The same letter describes a second hurricane, which damaged Jeaffreson's new buildings on 4th October 1681. Jeaffreson wrote,

> As soone as the storme began to cease, I went up to my house which I found miserably torne, and flat with the ground. My sugar-worke, in like manner, and all my buildings. I walked downe to my new sugar worke, which I had built not long before, about a quarter of a mile or more from my house, towards the sea, to make my tenants' sugar canes; to whom I had leased fifty acres of land, and had newly begun to make sugar at it, and was then boiling at it, when the storme began. I found that likewise flatt with the ground – the stone wall overturned, and the timber scattered in divers places, farre distant from the house (see Appendix 1).

The description fits well with the exposed position of Jeaffreson's works to the north-west of modern Wingfield. The 'new sugar worke' which he 'walks down to', 'about a quarter of a mile or more from my house, towards the sea' is suggestive. Walking towards the sea from Jeaffreson's works would have been done by following the main road across the island, which headed down to the Matthews enclosure. The probability is that Jeaffreson's boiling house and curing house were located in the area of the surviving factory, with a cattle mill nearby. No standing building

---

16 Poyntz was 'an upholsterer of Cornhill', and relative of General Poyntz, who was Governor of St Kitts during the Commonwealth (Jeaffreson *ibid*).

remains relating to these boiling- and curing-houses were identified during the fieldwork at Wingfield. Since these structures were apparently so comprehensively destroyed by the hurricane, this is perhaps to be expected.

Two aspects of the events of 1681 may be highlighted. Firstly, it is notable that the description of Jeaffreson's destroyed works is that it was built 'to make my tenants' sugar canes' – clear evidence that Jeaffreson's sugar works were built to process tenants' sugar rather than just his own (cf. Higham 1921, 178). Secondly, Governor Matthews died in this year (Jeaffreson to Madam Brett of Channall Row, Westminster, 5 May 1681. Jeaffreson 1878, Vol. 1, 260-262). This appears to have provided an opportunity for Jeaffreson to expand the land he claimed as his own. Within months of arriving in 1676, Jeaffreson had written about his frustration over the confusion which evidently existed over the precise boundaries of his inherited land. He complained about the lack of a Deed for the 1000 acres granted to his father by the Earl of Carlisle: Jeaffreson writes,

> But I admite that I have never had nor seene any deed, by which my father held this manor of Wingfield, but only that from the Lord Carlisle, which nominates only a thousand acres. After he had made choice of which plantation, I suppose there was (or ought to have beene) some deed from the Lord Carlisle or Sir Thomas Warner, setting forth the bounds of the said plantations. For I finde the lease of Serjent Delve bounding this manor, with the river to the east, and Merrifield's Gutt to the west. Notwithstanding which, one Mr Garbrants holdes a large slip of land, between mee and the gutt, which he had by marrying the daughter of one Mr Partridge, to whom some say my father gave that plantation for his life, who is now dead. But Mr Garbrants pretends to hold it by deed from the Earl of Carlisle. He likewise holdes the Red House Plantation, where Captain Samuel Jeaffreson lived, which his son, my cousen Samuell (who is now at Antegoa, and whom I have never yet seene) solde to Delve who, when the island was lost, gave it to his god-daughter, the child of Mr Garbrants, a Dutchman. Mr Garbrants saith that you satisfied Delve, when he was in England, that he might safely buy it. Upon which grounds he made up the bargain. Pray give me what instructions you can in these concerns in your next letter, as alsoe concerning a plantation which my father had on the wineward side of the island, called the Grange, which my cousin Robert Jeaffreson, as some say, solde to Mr Watkins, and that the mone was payd. Some call it mine. Soe many people are buzzing these things in my ears, I would gladly know as much as they; not that I have any intention of being troublesome (Jeaffreson to Jeaffreson 11 November 1676; Jeaffreson 1878 Vol. 1, 199-200).

It is clear that Jeaffreson considered a large swathe of land, between Wingfield River and Merrifield's Gut, to be his – including the land which Matthews owned. This pattern of land ownership would be in keeping with the Pares model described above.

The creation of 'Wingfield Manor'

This section considers the documentary and archaeological evidence for the development of Wingfield after the hurricane of 1681, up to a detailed inventory of the estate in August 1685. Jeaffreson permanently returned to London in August 1682, soon becoming the London agent for St Kitts (Higham 1921, 155-6). Jeaffreson vividly described his return to London after 6 years in the tropics

> I have found it inconvenient for me – who was in health – to arrive in so colde a season as I did. I presently got a great colde, which at best I feare will keepe me company this winter, though I have been and am very carefull of myselfe. It was bitter cold at my first coming to England. Nay, we had snow with raine some tyme before we came neare the channell, and that for severall days. (Jeaffreson to James Phipps (in St Kitts) 15 November 1682. Jeaffreson 1878, Vol. 1, 309-322).

Jeaffreson clearly rebuilt his sugar works swiftly in 1681-2, before his departure for London, and in such a way as to build up his earlier descriptions of the plantation as 'Wingfield Manor'. He appropriated land which he considered his own, including the walled enclosure at Wingfield, as part of this rebuilding process. The double- or triple-gabled Jacobean house shown within the walled enclosure on the plan of 1682 appears to be the same house which he now referred to as his 'Manor House'. This appropriation of the former Governor's residence was a powerful statement by Jeaffreson of his status. This attitude is further demonstrated by a letter of 9 October 1682 from Jeaffreson in London to his agent at Wingfield whom he referred to as 'Ensign Thorn'. The cautiousness of Jeaffreson's negotiation of this new identity is perhaps hinted at by the labelling of this letter 'not sent'. The letter reads

> the newly selected Governor of the Island and his Lady have hinted broadly to the Writer, how gladly they would accept the loan of his house on Wingfield Manor, as a residence, till they should have time to hire a suitable residence. They would like to have the Manor House for three or four months. To this suggestion, or rather this open request, the Writer has replied that he has by agreement surrendered the residence on his plantation to his steward's use, and that it rests with him to decide whether they may have their wish (Jeaffreson to Thorn, marked 'NOT SENT', 9 October 1682. Jeaffreson 1878, 307-8).

The inventory of Wingfield in August 1685 lists a 'dwelling house with three rooms, six leather chairs, one gable and frame' and other household items, and is presented in full in *Appendix 2*. It is probable that this is the 'Manor House'. Despite his suggestion in a letter of 16 November 1682, that the production of indigo may be preferable to further sugar production (Jeaffreson to Ensign Thorn 16 November 1682. Jeaffreson 1878, Vol. 1, 322-3), the same month saw him send out from London 'some new disbursements for the advantage of my plantation, in the hope it will repay me in tyme for all charge and trouble' (Jeaffreson to Ensign Thorn 16 November 1682. Jeaffreson 1878, Vol. 1, 324-5). A detailed list of these parts, which comprise parts for a sugar boiling house and still – coppers and 'wormes' – are listed in *Appendix 3*.

The death of Matthews provided more than simply an opportunity for Jeaffreson to take the land that he claimed as his own. Matthews also appears to have been granted the 'royalitie to' Wingfield River, including 'ye sole Power of fowleing & fishing in ye same'. A Grant from Governor Stapleton was procured by Jeaffreson in 1685, granting him the right to 'make erect or build Water Mills Indego Works or any other Conveniences' at Wingfield.[17] The water mill was constructed at some point after the plan of 1682: drawn up in the year in which Jeaffreson returned to England, the plan showing the enclosure does not show the water mill. However, the remarkable accuracy of the plan, especially the course of the river, suggests that part of the reason for commissioning the survey was to inform the construction of a dam and leat. The water mill had been constructed by 27 August 1685. An inventory of Wingfield of this date listed

> one waterworke vizt. A cassada mill, a boyling house, eight coppers, three skimmers, one ladle, one scoupe, ...one copper cooler, two wooden coolers, one large wooden trough, two stills wth heads wormes and wormes Caske (see Appendix 2).[18]

A list of recent expenses in the same document includes several references to timber, 'sloop loads of limestones' and lime from Nevis, and the payment of wages to carpenters and to Alexander Merrefeild, a mason, for 37 days' work. These items were presumably needed for the construction of the water mill and the separately listed 'Boiling house shingled'.

Further confirmation that Jeaffreson was crushing and boiling sugar during this period is provided later in the inventory, where a list of items on the estate which have been lost or worn out in recent years includes 'one Cas'a mill and appur'ts; Three iron hoopes for the Rollers – wooden in the middle'. The accompanying list of expenses includes 'a new sett of Rollers', wages to one John Ellis and 'a Ffrenchman' and 'Louis, a Free Negro' for 'Boyling'.

Perhaps most evocative of the 24-hour working regime of boiling sugar is the purchase of '20 candles for the boyling house' (*Appendix 2*).

Significant above-ground remains of the 1680s water mill were identified during survey at Wingfield, incorporated into the fabric of the later factory. The earliest surviving building within the sugar works was a crushing house: a well built rectangular stone building, placed adjacent to the wheel pit, and integral with its primary construction. The crushing house measured 7m east/west and 4.5m north/south. The building was entered through an open archway, with brick dressings. It had a brick barrel-vaulted ceiling and was open-ended to the south. The floor was covered in concrete so the original arrangement of how the crushing machinery was set was not visible. There was evidence of where the shafting for the wheel had passed through the wall, but this had been later filled in (**Figure 6**).

The boiling house clearly originally extended to the south of the crushing area, as the springer of a arch was visible on the west wall, but at a lower level. This lower part was interpreted as the primary boiling house: but this area was covered by later construction. Part of the primary boiling house's flue system – three brick arches within a wall aligned roughly east-west – was identified in Trench 6. A fragment of standing masonry – the corner of a structure on the same alignment as the boiling house – was interpreted as part of the primary curing house. This was aligned with the crushing/boiling house (and at a slightly different angle to the later complex), and was of similar construction. The arrangement of the water supply in this early period seems to have been by a wooden launder, running for some distance from the original water overflow. The primary phase of sugar works appears, therefore, to have consisted of two substantial stone buildings, incorporating some brickwork, set into the side of the hill, and a water system.

At an early point in these buildings' history, a substantial battered perimeter wall was provided. This wall enclosed the principal buildings, and the subsequent works developed around it. This substantial wall appears to represent an attempt to serve a defensive function, with access to the works provided only through the northern (presumably gated) entrance to the crushing house.

Jeaffreson's works above Wingfield had been destroyed by hurricane in 1681, and his rebuilding appears to have been centred on modern Wingfield, with a new house in the Matthews enclosure. Having restored his claim to a large sweep of land, to the north of Old Road up the mountain between the River and Merrifield's Gut, Jeaffreson's focus turned to the area at Balcony Hill. In a letter from London dated 15 November 1682, Jeaffreson refers to some tenants beginning 'to clear and settle above Balcony-Hill', some of whom

> would willingly rent land at 800lb per acre, for seven
> years, provided they might be secured to have their canes

---

[17] Any use by Jeaffreson of the water from Wingfield River for indigo production is unclear, although some of the buildings at Wingfield may have been used for this purpose. In particular, a series of three paved terraces which survive as 19th-century garden features could possibly have originally held indigo tanks. These would have lain within the enclosure, but further investigation would be necessary to confirm this.

[18] The term 'cassada mill' in the inventory requires brief clarification. The rest of the description clearly refers to sugar boiling-, curing- and still-houses. Cassada (= cassava or manioc root) was used to make 'cassava bread' – a process which required the grating of the root and pressing out the juice. The term 'cassada mill' therefore clearly refers to a crushing mill appropriate for sugar, rather than a mill used for cassava.

made to halves. (Jeaffreson to James Phipps in St Kitts, 15 November 1682; Jeaffreson 1878, Vol. 1, 315-316)

Jeaffreson's comment that

> I am somewhat backward in [this proposition], being willing that the old workes should be cleared, and put in a posture of making some returnes, before I launche for the upon a new one. (*ibid.*)

again indicates that he aimed to build and control a sugar works, and lease land to tenants who would grow sugar.

Enclosure and Exchange

It was suggested above that the shift to sugar in the Leeward Islands was closely related to the opportunities brought by London-based merchant companies from the middle of the 17th century. In this section, I want to explore how such impulses were worked out in local situations. One striking aspect of the creation of 'Wingfield Estate' is the continuity between the earlier enclosed landscapes described in Chapter 2 and the new situations of the shift to sugar. Practices of enclosure and agricultural production are the most visible archaeologically, but the role of trade and exchange are also important. The Jeaffreson archives are filled not only with details of the construction and maintenance of the sugar works, but also with detailed inventories of his purchases and sales of European commodities sold by Jeaffreson. On his first journey to St Kitts in 1676, Jeaffreson brought with him such large amounts of saleable items – Madeira wine, 'baizes, searges, that is perpetuanes, hatts' as well as 'cheese, butter, white and red herrings, pilchards and beefe'. His letter also underlines the necessity for good tools, and asks for soap, candles, hats and beef for himself (Jeaffreson to Poyntz, 5 June 1676; Jeaffreson 1878 Volume 1, 183-186).

Such were the quantities of cloth and clothing, food, and wine brought by Jeaffreson that his biographer has suggested that he set up a 'store' at Wingfield (Jeaffreson 1878). Similarly, a note enclosed with a letter of 23 July 1678 to his cousin and agent Poyntz – 'an upholsterer of Cornhill', and relative of General Poyntz, who had been Governor of St Kitts (Jeaffreson 1878, 67) – in London lists a range of commodities, including candles, soap, knives, dominated by material, thread, '4 grosse of silver, and 5 gross of silke coat-buttons suitable', and clothes (felt hats, 'plaine shoes'). The note lists cloth, silk, 'greene searge for livery', 'deep red tammy', 'yellow tammy', 'browne thread', 'ells of Holland', 'blew lining', 'Kenting', 'canvas', brown and white 'ossenburgs', 'broad Dowlas', 'German linen', 'Callico', 'cullered noxed searges', 'Irish freeze of an ordinary sort' and 'persion taffety suitable for lineing' (Jeaffreson 1878, Vol. 1, 233-6). Some of these items were necessary for the everyday running of a plantation: indentured labourers and slaves needed clothing, and indeed some English West Indian colonies

even passed Acts of Assembly prescribing the amounts of food and clothing allowed to indentured servants. For example, in 1669 Antigua prescribed 'three pairs of shoes, three shirts, pairs of drawes and one cap per annum' (Emerson Smith 1947, 237). Other items were clearly for sale to other colonial residents – such as the fine furniture, carpets and drapes that Jeaffreson describes (*Appendix 2*). The supplies of such commodities continued throughout Jeaffreson's involvement with Wingfield: even after his return to London (see lists in *Appendix 2*). In this case, Jeaffreson was increasingly reliant on his agent in St Kitts – Ensign Thorn.

Such is the richness of the documentary record for Wingfield that details of items which Jeaffreson ordered for himself also survive. For instance, a note of 1678 requests 'one paire of silk stockins with sowing and stitching silke', 'ribbonds to make a fashionable trimeing and to tye the sleeves' and 'one lace cravatt and cuffs genteele, but not too riche'. The accompanying letter asks that

> only as to those that concerne my owne weareing apparell, especially the ribbonds and cravat, I would bee assisted by the fancy of my sister, which I always approved very well (Jeaffreson to Poyntz 23 July 1678. Jeaffreson 1878, Vol. 1, 233).

A similar note from 25 July 1681 requests

> a demi-castor hatt which, if good will do almost as much credit as a better in this island; a good perrewig; a laced cravat and cuffs; as much broad cloth as will make me a fashionable suit; a suiteable lining and trimming of any colour, except blew or yellow, which I now weare; a douzaine yards at least of ribbons for cravatt and cuffs; a fashionable and handsome belt (the last one was a very good one, but is decayed now); a payer of silke, and 4 payer of thread stockings, larger and stronger than the last; enough gold and silver to lace my hatt round; sewing and stitching silke, white dimmety to make 2 payer of linings, and whatever else is necessary. Only skins for pocketts are not serviceable here; 8 payer of shoes, which is more, I hope, than I shall weare out here, after the arrival of these things, which I shall expect around Christmasse; if sooner the better (Jeaffreson to Poyntz 25 July 1681. Jeaffreson 1878, Vol. 1, 269-70).

The image conjured up by this costume's description is very powerful. Having spent 5 years in the West Indies, Jeaffreson's clothing and the attitudes is suggests are in keeping with his attempt to expand his wealth and influence: exemplified by his creation of a personal 'Manor'.

Early, enclosed sugar works functioned, then, as places of trade, exchange and consumption as well as agricultural production – just as the Carib enclosures had done. Acknowledging how sugar 'factories' were often also merchant 'factories' brings several interpretive consequences.

Firstly, it highlights how the establishment of sugar works was an enterprise restricted to a certain class of merchant or planter. Dalby Thomas, writing in 1690, estimated the costs of establishing a 100-acre sugar plantation in Barbados to be £5600 (Thomas 1690, 14-15). As well as the large capital requirements, procuring the necessary processing paraphernalia – rollers, coppers, etc. – required strong contacts with industrial sources in England. And there was no point in establishing a sugar works if one did not have the considerable resources required to ship this bulk item back to England. Moreover, the shipment of loads of sugar to England was closely bound up with the counter trade in European commodities such as cloth, iron tools and Madeira wine.

Secondly, it underlines how during the 17th century, the value of sugar for Caribbean planters changed radically. In the 1630s, taxes in the English Leeward Islands were payable in tobacco. Williamson (1926, 85), referring to a contemporary source, states that

> a planter who went [to St Kitts] in 1630 deposed that there was a yearly levy of 20lbs [of tobacco] per head to the Proprietor, 20lbs to the Governor, 10lbs to the Church, 20lbs to the Captain of the Train Bands, and 40lbs to maintain guards against Carib attacks for six years

In contrast, by the 1670s sugar was developing as the dominant currency in this near-moneyless society. Some coinage was used during the 17th-century in the Leeward Islands: including the New England coins which were minted from 1652, but the vast majority of trade occurred by credit and barter (Higham 1921, 195). Sugar was used for the payment of wages, of taxes, and especially for the purchase of European commodities.[19]

Thirdly, and most radically, it encourages us to see the landscapes of St Kitts and the other islands in the late 17th-century English eastern Caribbean as dominated by places of both material exchange and technological production – enclosed factories and heavily-defended trading towns – in which strong continuities with earlier Carib enclosed landscapes were visible.

Conclusions

This chapter has used the highly-documented example of Wingfield Estate on St Kitts to sketch some of the landscape changes that occurred during the shift to sugar in the English Leeward Islands during the closing decades of the 17th century. The picture presented suggests that previous Barbados-based historical models have failed to capture the local complexities of the shift to sugar. On St Kitts, three main aspects of the shift to sugar have been highlighted: the role of trade and exchange in the

development of sugar works, the 'feudal' rhetoric of the owners of early sugar works, and the persistence of earlier modes of production and exchange within enclosures.

As these impulses came together in the late 17th century, earlier enclosed landscapes were increasingly remodelled by planters who drew upon English ideas of feudal power in relation to the landscape.[20] The activities of Jeaffreson were in some ways a continuation of a process begun by his father's purchase of Dullingham Hall: an appropriation of established symbols of power. At Wingfield, after the death of Governor Matthews, Jeaffreson shifted his base into the Governor's enclosure, and created the new, pretentious 'Wingfield Manor' – a newly-created New World feudal manor, which even had tenant farmers and servants. The close kin relations between the pioneers of St Kitts – the minor aristocracy of Suffolk and Cambridgeshire, on the periphery of London, brought into the circles of merchants – also appear self-consciously to have attempted to reproduce a feudal model. The self-creation demonstrated in Jeaffreson's orders for clothes is palpable.

This agro-industrial feudalism bears strong similarities to the 'aristocratic capitalism' described by Mason (1993, 103) as a Caribbean-specific alternative to Cain and Hopkins' (1986) influential model of 'gentlemanly capitalism'. While Mason uses the term in the context of early 18th-century Leeward Island planters, it is perhaps most appropriate to the situation in the closing decades of the 17th century – bound up with the urge among provincial men like Jeaffreson to draw upon English models of landscape power. Such feudal impulses were not new in New World settings, of course: European settler colonialism in the Caribbean was after all in origin a late medieval (late 15th-century) phenomenon. Here, the 'feudal' rhetoric seen at Wingfield reminds us of the tendency for the distinctive developments of the late 17th-century Caribbean to be missed, as the better-documented Georgian attitudes and circumstances of the developed economies of 18th-century sugar and slavery are projected back (e.g. Mintz 1985). Thus, the aesthetic views of landscapes described by Lydia Pulsipher during the 17th century are in fact a more accurate reflection of the 18th century:

> The high value Europeans placed on clearing the tropical landscape...developed from their aesthetic views that there should be open vistas in the far and middle distances and that there be fields and meadows in which men could dwell (Pulsipher 1977, 96).

The empirical dimensions of the landscape perspective adopted here underlines how the shift to sugar in the Leewards was a situated and contingent development, and one that contrasted with later landscapes.

---

[19] Trading tokens were used to some extent during the 18th century, but the widespread use of currency in the British West Indies did not occur until the 19th century. On sugar as currency in the Caribbean (see Merrill 1957, 54; CSPC 9/1/1674, 1669-1674, #1201.)

[20] These are perhaps also seen in a failed 17th-century proposal for the establishment of a University in the Leewards – by 'erecting a college or two' – reported by Higham (1921, 211-212).

Overall, then, the shift to sugar in the Leewards was developed by well-connected, capital-rich merchants deeply engaged in transatlantic networks that traded in both European objects, tropical products, and humans. In the late 17th century, at places such as Wingfield, they experimented with feudal models of landscape power. The provision of a wall around the new sugar works at Wingfield, and the appropriation of the Matthews enclosure, demonstrate strong continuities in the settlement layout, providing Jeaffreson with two large walled areas. The changes that they wrought in the landscapes of the Leeward Islands were fundamentally tied into the bilateral and developing triangular trades across the Atlantic: people like William Freeman, a contemporary of Christopher Jeaffreson on Nevis, St Kitts and Montserrat whose complex transatlantic networks are described by historian David Hancock (2000). The English elite in the eastern Caribbean at this time had a new confidence, seen in new scales of investment and new permanence in landscape projects. But their projects would have been impossible if they had not been able to build upon earlier Carib enclosed landscapes described in Chapter 2 – the practices of bringing together agricultural production and exchange within enclosed areas. Here, the importance of documenting the local contingencies of European settler colonialism is clear. Elsewhere, such a perspective suggests that generating accounts of the transition to sugar in Jamaica might acknowledge the contexts of Spanish clearance and cultivation, which had already been carried out for a century before it was annexed by the English through Cromwell's Western Design (Taylor 1965).

In time, however, the landscape forms and elite desires of sugar production began to change again. As sugar monoculture grew, from the first decades of the 18th century the 'manors' of tenant farmers or servants began to be displaced by impulses to recreate classical images of power: villas, ordered agricultural plantation, and a very marked increase in the numbers of slaves. This shift in landscape, settlement and scale is examined in Chapter 4.

'IMPROVED' LANDSCAPES (FROM *C*. AD 1713)

This chapter traces the landscape changes that came about as sugar monoculture developed across the British Leewards from around 1713, and then into the Windward Islands from the 1760s, with special reference to St Kitts and St Lucia. Historian Robin Blackburn's discussion of New World slavery is a useful starting point:

> The planters of the English Caribbean and North America … saw themselves as sovereigns of all they surveyed. …The Great Houses of the planters received African adornments, while echoing the Palladian mansions of the English or French aristocracy, the latter in turn being influenced by Versailles. Since plantation cultivation destroyed the forests, the planters has little difficulty finding sites with commanding views. They did not build fortresses or castles but theatres of gracious living. (Blackburn 1997, 21)

As Chapters 2 and 3 have shown, the early colonists of the eastern Caribbean did, *pace* Blackburn, develop landscapes that were not unlike 'fortresses and castles' – landscapes of military forts and redoubts, and of walled sugar factories and enclosures. However, as Blackburn's description above explains, the 18th century saw a radical shift in eastern Caribbean landscapes – an opening-up of former enclosures and the construction of new 'theatre' landscapes. This transition in plantation settlement occurred in the Leewards during the first decades of the 18th century, and similar impulses led to the development of sugar landscapes the Windward Islands after 1763. These shifts were closely bound up with the changing role of these sites and the Caribbean merchant-planter elite in a new Anglophone Atlantic world.

In this chapter, I shall describe the emergence and development of a range of new attitudes among the planter class to landscape, technology and social relations between *c*. AD 1713 and 1838. I shall discuss these through the notion of 'improvement'. The working-out of this 'package' of ideas and attitudes in particular landscapes will be explored at Wingfield, St Kitts (from *c*. AD 1713) and Balenbouche, St Lucia (from the 1770s). This will lead to a reconsideration of the geographies of sugar monoculture, and in particular the idea of planter 'absenteeism'.

Landscapes of Sugar Monoculture

Following the shift to sugar in the Leeward Islands, the development of sugar monoculture between *c*. AD 1713

and slave emancipation in AD 1838 brought a range of changes both to planters' ideas of landscape and also to the designed plantation landscapes that were actually constructed. Larger estates developed, on which planters grew and also processed their own cane. A crucial dimension of these changes was the massive rise in slave populations – a transition from the 'paternalistic hierarchy' of servants and fewer slaves to 'industrial slavery' (Olwig 1993, 35) which brought new abilities of planters to mobilise the labour required to effect fundamental changes in landscape form.

On St Kitts, from the 1720s the landscape of the former French land saw cattle mills replaced by new windmills dedicated to the processing of each estate's own sugar. By 1770s, 44,000 acres were reported as under sugar on St Kitts (Jeffreys 1780, 21), and although this is clearly an overestimate (since the total area of the island comprises only *c*. 42,000 acres) it is clear that every piece of cultivable land was being used. Each new, large plantation 'resemble[d] a small Town' (W. Smith 1745, 226), and plantation trades and shops developed alongside larger slave villages, slave burial grounds, well-constructed roads and pathways and field systems. Because of the complex earlier settlement landscape of St Kitts, this landscape of fewer, larger estates was achieved through hundreds of purchases through which planters bought up adjacent: creating estates like the Pinneys' on Nevis which ran 'from the sea to the mountain' (Pares 1960, 17-19; Pares 1950, 104). These enlarged estates in many ways represented attempts to reproduce the large grants of land given to a minority of wealthy early settlers in the 17th century. As the white population shrank proportionally, the size of plantations, slave populations and sugar output grew year on year.

On the plantations, larger fields and the new emphasis on sugar were accompanied by changes in labour organisation. Sugar cultivation, especially when compared with tobacco growing, brought new a demand for larger numbers of unskilled labourers, organised into gangs, and the numbers of slaves increased dramatically throughout the 18th century as it became unusual for indentured servants to work in the fields. Gang labour became synonymous with slavery, as white servants were increasingly unwilling to labour in the large gangs of regimented workers that hoed the ground, planted the sugar, weeded the fields, and cut the cane of the great plantations (Galenson 1981a, 151). New situations of industrialised racial slavery developed quickly (cf. Hicks 2000).

In parallel with the increase in slavery, there was an increasing tendency for plantation owners to spend time in Britain and elsewhere in the Atlantic world: a process known in the economic history literature as 'absenteeism', which has traditionally been seen as a process which sowed the seeds of the decline of the West Indian economy (a theme discussed further below). The growth of absenteeism among plantation owners also saw the emergence of new methods and ideas of the management of estate landscapes – technologies for absent planters to visualise and control their landscapes. Two new practices were particularly important: the appointment of resident overseers or agents to manage sugar plantations, and a new interest in the commissioning of numerous new estate plans. The sheer scale of mapping is remarkable: over 20,000 maps and plans survive in Jamaica alone (Higman 1988). As Barry Higman has observed, the phenomenon of estate mapping resulted in part from

> a large group of wealthy individuals resident in Great Britain anxious to visualise their plantations and capable of paying the charges of professional surveyors and planmakers (and, sometimes, pictorial artists) (Higman 1988, 1)

The new attitudes to landscape were particularly visible in changing methods and practices of landscape survey for estate plans, and in the development of 'ideal' plantation management literature.

Changing Methods of Landscape Survey

New methods of landscape survey developed during this period. Detailed surveys had been carried out from the earliest period of English settler colonialism in St Kitts, and there were precedents for such detailed survey in new colonial situations. As early as 1614, surveyor Richard Norwood (1590-1675) had started his survey of Bermuda which was to become the most famous of English colonial maps (Wilkinson 1933). Earlier landscape surveys has been carried out by 'direct measurement' – using line-measuring devices such as customary rods, chains, or wirelines (usually with a plane table) and the quantification of land by acre (=160 square rods). Chain surveying is depicted in a vignette on a 1729 copy of the Norwood map of Bermuda (Palmer 1988). The iron chain appears to have been first used in survey in the first decades of the 17th century (Richeson 1966, 104). Its continued popularity, and the discouragement in many late 18th-century surveying handbooks of using angle measurement (Richeson 1966, 158), appears to be due to the ease of its learning and use. Similar line-measurement was carried out with a perambulator or measuring-wheel from the 16th century. Both techniques of land survey continued well into the 20th century. On St Kitts, one of the earliest patents dates from 8th August 1637, is signed by Thomas Warner, and describes direct measurement by paces between fixed points in the landscape. Warner granted

unto Symon Gurdion of the said Island gentleman his heires and assignes for ever a certaine percell of Land er plantacon scituate In St Thomas parish in the middle division of this Island now in the tenure or Occupation of him the said Symon Gurdion bounded on the East wth the Land of William Warden and on the West wth the Land of Sargent Thomas Durant & John Mandaye Containing in latitude one hundred and twenty Geometricall paces both sides thereof poynting from the Seaside North East and by East and running from thence unto ye plantacon now in the possession of John Allen: plantacon unto ye Mountainds to have and To hold ye said percell of Land or Plantacon and every part & p'cell thereof...paying therefore Yearly unto the said Earle of Carlisle his heires and successors or assigns Lords Proprietaries of the said Island and to mee the said Sr Thomas Warner Knt & Governr...all such rents customes and duetys...for the time being as also one Couple of Capons or a Turkeye affatt Pigge or a Couple of Conneys Yearely at every feaste of Christmasse (Oliver 1908, 5).

A similar patent, dated 11 December 1648, was from the Earl of Carlisle for '240 geometrical paces of land' (Oliver *ibid.*). However, while direct measurement continued, the first decades of the 18th century saw a new use of triangulation in estate survey in the eastern Caribbean. As Michael Craton (1997, 52-54) has observed, many aspects of plantation life at this time were fundamentally influenced by maritime culture, and the technology of triangulated survey was closely associated with the military and maritime/navigation arenas. Indeed, the diary of the early 17th-century colonial surveyor Richard Norwood describes how he gained mathematical and surveying training as a young man at sea (Richeson 1966, 91-2). The principles of triangulation had been developed during the 16th century, and came gradually to be applied to surveying during the last decades of the 16th century especially in maritime- and military- as well as land-survey. Inspired by the sextant, a range of new surveying devices – from box compasses, quadrants, pairs of compasses, astrolabes, and geometrical squares to early angle measuring devices on tripods (theodolites or 'circumferentors') – came to be used by surveyors from around 1600. The 17th century saw significant developments in the measurement of height (including backsighting and tripods) and the practice of traversing (Taylor 1930, 140-161, 1934 158-176), it was in the 18th century that these techniques came to be adopted in the production of estate plans in the eastern Caribbean.

One particularly early example of a survey by angle in the West Indies (presumably with box compass and chain) is a patent dating from 1696 for a large French sugar plantation on St Kitts to William Stapleton of Nevis, which describes

The Plantation formerly belonging to the Father Hermit Lying in the Cayan Quarter Containing Two hundred and Forty Acres beginning at the Mouth of Kayan River and extending by the several Angles of the River to the intersection of the Common Path, Northwesterly Twenty Degrees one Chain and a half, Northwesterly Seaventy two Degrees two Chains, Northwesterly sixty two Degrees two Chains to Davies Line; Thence Northwesterly two degrees twenty Six Chains and a half; Thence West five Chains Forty Links to the Common Path; Thence Northesterly two Degrees Three Chain and a half Northeasterly six Degrees seven Chain sixty Five Links Northeasterly seven Degrees two Chains Eighty six Links Northesterly Three Degrees Eleven Chains Northwesterly Thirteen Degrees two Chain and a half Northwesterly twenty seven Degrees three Chains and a half Thence over the Path by the Intersection of the Chains Southwesterly Eighty Degrees two Chains Northwesterly Eighty Two Degrees Fouer Chains and a half Southwesterly Eighty Degrees Three Chain Northwesterly Eight Degrees Forty Five Chains to the Sea Side. Thence by The Several Angles of the sea side to the Mouth of the River which was the first station. Bounded to the North East with the sea to the south East with Kayan River to the West with the land of Davies Decoased the Common Path and part of Durres Together With all singular Messuages Houses Edifices Buildings Structures Mills Sugar Works Orchards Gardens Lands Tenements Pastures Foodings Mountain Lands Mars his Timber Trees Wood Underwoods Cains Cornes with the soyl and ground of the same Waters Water Courses Fishings and Fishing Places with all other Profits Commodities Emoluments and Appurtenances Whatsoever unto the said Plantations and Tract of Land in any wise belonging or appurtaining (Oliver 1908-17, Volume 5, 32-33).

The adoption of new technologies of survey led to a dramatic increase in the number of estate plans during the 18th century, and was closely related to new colonial attitudes to landscape. In particular, the shift from direct survey to triangulation was part of a more general shift in more abstracted conceptions of landscape form. Such impulses were perhaps most visible in the emerging plantation management literature.

The 'Ideal' Management of Plantation Landscapes

New attitudes to landscape were also visible in the rapid development of a new literature on ideal plantation management (*Table 3*). James Grainger's writings in St Kitts provide a good point of departure here. In 1764, soon after his return to St Kitts (where he would die two years later), Grainger published his didactic poem *The Sugar Cane!* relating to sugar cultivation in St Kitts, in which he put across 'the dream of Creole cultural idealism' in laboured 'georgic' diction (Sandiford 2000, 69; Gilmore 2000, 27-8, see Chapter 5 below). Grainger's idealism was part of a more general transition among Caribbean planters during the 18th century, which was reflected in the development – in contrast to 17th-century descriptions of the processes of sugar manufacture (Ligon 1657,

Thomas 1690) – of a new genre of 'georgic' discourses on plantation management (*Table 3*, Watts 1987, 384 ff; Goodwin 1987, 163). In British contexts, such literature has traditionally been attributed to the increased interest in Virgil's Georgics (Barrell 1980, 9) and classical ideals of agricultural practices. In the same year (1764) Grainger drawing on his medical training, published his *Essay on the more common West-India Diseases*: the 'first work from the English-speaking Caribbean specifically devoted to the diseases and treatment of slaves' (Gilmore 2000, 15). Such concern for the health of slaves – driven of course more by a desire for economic optimisation than by humanism or compassion – fitted well into the impulses towards the optimisation of production through science that informed the new ideal management literature.

Antiguan planter Samuel Martin's contribution to such efforts was his *Essay on Plantership* (1750). This publication was in its fifth edition by 1773, and Martin set up and ran a 'school of plantership' for Leeward Island planters at his 'Greencastle' Estate in Antigua from the late 1740s (Sheridan 1957; 1960). Martin not only outlined the 'art of managing' a plantation, but also encouraged planters who possessed 'proper qualifications', and engaged in public service. Martin's 'School of Plantership' paved the way for new advisory pamphlets to estate owners and island assemblies from Whitehall from the 1770s, and the development in the early 19th century of planter associations and horticultural societies: for example the Society for Improvement of Agriculture was established on Barbados in 1804.

This emerging plantation management genre provided detailed opinion and advice about the day-to-day business of running a plantation – much of which was aimed at overseers. Thus Belgrove (1755) provided a month-by-month schedule of activities (Goodwin 1987, 59-81). Many, such as Roughley, offered advice on the positioning and layout of an estate:

> a situation, uniting within itself the blessings of a plenteous supply of wholesome water, on a piede of ground sufficiently large to admit building an extensive set of works, overseer's house, hospital or hot house, &c., with a large mill-yard, and being central among the surrounding cane cultivation, is a place most desirable (Roughley 1823, 188).

Running throughout this literature was the idea of idealised plantation organisation and (especially) layout. Roughley went on to recommend that 'a well-contrived plan of the buildings, their relative, convenient and appropriate situations, one to another, should be digested, and laid out on a piece of paper, of a size sufficient to have the whole delineated upon it' (Roughley *ibid*). While plantation surveys were invaluable for the 'absentee' planter who desired documentary evidence of his West Indian possessions, during the mid 18th century this equation was turned around. As Barry Higman has argued, 'the

Drax, H.	1755 [1650-1682]	Instructions upon the Management of Drax Hall and the Irish Hope plantations. In Belgrove, W. (ed) A Treatise upon Husbandry or Planting 51-86
Chelsus, A. de	1719	Histoire naturelle du cacao et du sucre (Paris, Laurant d'Houry)
Labat, J.B.	1724	Nouveau voyage aux isles de l'Amerique (6 vols; The Hague)
Leslie, C.	1740	A new and exact account of Jamaica London
Martin, S.	1750	An essay upon plantership. London
Anon	1752	The art of making sugar. London
Pinney, J.	Mid 1700s	Manuscript sources/letters. Summarised in Pares 1950, Chapter 6
Belgrove, W.	1755	A treatise upon husbandry or planting. Boston: D. Fowles
Grainger, J.	1764a	Hints on the Management of Negroes. In Essay on the More Common West Indian Diseases
Grainger, J.	2000 [1764]	The Sugar Cane: A Poem in Four Books with Notes. In Gilmore (ed.), 86-198
du Monceau, D.	1764	Art de raffiner le sucre. Paris
Long, E.	1970 [1774]	The History of Jamaica. London: Frank Cass
Baker, J.P.	1775	An essay on the art of making muscovado sugar. London
Cazaud, M.	1779	Account of a New Method of Cultivating the Sugar Cane. Philosophical Transactions of the Royal Society of London. 69: 207 ff.
Ramsay, J.	1784	An Essay on the Treatment and Conversion of African Slaves in the British Sugar Colonies. London
Turnball, G.	1785	Letters to a young planter, or, observations on the management of a sugar plantation. London
Beckford, W.	1790	A descriptive account of the island of Jamaica (2 vols) London
La Couture, D.	1790	Precis sur la canne et sur les moyens d'en extraire le sel essential (Paris, Duplain)
Peterkin, J	1790	A treatise on planting (Basseterre, St Kitts)
Avalle, L.	1796	Table comparatif des productions des colonies francais aux Antilles, avec celles des colonies anglais, espagnoles et hollandaises de l'annee 1787 a 1788. Paris
Laborie, P.	1798	The Coffee Planter of Saint Domingo. London: Caddell and Davies
Orderson, J.W.	1800	Directions to young planters for their care and management of a sugar plantation in Barbados. London
Caines, C.	1801	Letters on the Cultivation of the Otaheite Cane: the manufacture of sugar and rum, the saving of melasses, the care and preservation of stock, with attention and anxiety which is due to Negroes: to those topics are added a few other particulars analogous to the subject of the letters, and also a speech on the slave trade, the most important feature in West Indian cultivation. London: Robinson
Collins, D.	1971 [1811]	Practical Rules for the Management and Medical Treatment of Negro Slaves, in the Sugar Colonies, by a professional planter. Freeport: Books for Libraries Press

Table 3 Examples of the Developing Plantation Management Literature, 1682-1811

plantation map sometimes preceded the reality, enabling planter and surveyor to impose their ideal models of order on the landscape' (Higman 1988, 80). Plantation landscapes were increasingly provided with the elements of designed landscapes recommended by such treatises. Grainger claimed to be reminded of 'the pillars of the Temple of the Sun at Palmyra' whenever he rode 'past the charming vista of royal palms on the Cayon-estate of Daniel Matthew Esq. Of St Christopher' (Grainger 2000 [1764], 196). In an extreme example in 1769, an idealised survey of Lucky Valley Estate, Jamaica was commissioned by Edward Long, which incorporates a series of concentric circles and arcs, drawn at quarter-mile intervals, superimposed over the layout of the estate and clearly centred on the mid-point of the works buildings (Higman 1988, 84).

The new focus on tightly-designed landscapes is clearest in the discussion of the arrangement of slave accommodation. Such concerns were in keeping with more general new concerns during the late 18th century with intervention in and regulation of slave lifestyles (Goveia 1965). Regulations included the imposition of carefully regulated time-management, and dramatically increased surveillance (Ramsay 1784, 74-7). Thus, Beckford (1790) recommended the laying out of slave quarters

> in strait lines, constructed with some degree of uniformity and strength, but totally divested of trees and shrubs (Beckford 1790, Volume 2, 20, quoted by Higman 1988, 248).

Similarly, Grainger (2000 [1764], 160) recommended planters to 'build thy Negroe-huts...in streets, at distance due'. Such arrangements set special slave quarters apart from the 'polite' landscape: in contrast with the earlier arrangements of smaller numbers of slaves and indentured servants living alongside planters. Complex changing attitudes (and nascent racism) towards slaves were written across the landscape of plantations in this way. As early as 1745, William Smith wrote of Nevis that slaves

> live in Huts, on the Western Side of our Dwelling Houses... because we breath the pure Eastern air, without being offended with the least nauseous smell; Our kitchens and Boyling-houses are on the same side, and for the same reason (Smith 1745, 226).

Changing Sugar Technologies

The technologies of maps, plans and management discussed above were intimately bound up with European colonial attitudes to landscape (Hauser and Hicks forthcoming). They formed part of a range of other technological changes relating to industrial (rather than purely agricultural) production. Whereas many traditional historical accounts of the West Indian sugar industry have characterised the technological processes of sugar production as persisting virtually unchanged from mid 17th-century Barbados, the 18th century was in fact characterised by continual experimentation and innovation with sugar technology (Watts 1987, 405-423). Such experimentation was fuelled by fast-developing new concerns with the application of scientific techniques to cultivation and processing, and, in particular, with productivity (Ward 1988, 61-118).

The practice of sugar cane planting developed in several ways. New Asian varieties of cane – such as Otaheite and Bourbon – were introduced during the 1780s, partly as a response to new concerns about the impact on harvests of pests such as caterpillars and sugar ants. Bourbon was

the 18th-century name for Mauritius, from which both varieties of sugar cane were brought (Watts 1987, 433). Irrigation systems were introduced to islands which had sufficient water: in Martinique, for instance, sugar estates were intercut by complex arrangements of irrigation trenches from the 1720s. The use of the plough and of dung as manure also appears to have occurred in some parts of the eastern Caribbean during the second half of the 18th century (Ward 1988, 75). While the use of the plough is documented as early as the 1750s – by Samuel Martin in Antigua (Sheridan 1961, 353) – it was in 'almost universal use' in Antigua, and presumably other islands, by 1820 (Ragatz 1931, 23).

The major change in the technology of sugar cane crushing was the invention of the more efficient horizontal crushing machine. The horizontal arrangement of rollers, secured by a headstock, allowed the cane to be crushed twice by being passed back from one side to the other. This arrangement appears to have been invented in 1754 by John Smeaton: but the widespread use of horizontal roller crushing machines in the eastern Caribbean did not occur until the 1790s (Deerr 1943; 1950 figures 1-2). The horizontal three-roller mill went through a series of complex developments, including the introduction of the tied headstock around 1830 (Deerr 1950, 539-41). Other developments of crushing technology included the invention of a device known a 'doubleuse' which automatically fed the sugar cane back through the rollers, and from 1721 the use of solid iron rollers (rather than iron-clad wooden rollers). The Patent (number 433) for this last innovation, granted to William Harding in 1721, describes

> sugar mills...being chiefly made with large timber and wooden cogs, only having a case of iron on the timber and an iron gudgeon through them. New models have been made of sugar mills engines and worms whereof the coggs and gudgeons are all iron (Deerr 1950, 537).

The efficient use of waste crushed cane or 'trash' was achieved through its use as a fuel for the boiling house furnaces. This practice, encouraged by the increasing local scarcity of furnace timber as the small islands were cleared, developed from the early 18th century (Sloane 1707, Labat 1722). 'Trash houses' were often built near to the boiling house to store this fuel.

Alongside the widespread cattle- and wind-mills, water power came gradually to be used for sugar mills – an arrangement requiring considerable investment in landscape design including the construction of dams and carefully surveyed water leats. The earliest water-powered sugar mills in the Leeward Islands appear to have been constructed during the 1670s: for example, a 'waterworck' shown on a 1673 map of Montserrat (Pulsipher 1977, 90).

While the technologies of steam power would have been available to English planters from the 1710s, the application of steam power to crushing machinery requires rotative action. While direct rotative action from a steam engine was the subject of a patent in 1766, it was not generally used until after the development of Watt's sun and planet motion from 1781. There is very little evidence of the use of steam power for crushing cane in the Caribbean until the early 19th century – and most such Caribbean steam engines on sugar estates are post-emancipation in date (ie after 1838). However, it is possible to convert bilateral power to rotative power by using a steam engine to raise water to drive a water wheel.[21] While histories of sugar processing technology do not mention the possibility of such an arrangement, a patent for the application of just such an arrangement to sugar crushing was taken out by one John Stewart in 1766, and described in a pamphlet of 1767 (Deerr 1950, Plate XXX). Stewart stated that he could provide 'a machine which performs its operations by the power of such common Fire Engines as are used for raising water out of Mine, which…will answer all the purposes of Wind, Water and Horse Mills'. There appear also to have been early experiments with the use of steam to heat the boiling house coppers. Evidence of a post-emancipation example of such an arrangement survives at Balenbouche, St Lucia (see Chapter 5 below). Between the crushing area and boiling house, cane juice came during the 18th century to be conveyed (sometimes pumped) through a gutter or pipe, sometimes being strained through a brass wire sieve (Martin 1750, 44), and into the first copper or clarifier. The use of clarifiers (or 'cold receivers'), and the mixture of juice with lime to promote crystallisation, also became far more common from the mid 18th century.

One widespread development in sugar boiling technology during the 18th century was the Jamaica train, which had originally been developed during the 1680s. Single-case 'coppers' came to replace the earlier cauldrons which were made up of smaller pieces rivetted together. Rather than a series of fires heating the coppers, this system consisted of a single furnace below the smallest (last) copper (the 'teache'), and a long flue which extended below the other coppers (Martin 1750, 43-5). This arrangement provided greater fuel economy and more precision in temperatures, and became the standard arrangement of a 'copper wall' from the early 18th century.

Other developments in boiling technology included from around 1775 the use of the hydrometer to measure specific gravity of cane syrup before transfer to the curing house (Watts 1987, 424), and the use of the vacuum pan (which increased the efficiency of evaporation by allowing it to take place under vacuum) after 1813. The vacuum pan was a new invention, patented in 1813 by on Edward Howard (Deerr and Brooks 1946, 4). Ward (1988, 102) even cites evidence of orders being placed in 1808 for microscopes to examine the effects of different procedures on sugar crystalisation. Finally, in the curing process centrifuges were introduced during the early 19th century. In these

systems, after boiling the cooled sugar was passed through the centrifuge to separate the molasses from the sugar granules: greatly speeding up the curing process. The complexity of these changes underlines the sustained nature of planters' attempts to maximise efficiency and output under sugar monoculture.

The Social 'Landscapes' of the Plantocracy

Distinctive 'social landscapes' of the eastern Caribbean planter class also emerged during the 18th and early 19th centuries. Here, the survival of the letter books of several planters makes it possible to make some judgements about the emerging social worlds of the planter elite. A number of such letter books have been published: notably the letters of William Stapleton of Nevis, the Mills family of St Kitts and London, the papers of the Tudways of Wells, Somerset, who held the Parham Estate on Antigua) and the Pinney family of Nevis and Bristol (Gay 1928, Johnson 1966, Mason 1993, Nuttall 1939, Ward 1988, 64-74; Pares 1950, Thoms 1969, see also Tudway mss, Pinney mss).

What shines through from such documents is the importance of descent and marriage alliances in planter social organisation in relation to land tenure. A small number of 'old' families tended to dominate the plantation ownership and power within each eastern Caribbean island society during the 18th century. The careful development of pedigrees through marriage relations was central to the development of West Indian landed dynasties, especially in the face of a new emerging Atlantic merchant class. Established families dominated the Islands' Assemblies and Councils, and had strong family and business connections with England, providing 'direct access...to the commodity and money markets of the metropolis' (Sheridan 1961, 344, 349; Sheridan 1974, 371; Olwig 1993, 23-5).

Kin relations were also central to the establishment of incoming merchants or planters to the Leewards in the 18th century. For instance, the medically-trained poet James Grainger (c. 1721-1766) married a wealthy heiress, Daniel Matthew Burt, soon after arriving on St Kitts in 1759. His wife's name was an amalgam of three of the planter families to whom she was related. This situation reflected her remarkable connections to an established plantocratic dynasty (Gilmore 2000, 13; Webb 1979, 486-7, 490). Her father was William Pym Burt, related to the Pyms who leased Wingfield Estate in the 18th century (see below), and her paternal grandfather was William Burt of Nevis (d. 1707). Her maternal grandfather was part of a significant local dynasty. He was William Matthew, a Governor of the Leeward Islands for a brief period during 1704. William had been the second son of Abednego Matthew, Governor of St Kitts 1678-81, and owner of the walled enclosure at Wingfield (see Chapter 3). Her maternal uncle, also William Matthew, was similarly Governor of the Leewards for only a brief period (1714-15), and was Deputy Governor of St Kitts 1715-1733. Her brother, William Matthew Burt,

[21] An arrangement pioneered at the Champion copper works in Bristol in 1752 (Deerr and Brooks 1943, 11).

47

was MP for Great Marlow in 1761, and Governor of the Leeward Islands 1776-81. Another Scottish doctor, Walter Tullideph, came to Antigua in 1726 and in 1736 wrote that he

> married an agreeable young widow by whom I gott Possession of a very fine Estate to which I am making additions and improvements and am likely to have an heir of my own.

Both James Grainger and Walter Tullideph had been introduced to the eastern Caribbean by friends who were already established there. The case of Tullideph is worth pursuing further as an example of the incoming bourgeois planter class. After arriving, he soon began to sell English commodities to planters as his brother's factor, worked as a doctor, and combined these trades by retailing medicines and drugs. He provided credit to planters by using his connections to borrow from London and lending at a higher rate of interest in Antigua. In 1736, Tullideph proceeded to enlarge the estate from 127 acres and 63 slaves to 536 acres and 271 slaves over the next 18 years (Sheridan 1957, 3; 1961, 350). Throughout his life in Antigua, Tullideph appears to have reproduced the plantocratic social structure – assisting a tight group of relatives and associates in a broad range of economic ventures, including overseeing plantations.

One planter who did not need to marry into West Indian society was Samuel Martin (1693-1776). He was heir to a substantial Antiguan estate, and was from a family that made much of its English aristocratic origins. Martin's ancestors had also been involved in the Elizabethan plantation of Ireland (Andrews and Andrews 1923; Sheridan 1961, 352). Having spent some years in England, Martin returned to Antigua in 1750, after which he began 'an ambitious program of reconstruction' of this sugar estate in a similar manner to Tullideph. Here, the close relationships between estate landscapes and social landscapes are clear: a theme that will be explored in the next section through the idea of 'improvement'.

Discussion: Improved Landscapes

As seen in the words of Walter Tullideph, writing in 1736, above, the white English and Scottish planter elite who brought about the transition to sugar monoculture between the early 18th and early 19th centuries saw the negotiation of both physical and social landscapes as requiring 'additions and improvements' (Sheridan 1957, 3). In the rest of this chapter, I want to explore how the idea of 'improvement' can be used as a point of entry in the examination of the emergence and development of sugar monoculture in the eastern Caribbean. The social 'improvement' of the incoming bourgeois merchants was clearly closely bound up with the urge to 'improve' plantations: increasing size and profitability through management. In this new situation where all planters processed their own sugar, 'additions and improvements' were interrelated:

economies of scale threw the balance in favour of the planter who possessed several hundred acres of arable land, and improved sugar works, and a labour force of [hundreds of] Negro slaves (Sheridan 1961, 343).

As we have seen, some of the new concerns with innovations in productivity and efficiency related to technological 'improvements' of plantation agriculture. For example, a committee of Antiguans wrote in 1788 that 'All…probable improvements in the Instruments of Husbandry have from time to time had a fair trial' (Ragatz 1931, 23). This included the 'improvement' of estates by enlarging their area (purchasing neighbouring estates and incorporating the land), their number of slaves and their overall productivity – and of course, by increasing profits. Improving activities often focused on the maintenance of healthy, productive slave labour through the use of (mainly Edinburgh-trained) doctors and a thriving import trade in medicines (Sheridan 1974, 372; 1985). 'Improvement' – in the sense of a demonstration or showing to be true – also involved survey, mapping and the commissioning of plans of West Indian estates. The 'improvement' of the accuracy of such plans through the application of new scientific survey techniques was important, and was also mirrored in the 'improvement' of landscapes through the implementation of 'ideal' landscape schemes on the ground. Constant changes in the technologies of agro-industrial sugar production also derived from impulses towards the 'improvement' of estates through the academic study and application of scientific principles and of plantation management. Meanwhile, new ideas of social respectability developed across all parts of West Indian society during the same period, especially after the Methodist missions from the 1780s (Coke 1808-11), which built upon earlier Moravian missionary activities that had begun in the 1730s (Olwig 1993, 71, 87). These ideas were closely linked with ideas of the self-'improvement' of an incoming bourgeois, international merchant class through marriage relations with an established landed planter elite, was bound up with these material processes.

From the 1780s, the idea of 'improvement' also came to incorporate the pernicious idea of the 'amelioration' of slave conditions (Ward 1988, 2). Crucial contexts for this development were the development of the Haitian Revolution (1791-1804), the slave insurrections that took place in St Lucia, Dominica, St Vincent and Grenada in the 1790s (Ward 1988, 97), and the growth of the anti-slavery movement in the North Atlantic world. The first legislative step towards amelioration was the Leeward Island Act of 1798, which aimed to prevent the physical abuse of slaves. The idea of amelioration 'gained currency from the 1790s as a professed policy for estate management' (Ward 1988, 97), and became particularly widespread after the abolition of the legal slave trade in 1807 as planters were encouraged to maintain slave populations through reproduction. While island legislatures passed a series of laws relating to slave treatment, and planters were prosecuted for cruelty, 'amelioration' was just the latest incarnation of the idea of improvement – which was from the outset bound up with the ideology of racial slavery.

My suggestion here is that the idea of improvement can be used to express the common attitudes held by male planters at this time to technologies, landscapes, and social relations. In such a model, the 'landscapes' of sugar monoculture brought a heterogeneous range of new concerns with improvement that were applied to environments, houses, mills, slaves and even marriage partners. And clearly, a central dimension of the idea of improvement in the eastern Caribbean was that it was accompanied by new extremes of horror and violence in racial slavery. As throughout this study, the archaeological question relates to how these ideas were worked out in particular situations. In the rest of this chapter, therefore, I shall present the archaeological and documentary evidence for the changing landscapes of Wingfield, St Kitts and Balenbouche, St Lucia during the 18th and early 19th centuries.

Improved Landscapes on St Kitts, from c. AD 1713

The accession of George I in 1714, and the end of the Stuart period, traditionally marks a watershed in the history of British activities in the Caribbean. By this time, all the English Leewards were fully on their way to sugar monoculture. Under the Treaty of Utrecht (1713), French St Kitts – an area almost certainly even more advanced in the transition to sugar monoculture – had been ceded to Britain.[22] Under the same Treaty, British involvement in the slave trade was radicalised. The decline of mercantilism had begun with the new involvement of private merchants in the slave trade after the withdrawal of the monopoly of the Royal African Company (RAC) in 1698 – an event which greatly affected the economy of Nevis, which had been the RAC's Leeward Islands entrepôt. This was consolidated through the granting of the slave *asiento*: the exclusive rights to supply slaves to the Spanish through the South Sea Company, and the continued development of the bilateral trade between Britain and the Americas. Some 2.8 million slaves were shipped by the British from Africa between 1701 and 1807 (D. Richardson 1987, 105-6).

The 50 years between the Treaty of Utrecht and the end of the Seven Years War saw the British Leeward Islands develop into the key sugar and trading islands of the eastern Caribbean. At the forefront was St Kitts. Any negative impact of the 1706 French attacks on the plantations in St Kitts and Nevis was more than offset by the payment of over £100,000 in compensation by the English government to the planters – around three quarters of which went to Nevis (National Archives, Kew, CO 243/2).

As Niddrie (1966) has observed, the response of the

colonial administration to the ceding of French St Kitts in 1713 is of interest. A significant proportion of the French population appear to have left for other French territories. The abandoned French lands were estimated to amount to around 30,000 acres, of which some 25,000 were cultivable. In correspondence with the Queen in May 1714, the Council for Trade and Plantations rejected the sale of the land in one tranche, despite the speculative interest of the South Sea Company. Rather, the Council proposed

> that no more than 2 or 300 acres of good manureable lands be granted or sold to any single family....[and] that the poorer sort of inhabitants may have some parcels of the worst land near the seaside given to them gratis... The better to perform this work...it will be necessary that Commissioners of known probity and ability not exceeding three with Surveyors under them, be sent from hence (CSPC 1712-14, #662. Quoted by Niddrie 1966, 7-8)

In order to divide the land into small lots, the Governor of the Leeward Islands proposed in April 1716 that since

> most of the French plantations have very irregular bounds...therefore it would be necessary that whenever there be directions from H.M. for the settling of that part of the island, that orders should be given to the Surveyors, that an East and West and North and South line should be struck through the two former French parts (they being in the East and West parts of the island), that from hence all plantations might be laid out in such square tracts or quantity of acres that should be granted by the Crown to particular persons; this would not only make the island look like a garden but prevent in time to come any vexatious law suits or wranglings which might otherwise of necessity ensue but will prove vastly to the quieting of the inhabitants (CSPC 1716-17 #118. Quoted by Niddrie 1966, 8-9).

However, British attempts to handle the sale of the French lands in such a way as to encourage the growth of a small landowning 'yeoman' class appears to have failed. Provisional grants were made – apparently by the St Kitts Assembly – in the decade after the 1713 with no action from London. It was not until 1726 that three 'commissioners' were appointed, the provisional grants were cancelled and the land was sold. However, on the eventual completion of the sale process in 1728, 'most of the plantations remained in the hands of local settlers long established in the island' (Niddrie 1966).[23] A similar attempt to encourage the development of a yeoman class occurred on Antigua in 1700, when the Assembly passed an Act which created '10 acre lands' described by Douglas Hall, which

---

[22] The French Companie des Isles had begun 'a definite policy of encouraging the cultivation of the sugar cane' from its formation in 1635 (Higham 1921, 30; Mims 1912, 30-36).

[23] See National Archives T 1/275 ff. 248-249 (1729) *List of contracts made by the Commisioners for Sale of Lands in St Christopher's that formerly belonged to the French*. See also National Archives CO 152/13, ff. 253-256. (1721) *A List of the present possessors of the French land in Basseterra and Cabesterre divisions*).

call[ed] upon the owners of undeveloped land on which they had neglected to pay taxes to pay the arrears or forfeit the land to the Crown. Any land so forfeited was to be granted, in small lots, by the local legislature who would give a preference to disbanded soldiers. Each grantee was to receive £3, a baron of beef, and a cask of flour, and was to be exempted from levy for debt, and from taxation. His title was to be recorded, and he was to have the vote... If any grantee, or any of his heirs, did not settle on and develop his grant, of if a grantee died without heir, the land was to revert to the Crown (Hall 1971, 41-2).

However, the Antiguan scheme failed: the majority of the land being annexed by larger estates during the 18th century. The similar failure of the Commissioners' planned scheme of settlement of the ceded French land in St Kitts is demonstrated by the cartographic evidence. The Moll maps of 1708 and 1729 show great continuity in the locations of sugar works between the French and English phases of occupation.[24] The land boundaries recorded by Anthony Ravell (1780 [1775]) – the 'Surveyor General of St Christophers, Nevis and Montserrat' – demonstrate some of the 'square tracts' encouraged by the Commissioners but new large estates were formed, centred on sugar works. The failure of these schemes was clearly due to the power of the planters, and their alternative conceptions of the future of plantation landscapes.

Wingfield Estate, St Kitts, c. AD 1713-1838

In Chapter 3, the establishment of Jeaffreson's new water-powered sugar works at Wingfield, and his adoption of Matthews' enclosure, house and associated buildings (probably indigo works) in the 1680s, was described. The new 'Wingfield Manor' – a name which persists to this day – was damaged in the French attacks of 1706, and by the 1720s the surrounding landscape was much changed. The ceding of French lands in 1713 saw the British administrative centre shift from Old Road to the old French capital of Basseterre, which has remained the administrative capital of St Kitts ever since. The paucity of documentary references to the town and cartographic evidence points to the partial abandonment and contraction of the settlement at Old Road after this date, although significant free black population developed in Old Road during the 18th century (Cox 1984, 1988).

Up until 1713, Christopher Jeaffreson (1650-1725) managed the Wingfield estate from Cambridgeshire through his Ensign in St Kitts, Mr Thorn. From 1713 Jeaffreson leased Wingfield to one General L. Lambert between 1713 and 1728, and to then the estate was leased to one Charles Pym between 1728 and 1758. An inventory of Wingfield taken in 1713 before the lease portrays a markedly different image of Wingfield from the 1680s estate. It lists only a few slaves, 'an old boiling house and

walls', 'four mill posts and one bridge tree of the island wood' and 'one deal water spout rotten & of no value', along with 'a few negro houses' (*Appendix 4*).

A complex sequence of industrial development took place in the sugar works in the early 18th century, and these changes are in keeping with the change in management after 1713 (Hicks and Horton 2001b). A massive brick and stone aqueduct was constructed to replace an earlier wooden launder, and its impressive arches and fine brick dressings now dominated appearance of the estate. Above the northern entrance to the crushing area, a small bell tower, built of brick, was added. The pre-existing wall around the works was retained, but in the first phase of investment and change the boiling house was extended, with the mouths of the flues (small openings with brick voissours) facing east from their current locations, but with the building extended further to the west than at present (**Figure 6**).

In a second phase of development at the works, a completely new boiling house arrangement was provided: the building was 'flipped over' from west to east, keeping the coppers in the same position. Four coppers survive in what would originally have been a row of six coppers, with open windows above. The old east-facing flues were covered over by a new south-north flue system, and the western part of the earlier boiling house was demolished. The new flue arrangement incorporated a corridor running in below the boiling house from the south. In an interesting development, this corridor controlled movement around the works, now forming the only entrance within the walls apart from through the sugar crushing area into the boiling house (Hicks and Horton 2001b).

The dating of this second phase of works development is difficult from the building sequence, but one significant piece of evidence is that below this changed arrangement a new culvert was provided from the water wheel, through which the water passed, before being channelled along the side of the road to Romney, and being used for the water wheel there. A substantial stone bridge between the Wingfield and Romney works also appears to have been constructed at this time.[25]

A documentary reference describes the pulling down of the boiling house at Wingfield in 1795: presumably another later change:

> The evidence of Mr Spence, who states that his father (Robert Spence) lived as Manager on Lord Romney's Estate between the years 1797 and 1801. That he

---

[24] Herman Moll *The Island of St Christophers, alias St Kitts.* National Archives CO 700/St. Christopher and Nevis3.

[25] The road from Wingfield to Romney which passes below the aqueduct, around the works, crossing the river the stone bridge, and following along the side of the valley, is flanked by impressive stone terrace walls. While the bridge over river has the appearance of an 18th-century carriage-way bridge, it in fact has a date stone of 1871. This may be from a reconstruction, after a flood: date stones can be an unreliable indicator of the date of first construction.

recollected several Negroes about Males and Females (young and old) having the Surname of Jeaffreson. There were Negro houses on the lands let by the General to Lord Romney, in which houses he recollects that the Negroes names Jeaffreson resided. That his Father always considered them so and that the reason why the General's Lands were rented out was because he had too few Negroes to work them himself. That there is a Water Mill now on the General's Lands, and there was a Boiling House which was pulled down in 1795. (Jeaffreson Papers: Case between Romney and Jeaffreson 17 December 1823)

Since no dams survive for the Romney works, this arrangement is clearly contemporary with the construction of the water works at Romney. The only evidence for this is that water works are shown at both Romney and Wingfield on the Baker map of 1756. However, this is two years before the lease of Wingfield was taken over by the Earl of Romney (Robert Marsham, 1712-93), who had married Charles Pym's daughter and heiress Priscilla in 1742. The works at 'Romney Manor' appear to have been developed soon after the marriage. Romney held the lease until 1819.[26]

The new boiling house is marked with a cross on the Baker map of 1756 (**Figure 14**) – a fact that requires brief discussion. This may be the result of a surveying mistaking the distinctive brick bell tower (used for ringing out the daily divisions of plantation routine) above the boiling house for an old church. Boiling houses and churches are similar in form: an observation supported by a description of a Tobago sugar estate in 1793: 'the works have the appearance of a church.' (Young 1793, 276-7, quoted in Eubanks 1992, 112). However, Christianity among slaves was being encouraged by increasing numbers of planters during the late 18th century who would receive missionaries at plantations. An account from around 1830 describes such meetings as taking place either under a large tree or 'in the boiling house, which was fitted into a chapel for the occasion' (Olwig 1993, 72). Since boiling houses were only used during the harvesting seasons, it would be strange if such substantial buildings were left unused for the rest of the time. The possibility that the boiling house at Wingfield was used as a chapel during the 1750s is intriguing: and would be important evidence in the obscure history of the promotion of Christianity among slave populations. The proximity of Wingfield to Old Road, and the distance of the 17th-century Anglican parish Church at Middle Island, to the west of Old Road, raises the possibility that such a chapel would have served a wider community.

[26] Romney had a large house in Maidstone called The Mote, and the history of the Marsham family and their involvement in the development of Wingfield and Romney Manor benefits from a substantial archive in The Centre for Kentish Studies, Maidstone, Kent, England (See also Gilmore 2000, 275).

The often fraught business relationship between the Marshams and Jeaffreson is detailed by correspondence in the Jeaffreson papers. A document of 1823 describes the history of the leasing of Wingfield:

General Jeaffreson is the Owner of a large Sugar Plantation called the Wingfield Manor Estate situate at St Kitts in the West Indies. This Estate was let by the General's Ancestors by a Lease dated in Mar 1713 to Major General L. Lambert, who was an ancestor of the present Lord Romney & who had an Estate adjoining ;and immediately on the expiration of that Lease (in Nov'r 1728) the same Estate was let on Lease to Charles Pym also an ancestor of Lord Romney; immediately on expiration of which a second Lease was granted thereof, on the 25th of March 1758, to the late Lord Romney before or immediately on the expiration of which a second Lease was granted to his Lordship of the same Estate on the 20th of Oct'r 1781 which last Lease exp. At Michaelmas 1818 so that the Estate was in the Continued possession of Lord Romney and his Ancestors from 1713 to 1818 (when after some negotiation) bettween Lord Romney and the General, as to the terms of renewal, in which they could not agree, Lord Romney's Agent in the Island gave over the Estate to Gen. Jeaffreson's Agent. (Jeaffreson Papers: Case between Romney and Jeaffreson 17 December 1823)

An argument in 1823 between Jeaffreson and Romney over the ownership of a group of slaves which appear to have shifted from working at Wingfield to Romney when the estates were under joint management:

Jeaffreson Mr Tyson, the present Tenant there, was a gang of Slaves on Lord Romney's Estate which were reputed to be the Descendants of some Slaves that formerly belonged to the General's Estate, but which had been removed off it to Lord Romney's. Mr Tyson also obtained from an old Gentleman who many years ago resided on Lord Romney's Est'e a list of the Negroes on his Lordship's Estate in the years 1779 & 1780; in those lists the following names appear vizt Cate Jeaffreson, [illegible]y Jeaffreson, Mina Jeaffreson, Nanny Jeaffreson, Bender Jeaffreson, Betty Jeaffreson, Eve Jeaffreson, Flamm. Jeaffreson, Neddy Jeaffreson & Diana Jeaffreson. Of the above slaves only Bender Jeaffreson is now alive; but their descendants are the Slaves who are now supposed to be the property of General Jeaffreson. In consequence of this information, from Mr Tyson, the General directed an Enquiry to be made in the Island as to the Evidence he could obtain of these Slaves being his Property; and on searching the Register Office of Slaves the undermentioned equal return of Slaves with the surname Jeaffreson (Jeaffreson Papers: Case between Romney and Jeaffreson 17 December 1823).

Clearly, then, at some point – presumably under the Pym lease – the Romney and Wingfield works came to be managed as a single enterprise. The considerable double-investment in Wingfield and Romney demonstrates a confidence in a long-term situation in which the plantations were managed together.

Apart from the investment in and development of the sugar works, a new Estate House – shown on the Baker map of 1756 – was provided at some point during the first half of the 18th century. This new house was situated to the north, high up above the works, and commanded wide views. Archaeological landscape survey identified the earthwork remains of a stone terrace which carried a road to the site of this house, and a set of earthworks which form a terrace and a house platform (**Figure 7**, **House 2**). Downhill, the area of the Matthews enclosure appears to have been abandoned, continuing as an area of barns and storehouses, with the enclosure walls and house demolished. In 1756, the Baker map shows that Jeaffreson continued to own two other works in the vicinity of Wingfield: one on what appears to be the site of his first works, and a third further uphill to the north.

The development of the Wingfield landscape in the later 18th and early 19th centuries can be traced by comparing the Baker map with the McMahon of 1828 (**Figure 15**), in combination with the evidence of landscape survey and building recording (**Figure 6**). Several radical changes are visible in the plantation landscape. Firstly, while the sugar works remained in the same location, a new plantation house was provided (**Figures 6 & 7, House 3**), re-using the site of the Matthews enclosure, and even using the massive enclosure wall as part of its foundation. Secondly, the two works to the north of Wingfield which were still in use in 1756 are shown as under cane in 1828: all the sugar processing being brought together at Wingfield and Romney. The road across the island, which had run through the Matthews enclosure in the 1680s, was diverted around the other side of the remains of the enclosure by 1828. The abandonment of the road across the island apart from for access to higher plantations during the 18th century is underlined by a description from 1854 of a journey from Basseterre to Spooner's Level:

> since…the island has become a British possession [the road] has been considered of little moment, and has been much neglected, indeed I have never travelled in any country, not even in the wilds of Ceylon, a road less deserving of the name of road, or ever rode down a descent comparable for difficulty with the 'nine turn gut' as the steepest part of the road is called, leading towards Old Road' (Davy 1854, 469).

Thirdly, the McMahon map also provides a detail omitted from the Baker map – the location of an area of 'Negro Houses', in low-lying land near the banks of the Wingfield River, and out of sight from the main estate.

After this complex sequence of landscape change, in 1819, the lease for the much-'improved' Wingfield was advertised:

> To Let: The Plantation called *Wingfield Manor* situated in the Parish of St Thomas, Middle Island to the westward of Little River in the Town of Old-Road, the Property of Major John Jeaffreson, and now in the occupation of the Right Honourable Earl Romney, consisting of 960 Acres of Land, of which the Cane Land and Pasturage are inferior to none in the Island. The Cane Mill is turned by an abundant Stream of Water, and the Estate commands peculiar advantages. Immediate possession, with the standing Crop of Canes and Provisions, may be had. For the Terms and Particulars, apply to R.W. Pickwoad (*The Godwin* January 19 1819).

Sugar Landscapes on St Lucia, from c. AD 1763

The history and archaeology of the 17th-century landscapes of southern St Lucia were explored in Chapter 2 above, and similar situations persisted into the 18th century. Despite the existence of a governor system since 1651 (Breen 1972 [1844], 420-21), St Lucia had oscillated violently between British and French ownership: changing hands 14 times before being ceded to the British (unusually as a Crown colony) in 1814-15 (Burns 1954, 454-466). Permanent French settlement, centred in the north and west of the country, close to the French stronghold of Martinique, developed after 1713. After the Treaty of Utrecht (1713), the French population of St Lucia was reportedly increased by a number of French deserters (Jesse 1969, 18), and on March 23 1719, a formal Prise de possession – a ceremony of formal occupation – was conducted at Pointe St Victor on the Carénage (Castries Harbour). However, this French colony was apparently short-lived. Yet another British settlement venture was launched in 1722: but the Treaty of Aix-la-Chapelle (1748) defined St Lucia, along with St Vincent, Dominica and Tobago, which all had strong Carib populations, as reserved for the Caribs 'forever' (Watts 1987, 250).

St Lucia was taken again by the British in 1778, but was handed back to the French with the Treaty of Versailles in 1783. St Lucia was annexed by the British in 1793 on the wishes of French planters who were concerned about the consequences of the French and Haitian Revolutions, but the island was immediately re-captured under Victor Hugues, who then brought about slave emancipation on the island. Similar revolutionary activities took place in Grenada in 1795. St Lucia was re-captured by the British in 1795, who swiftly re-instated slavery (Craton 1982). St Lucia was permanently returned to British control with the Treaty of Paris in 1814 (until independence in 1979).

West Indian histories of the Windward Islands conventionally carefully trace such broad changes and conflicts, but offer little further detail, since very few documents survived the endless administrative changes. But as suggested in Chapter 2 above, accounts of landscape change are more helpful in exploring the archaeology of colonial St Lucia than nationalist stories of European settlement and warfare. The broader context of British and French plantation landscapes in the eastern Caribbean is helpful in understanding the changes wrought in the second half of the 18th century. The 1760s saw a dramatic new confidence of British and French investment in the Windward Islands, and developments that brought to the Windwards the earlier process that was vividly described by one William Byam in 1668 as 'hewing a new fortune out of the wild woods' (describing his arrival from Surinam to establish a new plantation in Antigua, quoted by Sheridan 1961, 347).

In British contexts, by the mid 18th century, sugar monoculture and the larger estates meant that it was very difficult for incoming merchants to obtain arable land in the old British sugar islands of the Leewards, Barbados and Jamaica. By the 1750s, aspiring planters had started to establish plantations in non-British islands, and to smuggle the sugar into the British market (Pitman 1967, 337-338). Planter interests from the Leewards had actively opposed the extension of sugar production elsewhere in the eastern Caribbean – especially St Lucia – since the 1720s (Pitman 1967, 336), and it had previously been proposed that St Lucia could be settled with a ban on sugar production (Gordon 1720), but the new security of the 1760s led to an explosion of investment. Aspiring planters sought out the especially desirable fertile, coastal areas of flat land that characterised these islands. This feeling was expressed in April 1763, just two months after the Treaty of Paris, by James Grainger, who wrote from St Kitts to London that 'Mr Bourryau has bought a vast estate in Grenada...[and] many of my friends have purchased large plantations' there. Grainger continued by expressing regret that he had not the resources to buy land in Grenada or St Vincent (Grainger to Percy 18 April 1763; Gilmore 2000, 17). The success of the new plantations was reflected by the imposition from 1764 of the same 4.5% duty on exports from the British Windward Islands as had been paid in the Leewards and Barbados since 1664 (Burns 1954, 507).

The social and agricultural landscapes of each of the Windward Islands into which British and French planters moved in 1763 were varied: a diversity that was acknowledged at the time in statements of the *Considerations which may tend to promote the Settlement of our New West-India Colonies* (Pitman 1969, 355, cf. Campbell 1763). The French sugar economy on Grenada was (*pace* Ward 1988, 38) well established at this time, with some 82 sugar plantations (Pitman 1969, 355). Small cotton, coffee and cocoa plantations had been established by European and Carib populations on St Lucia, Dominica and St Vincent, while there is little documentary evidence of any permanent settlement in the Grenadines and Tobago. The long-term changes in landscape in the Windwards will be examined in the rest of this section with special reference to the south coast of St Lucia.

A shift in St Lucia's agricultural situation had occurred from the 1730s: after which, a mixed frontier economy of small-scale production of tobacco, ginger, cotton, coffee and sugar was replaced by a new, widespread emphasis on coffee and cotton. Between *c*. 1730 and 1745 the island's documented population had expanded from 463 (of whom 175 were slaves) to 3455 (of whom 2573 were slaves). While no agriculture is recorded in 1730, the 946 hectares were recorded as under coffee and 414 under cotton by 1760 (Rennard nd).

Suddenly, from the mid 1760s, large sugar estates began to be developed. A permanent government was established at Souffrière in 1765, and by 1787, a highly detailed survey by Lefort de Latour depicted an intensively cleared landscape of sugar, coffee, cotton and cocoa plantations (De Latour 1787; see also Campbell 1763). Between 1765 and 1780, at least 50 large sugar plantations were established (Breen 1972 [1844], 275). Another source suggests that on 1st January 1769, 16 sugar works, and 18 nearly completed, were recorded on St Lucia, alongside 1279680 plants of cocoa, 2463880 plants of coffee, 681 squares of cotton and 454 of canes (Jeffreys 1780, 26).

In 1780, the damage of a hurricane on St Lucia reportedly 'destroyed most of the estates' works' (Breen 1972 [1844], 277), and meant that the establishment of a road system was 'a job which must be done all over again as though the island had only just been colonised' (de Latour 1787). However, another source records that by 1789, 32 water mills, 18 cattle mills and 3 wind mills existed on the island (Breen 1972 [1844], 291-2, quoting the St Lucia Almanac for 1789). While there is some evidence of the abandonment of some St Lucian plantations in the early 1800s (Watts 1987, 282, National Archives CO 253, 11), the recorded numbers had grown to 51 water mills, 26 cattle mills, 6 windmills and 14 steam engines by 1843, and the number of sugar estates grew from 43 to 81 during the same period (Breen *ibid*). Another source lists 73 sugar works, 313 coffee plantations, 150 cocoa plantations, and 459 cotton plantations in 1789 (de Latour 1787, Appendix: Récapitulation des onze quartier qui composent l'Ile). The landscape contexts of such agricultural changes in St Lucia is most easily described through a detailed examination of particular plantation landscapes, and the next section considers the documentary and archaeological evidence for landscape change at Balenbouche estate from *c*. AD 1770 (**Figures 3, 12 & 18**)

Balenbouche Estate, c. AD 1770-1838

Despite the paucity of documentary sources for colonial St Lucia, some evidence of the planters and slaves of Balenbouche Estate can be drawn together. The earliest identified documentary evidence relating to Balenbouche are two plans of the Quartier de l'Islet a Caret (the modern quarter of Laborie) dating from AD 1770 and 1780 (St Lucia National Archives, uncatalogued documents: de Latour 1787). Both plans show the area owned by Martin, with an estate to the west of modern Balenbouche, bounded by River Dorée on the west, owned by 'Héritiers Degatieres'. More detailed documentary resources relating to the proprietors and slaves at Balenbouche survive

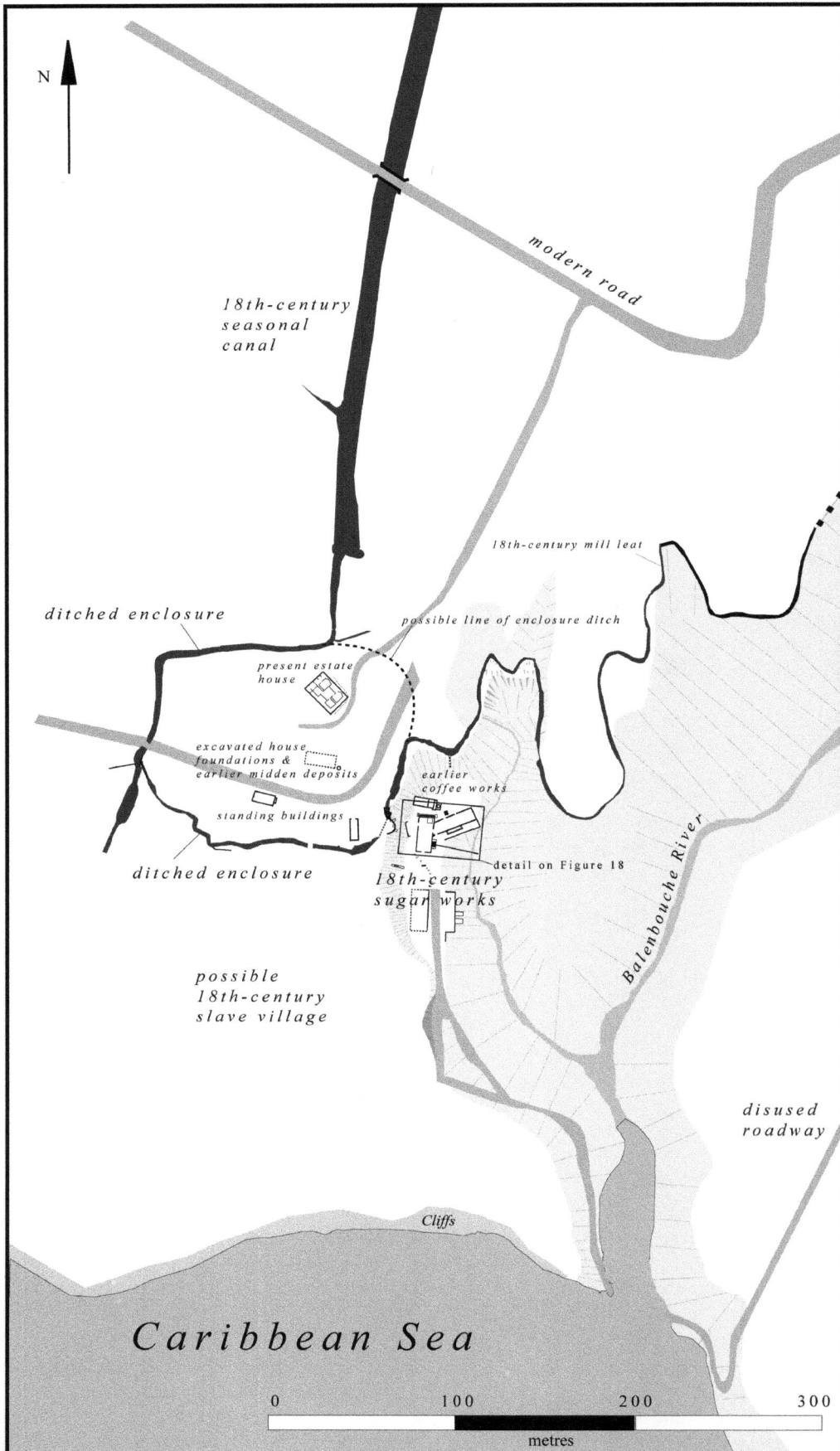

N

modern road

18th-century
seasonal
canal

18th-century mill leat

ditched enclosure

possible line of enclosure ditch

present estate
house

excavated house
foundations &
earlier midden deposits

earlier
coffee works

standing buildings

detail on Figure 18

ditched enclosure

18th-century
sugar works

Balenbouche River

possible
18th-century
slave village

disused
roadway

Cliffs

Caribbean Sea

| 0 | 100 | 200 | 300 |

metres

FIGURE 12. LANDSCAPE SURVEY AT BALENBOUCHE, ST LUCIA (MULTI-PERIOD)

Year	Number of slaves
1815	203
1819	185
1822	167
1828	182
1834	166

Table 4. Number of slaves at Balenbouche Estate, 1815-1834 (National Archives, Kew. Abstracts of returns (plantation slaves): T71/379, T71/381, T71/383, T71/387, T71/390)

after 1815 (*Tables 4* and *5*). Throughout this period, the 'Ballambouche' slave returns are in French, unlike the majority of St Lucian slave returns. The estate therefore appears to have remained in French-speaking ownership after the ceding of St Lucia to Britain in 1813 until at least 1834. In 1815, the proprietors of the estate are named as Louis Marie Duval and Jacques Marie Dogigny Lacaze (T71/379). By 1822, the proprietors were listed as 'Veuve Duval et D. Lacaze'. Presumably this is the widow of Louis Marie Duval and the overseer J.M. Dogigny Lacaze (T71/383). In 1828, the entry reads 'Duval et D.D. Drivon', while in 1834 the entry is 'Sr et Dame Dominique Drivon'

(T71/387, T71/390). The Duval in 1828-1834 is probably Louise Catherine Duval, who was born on 3rd December 1800, who is recorded as owning Balenbouche Estate before emigrating to New Orleans (St Lucia National Archives, uncatalogued documents).

Two hundred and three slaves were recorded at 'Ballambouche' estate on the 13th December 1815 (National Archives T71/379). These included 31 families, and their names, occupations, ages, and countries of birth are listed in full in *Appendix 5* (see *Tables 4* and *5*). Forty two of these were recorded as born in Africa, while six were born elsewhere in the Caribbean (Dominica, Montserrat, Martinique, Grenada and Guadeloupe). A sample of the number of slaves held at Balenbouche between 1815 and 1834 is presented below. The slave numbers represent a large estate, compared, for example, with 63 slaves held at the adjacent sugar estate of Degatieres in 1834. These slaves were held by 'Veuve Alexander, ci devant widow and heir of the late W. Alexander' at the adjacent estate of the 'Desgatiers' estate in 1834 (National Archives, Kew T71/390). This is probably a reference to the same family as the 'Wme Alexander' listed as owning a sugar factory adjacent to Balenbouche in 1787 (de Latour 1787). When 'Balambouche' was sold on 18 February 1836 by judicial sale through the St Lucia Incumbered Estates Commission, it was the most expensive of any of

French	English Translation	Number recorded in 1815
charpentiere	carpenter	6
macon	builder	3
cuisinier	cook	1
rumier	distiller	2
guardien	guardian (of young children)	10
cultivateur	cane worker	117
matelot	seaman	4
commandeur	gang leaders	2
point	none	30
pecheur	fisherman	1
infirme	infirm	3
domestique	domestic	13
hospitalisse	nurse	2
petit atelier	workshop (pottery?, textiles?)	4
tonnelier	cooper	3
rafineur	sugar refiner	1
mousse	ship's boy	1
TOTAL		203

Table 5. Slave Occupations at Balenbouche 1815

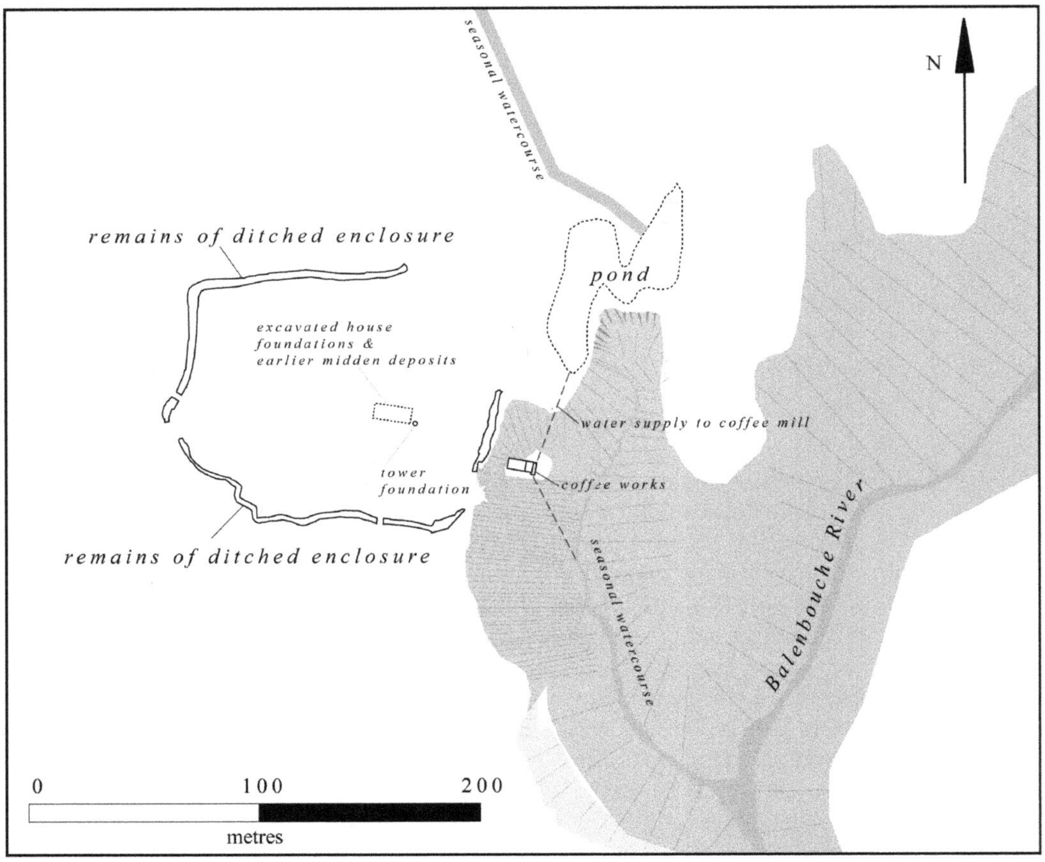

FIGURE 13. DETAIL OF PRE-SUGAR ESTATE LANDSCAPE AT BALENBOUCHE, ST LUCIA, SHOWING REMAINS OF DITCHED ENCLOSURE

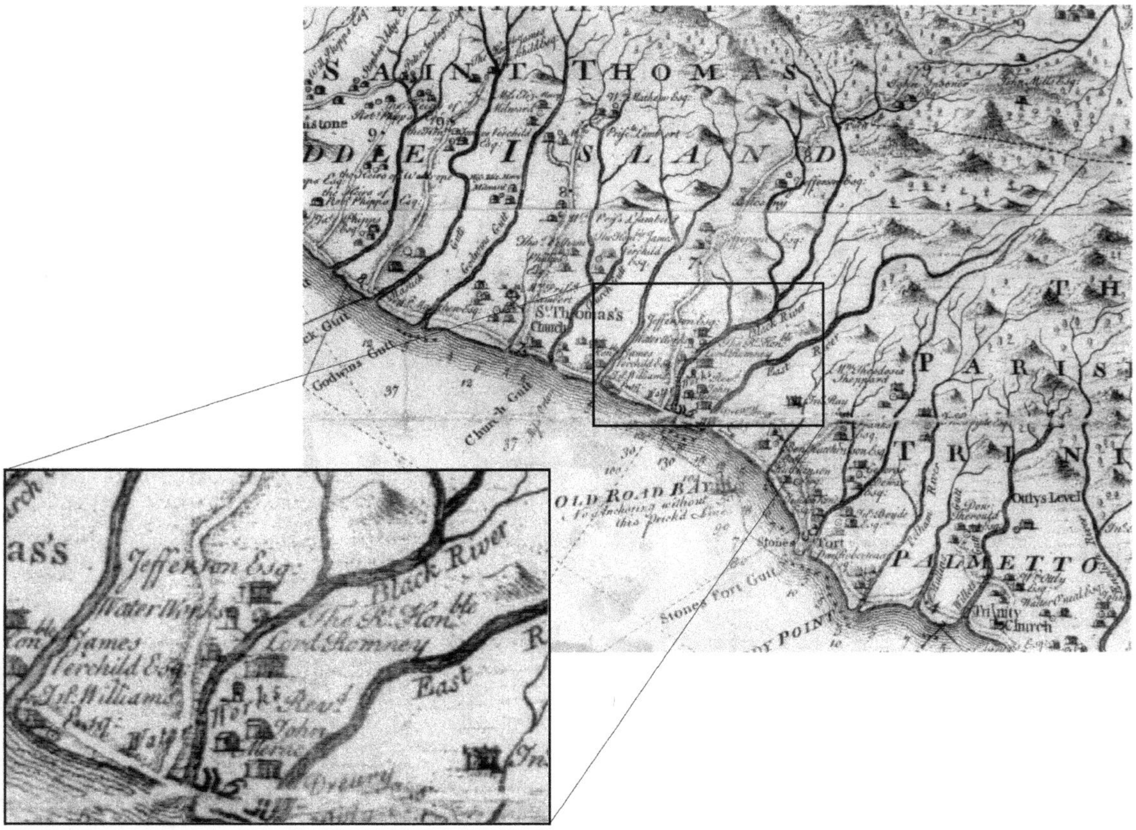

FIGURE 14. DETAIL OF BAKER MAP OF ST KITTS (1756), SHOWING WINGFIELD AND ROMNEY WORKS

FIGURE 15. DETAIL FROM MCMAHON MAP OF ST KITTS (1828), SHOWING WINGFIELD AND ROMNEY

the 77 sugar plantations sold in this way between 1833 and 1844. At that time the estate comprised 587 acres, and was sold for £6640, while the Degatieres estate comprised 430 acres when it was sold on 26 January 1837 for £2560 (Breen 1972 [1844], 317).

The archaeological evidence for the pre-sugar landscape at Balenbouche was considered in Chapter 2 above (**Figures 13 & 16**). In addition to this documentary evidence, two major phases of sugar works were identified during archaeological survey. These are summarised below (**Figures 12 & 18**).

Balenbouche: Sugar Works 1
In a plan of 1770, the French-constructed island road – the *Chemin Royal* – is shown as running straight across the area of the modern Balenbouche estate, from the mouth of the Balenbouche River, to the north-west. In contrast, by 1780, the *Chemin Royal* is shown running further to the south, before following the western estate boundary with the Degatieres estate northwards and picking up its former course running west across Degatieres. The most probable interpretation of this evidence is that the apparent

diversion of the *Chemin Royal* represents evidence of the large-scale construction of the Balenbouche estate at some point between 1770 and 1780 (St Lucia National Archives, uncatalogued documents: de Latour 1787).

The 1780 survey of St Lucia lists Martin as owning land on the site of Balenbouche under sugar cultivation, and V. Duval as owning adjacent land under cotton. 'Wme Alexander' is listed as the proprietor of the Degatieres estate (de Latour 1787). Other cartographic evidence is confusing, in that no estate is shown at Balenbouche on the Bellin (1758), Ravell (1780 [1775]), any of the in any of the reprints of Jeffreys (1780) (Laurie and Whittle 1794, 1810, 1872), Thomson (1821) or the Admiralty chart (1859). However, the Chemin Royal and later roads are also not shown on these maps, and it is probable that the isolated southern coast of the island was not seen as important by cartographers at this date.

Survey identified a highly ambitious water system that made use of the perennial water supply of the Balenbouche River, one of the largest rivers on St Lucia, to power the sugar works. A massive stone dam, 5 m in thickness and

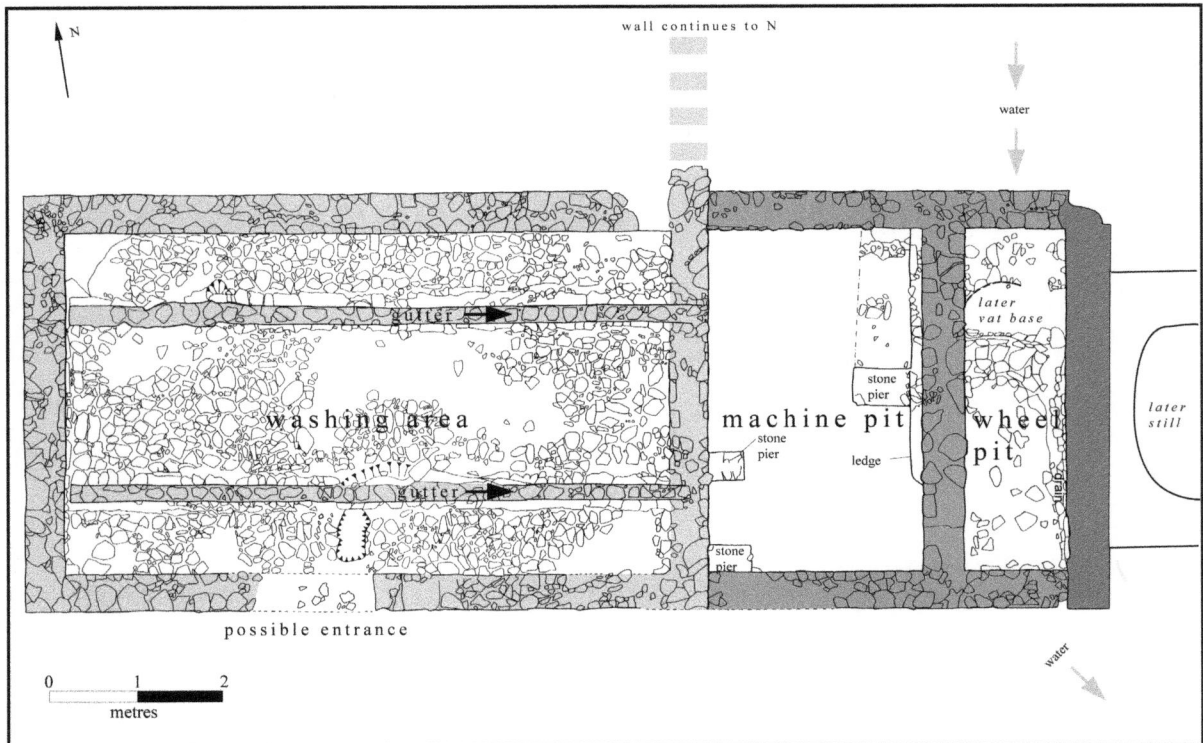

FIGURE 16. COFFEE PROCESSING BUILDING, MACHINE HOUSING AND WHEEL PIT AT BALENBOUCHE, WITH LATER (EARLY 19TH-CENTURY) STILL TO THE EAST.

7 m in height, was constructed and survives today. The purpose of the dam was to store water in case of fluctuations in water flow, forming a lake on the gorge behind, rather than to gain a head of water, as the outlet to the leat was at ground level. Running from the dam, a stone-lined leat measuring some 4 km in length, twisted and turned in order to follow the contour precisely.

A second water source was provided by an artificial canal/millpond 2 km in length, which made use of the seasonal watercourse which had been used for the coffee works' water system. This second canal is clearly visible on mid 20th-century air photographs (**Figure 17**). A leat was constructed using the remains of the earlier ditched enclosure to provide a second water source. (**Figure 12***)*.

A new estate house was constructed within the earlier enclosure on the site of the present estate house (**Figure 12**): an outward-looking site, provided with wide, 'borrowed' views of neighbours' lands and of the sea. Behind the house, an area of primary slave accommodation was identified in the north-west part of this area, and the post-pads of a timber structure were excavated. At this stage, slave accommodation appears to have been located within the leat – continuing to use the former enclosure. Indeed, the moated area may have served to control slaves' movement around the estate (Hicks and Horton 2001a).

This first phase of sugar manufacture saw a change in the whole scale of industrial operations on the estate, involving

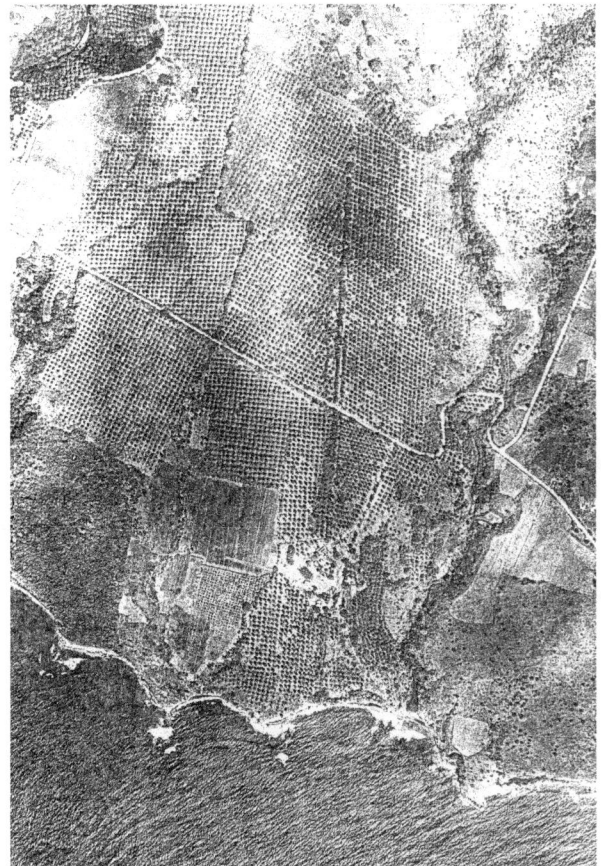

FIGURE 17. AIR PHOTOGRAPH OF BALENBOUCHE ESTATE (1946)

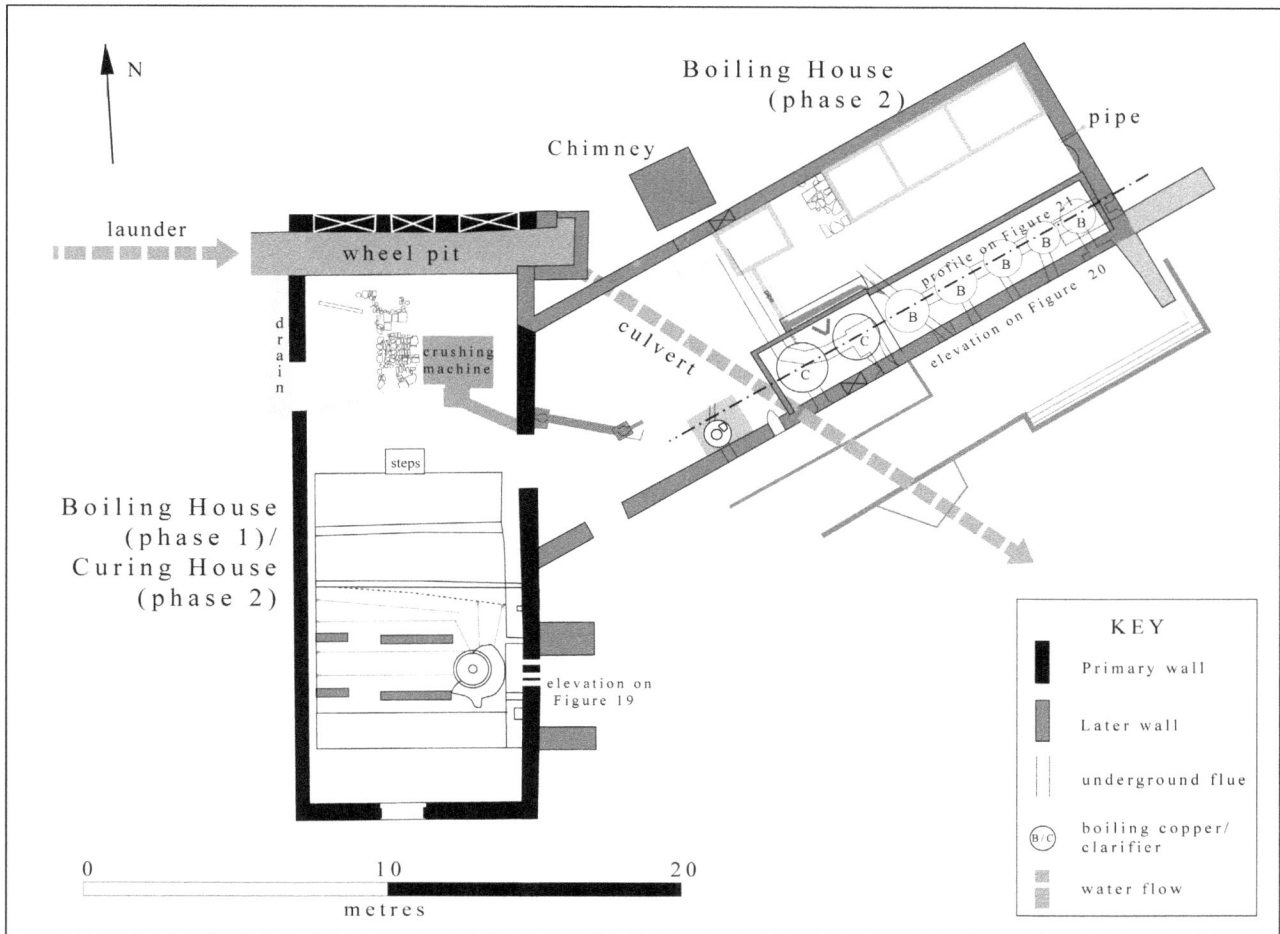

FIGURE 18. DETAIL OF LATE 18TH-CENTURY SUGAR WORKS BUILDINGS AT BALENBOUCHE, ST LUCIA, SHOWING PHASE 1 BOILING HOUSE AND ITS CONVERSION INTO PHASE 2 CURING HOUSE, PHASE 2 BOILING HOUSE (BUILT ACROSS THE RIVER GORGE TO THE EAST), WATER CULVERT AND MILL LAUNDER, CRUSHING MACHINE AND WHEEL, AND LOCATIONS OF FIGURES 19-21

the construction of two massive industrial buildings – a boiling and crushing house with wheel house, and a curing house (**Figure 18**). The creation of the sugar estate involved massive amounts of earth-moving, as buildings, roads and water systems were sculpted into the side of a steep ravine. A platform for the mill buildings, 80 m long and 20 m wide, was cut out from the side of the valley wall, and a massive retaining wall was built up along the eastern edge of the terrace from the valley bottom (**Figure 18**). Further retaining walls were built above the works buildings' terrace to the west. The standing building remains of the primary boiling house, which measured around 21 m north/south and 8.3 m east/west, were recorded. The dimensions of the primary curing house, which survives as buried remains, were almost exactly the same as the boiling house. The platform on which they stood widened at a position – possibly forming a storage area – which reflected that of the curing house (**Figure 18**). It is unclear whether a distillery was provided in this Phase.

Balenbouche: Sugar Works 2
During the 1790s or possibly the early 19th century,

the sugar works were radically altered. The first Curing House was abandoned and demolished (**Figure 18**). Large amounts of earth were piled around the boiling house, partially burying it, and covering the flues: thus facilitating its conversion into a curing house (**Figure 19**). Meanwhile, in a truly remarkable expenditure of effort, a new boiling house was built on a massive artificial building platform built from the valley floor out across the ravine. As the wheel pit from Boiling House 1 was retained, a stone-lined culvert was constructed before the artificial platform of Boiling House 2 was built (**Figures 12 & 18**). The new boiling house was provided with a 'jamaica train' boiling system, and a separate flue system for clarifiers (**Figures 19, 20 & 21**). A large new chimney was constructed to the north of Boiling House 2 to draw the fires. Another radical change occurred across the rest of the plantation as a result of the provision of a new road to the north of the estate during the last years of the 18th century. As a result, the plantation 'turned around' to face north.

While the estate house remained in the same location, slave accommodation appears to have shifted to the south,

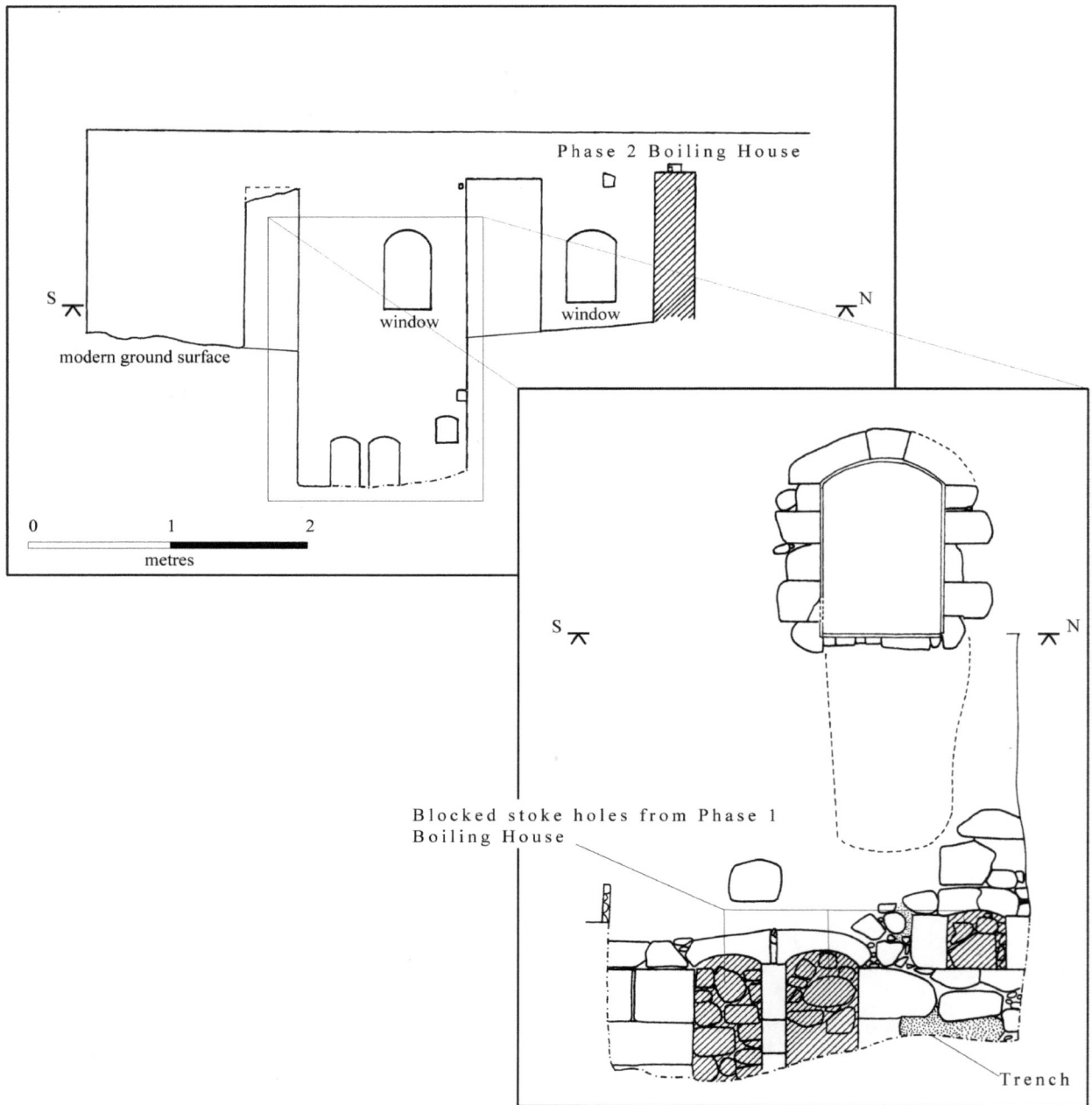

FIGURE 19. DRAWN ELEVATION OF EAST-FACING WALL OF PHASE 2 CURING HOUSE AT BALENBOUCHE, WITH DETAIL SHOWING TRENCH (TRENCH 8) REVEALING SURVIVING BLOCKED STOKE HOLES FROM PHASE 1 BOILING HOUSE

behind the 'polite' part of the landscape: a change which opened up the enclosure area and provided the possibility of looking down on the impressive works from a new landscape which may be characterised as both polite and industrial: combining the area from which cane was sent down stone chutes to the crushing house with an area in which the estate house lay.

Discussion

The results of documentary and archaeological research into the changing landscapes of Wingfield (after *c.* AD 1713) and Balenbouche (from the 1770s) allow us to

nuance our understanding of how the 'improving' impulses sketched above were worked out in practice.

Throughout the sequence at Wingfield, the sugar works were continually enlarged – in a very complex sequence of construction. There was constant experimentation with the arrangement of coppers, flues and curing houses: apparently in a constant impulse towards increased capacity, efficiency and productivity. The provision of a corridor into the works – apparently controlling access in and out of the factory – suggests that the architectural design was concerned with the control of labour. The estate was also subject to absentee leasing, leading to its enlargement through being

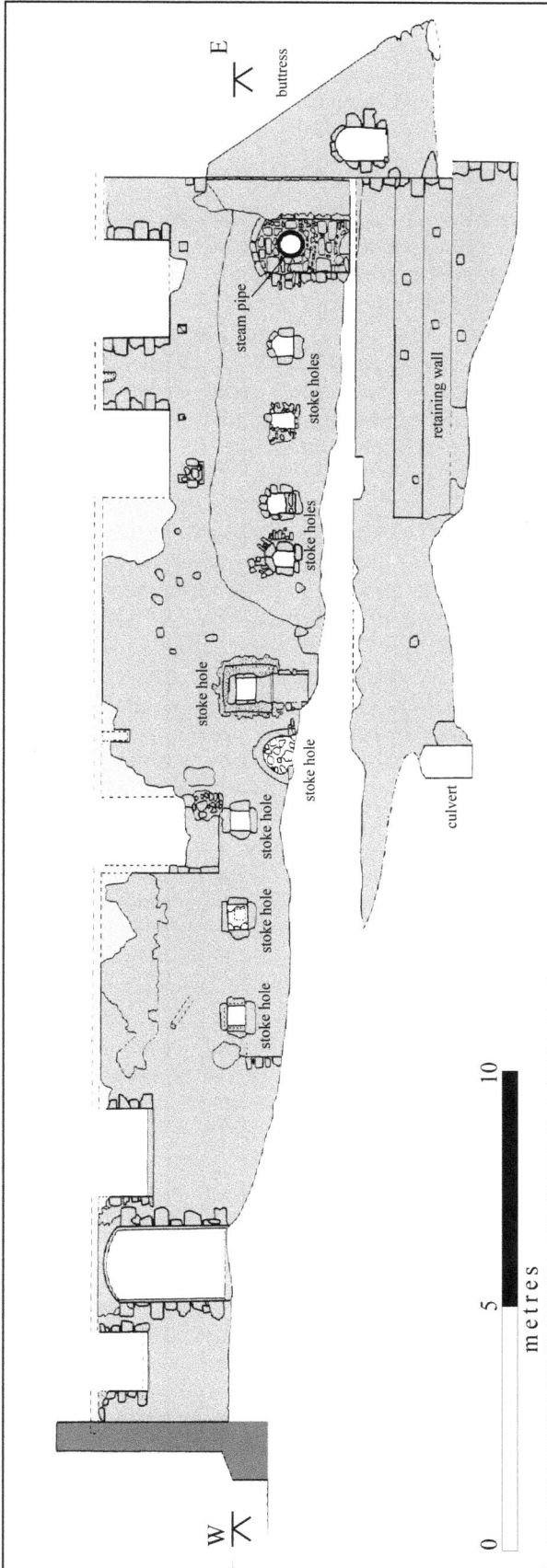

FIGURE 20. DRAWN ELEVATION OF SOUTH-FACING WALL OF PHASE 2 BOILING HOUSE AT BALENBOUCHE

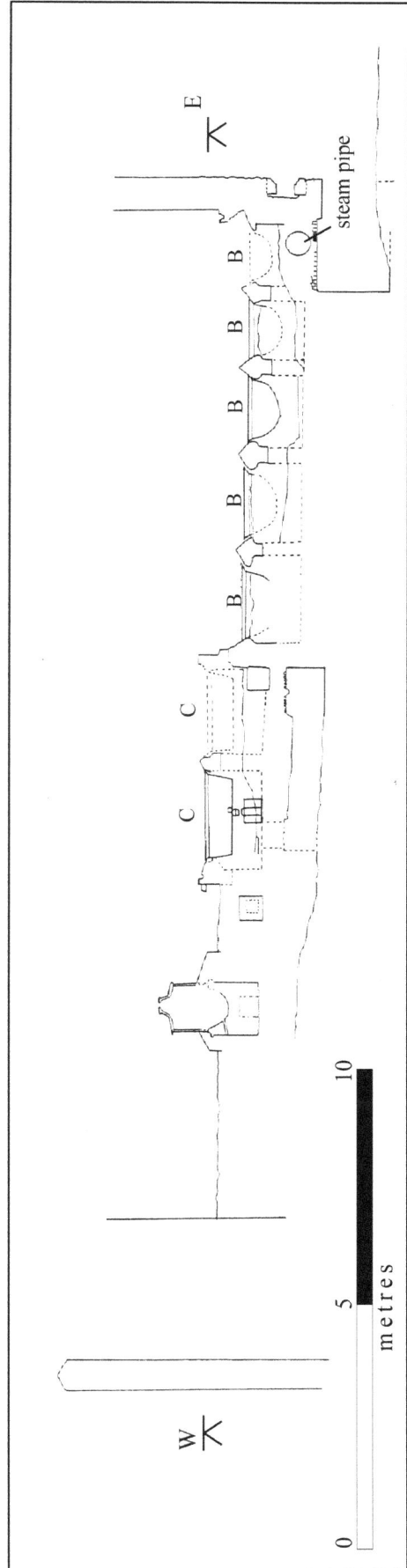

FIGURE 21. PROFILE ACROSS INTERNAL FEATURES OF PHASE 2 BOILING HOUSE, BALENBOUCHE, ST LUCIA

managed with Romney: increasing the processing capacity of the estate. The abandonment of the cattle mill-powered works on higher ground to the north, was in keeping with the tendencies towards consolidation and new expansion. Equally, from *c.* 1713 the changing plantation landscape of Wingfield demonstrated new and increasing concerns with design and planning. From the first phase of alterations to the works, the 'front' – the eastern elevation – became by far the most impressive, with the dramatic brickwork of the boiling house and aqueduct. The construction of the new Great House high up above the works, and an impressive terraced road winding uphill towards it, meant that visitors to the house would pass by the impressive works facade on their approach. The location of the slave accommodation in an out-of-sight area, below the crest of the hill on which the plantation house was built, is also suggestive of a designed landscape: and demonstrates an active distancing of the planter and his slaves. Similarly, with the construction of two estate houses: one on higher ground commanding wide, borrowed views (House 2), and a second plantation house on the foundations of the Matthew enclosure (House 3), the 'polite' and industrial parts of the estate were separated (by height, or by the main estate road, respectively) (**Figure 7**).

At Balenbouche, the contrast between the construction in the 1770s of the sugar works and the earlier coffee works was striking. A relatively simple investment in landscape change making use of a seasonal watercourse, and arranging a series of stone buildings set on small terraces in the side of the valley, was swept away by a phenomenal investment of labour over two phases: combining massive excavations and construction programmes for the works, and a highly complex feat of engineering in the provision of the water system and the situating of the works buildings. A new plantation landscape was created with no concern for the earlier infrastructure, and presumably the survival of the remains of the enclosure as a leat and the digging of a canal from the seasonal watercourse to the north resulted from concerns that trying to remove these features would lead to flooding.

The shift between Phase 1 and Phase 2 at Balenbouche is particularly revealing. The initial layout of the works was in keeping with the latest idealised treatises on sugar planting: the boiling house flues facing east as universally directed, to take advantage of the prevailing West Indian wind direction. However, the works are located in a deep valley: making the prevailing wind direction run from the seas from south to north. The changes in Phase 2 were clearly perceived as of great importance, since the task of floating a massive industrial building across a ravine is a major feat of engineering, comparable with the provision of the enormous dam in the previous phase. The new arrangement of flues and chimney was perfectly aligned to position that maximised the wind coming up the valley. The resulting T-shaped arrangement, with the awkward arrangement of a crushing area in the curing house, requiring a pipe running into the boiling house, appear to exemplify an emphasis

not on the idealised plan-view landscapes of Phase 1, but new concerns with increased efficiency and responsiveness to local natural environments. While some elements of the resulting arrangement are awkward, it should also be noted that the resulting T-shape arrangement was a variation on the recommended layout of boiling and curing houses in several contemporary treatises on sugar, most notably William Beckford's (1790, 28).

The sequences at Wingfield and Balenbouche highlight the material consequences of the new ideas of 'improvement' that informed the growth of sugar monoculture in the Leewards, and its confident expansion to the Windwards, during the 18th century. Improved landscapes were developed in local and contingent circumstances, and yet aimed to remove the traces of earlier enclosed landscape forms. In the Leewards, plantations were increasingly extended by land purchases, and so that fewer individuals came to own larger estates. Thus in St Kitts and Nevis, a major influence on the financial basis of these new ventures was the injection of substantial sums of compensation for the 1706 attacks, in combination with the new availability of French lands after 1713. These factors drove forward the establishment of the new landscape of windmills and factories across St Kitts. But the principles of designed plantation landscapes which had been worked out in the small islands of the Leewards and Barbados had been heavily restricted by the availability of land. The creation of large estates had been partially successful through complex series of land purchases, but where in the Leewards the impulse of the planter class towards 'improvement' in the landscape was physically limited by the very small and already complex landscape of land ownership, the ceding of several of the Windward Islands to the British in 1763 provided an opportunity to expand into new landscapes. Thus, even in the last years of the 18th century, Tobago remained for one commentator 'not a twentieth part cultivated, yet it is all, or for the most part, improvable' (Young 1793, 279; quoted in Eubanks 1992, 190). The new opportunities in the Windwards offered new possibilities – formerly restricted to the larger Greater Antillean island of Jamaica – to develop large plantations. Rather like the shift to Jamaica a century earlier in 1655, the 1760s saw new investments in the Windwards: except now highly formalised attitudes to plantation landscape design had developed.

In the Leewards then, and most visibly from the 1760s in the apparently empty landscapes of Windwards (where Indigenous or other earlier settlement was ignored), the landscape was treated as uncultivated and natural (a *terra nullius*'), and controlled, designed plantation landscapes were presented by the planter class as rural idylls. Through this sleight of hand the extreme power relations of racial slavery were partially obscured.

Technological change, larger estates and large increases in the number of slaves accompanied the industrialisation of sugar production on a new scale (Goodwin 1987, 17).

But such transitions were also part a new set of attitudes and values held by planters. The 'package' of ideas, values and attitudes associated with the idea of 'improvement' produced new kinds of material and social landscape. These made use of classical images that were in stark contrast with the neo-feudalism of 17th-century sugar planters: slaves replaced servants, the agricultural productivity of single estates was preferred to numerous tenants, and grand Palladian villas were preferred to the castles or 'Manors' of a previous generation of West Indian planter. New improved landscapes – what Blackburn (above) called 'theatres of gracious living' – were places at which the material, ideational and transatlantic landscapes of the planter elite were imagined and worked out. The creation of such plantation spaces across the Windwards, as described for instance by Seymour *et al.* (1998, 330-341) on the La Taste plantation, Grenada, is vividly portrayed in a description of Betsy's Hope Estate in Tobago dating from 1793:

> On the beach at Queen's-bay are brick and stone pillars, not unlike the great gate of an English park, whence the eye is directed up an avenue of coconut trees, and from thence, in the same straight line, through a broad and regular street of negro houses, at a mile from the gate, to the works, which terminate the avenue, and have the appearance of a church built in the form of the letter T, with a tower raised at the centre. Over the works rises a precipice, on which stands the Mansion-house, nobly commanding the whole vale. A fine river winds from the back mountains, under the point of the great ridge on which the house stands, and then pours in a direct line, nearly by the east of the negro village into the sea. In its course it supplies a canal for turning the water wheel. (Young 1793, 276-7; Quoted in Eubanks 1992, 112)

Another Great House in 1790s Tobago was

> an excellent building, framed in England, and placed on the very pinnacle of the highest mountain in Tobago, with garden and shrubberies, abounding with birds of the most splendid plumage (Young *ibid*. Quoted in Eubanks 1992, 190).

The new designed landscapes of improvement were characterised by open aspects. The surveillance of slaves was an increasing concern: made more possible by open landscapes. The worlds created by planters combined outward-looking architecture with avenues of trees, running water (at both Wingfield and Balenbouche), and the 'pastoral setting' of the surrounding fields of cane. The 'open' character of these new, improved landscapes operated in other ways, however, as will be considered in the final two sections of this chapter: through the performative and geographical dimensions of improvement.

Performing Improvements

In this section, I want to explore the performative dimensions of improvement in the 18th-century eastern Caribbean, focusing in particular on how these brought new attitudes to material things that were closely bound up with the emergence of the ideology of racial slavery. I want to suggest that the 'improving' impulses documented above served to make new connections between natural, material and social landscapes.

Personal improvement was worked out through new elite social landscapes in the eastern Caribbean as the planters' oligarchy strengthened. Complex social hierarchies developed, and were expressed through sometimes bizarre images of power and prestige: including new and minute distinctions in skin colour, conventions of dress and social behaviour (Bayly 1989, 90-91). Such changes formed part of a more general 'rise of provincial elites' across the nascent British empire (Bayly 1989, 32-34), and images of engagement in the wider Atlantic came to hold power and prestige as planters increasingly developed linked interests around the world (Porter 1995, 85).

Conspicuous consumption – described by Janet Shaw in the mid 1770s as 'the extravagant style of entertainment, which prevails in the West Indies...an ostentatious profusion, a load and waste of victuals disgrac[ing] the table of every planter' – had characterised the eastern Caribbean plantocracy since the 17th century, and had throughout been characterised by the consumption of imported items – meat, butter, cheese, Madeira wine, etc (Andrews and Andrews 1939, 85-6). At the same time, in the export economies of the Caribbean, and the increasingly complex networks of middlemen and overseers, the negotiation of social relations in an international arena was the source of wealth. The material demonstration of these skilful connections, of the cosmopolitan nature of the planter, was increasingly important in local systems of prestige.

Such material enactments of improvement were most visible in the estate landscapes which became the 'theatres of gracious living' described by Robin Blackburn above (1997, 21). Samuel Martin's *Essay on Plantership* (1750) – itself described by James Grainger as 'an excellent performance' (Gilmore 2000, 89) – argued that the properly managed plantation

> ought to be considered as a well-constructed machine, compounded of various wheels, turning different ways, and yet all contributing to the great end proposed (Martin 1750, 37)

Thus, the day-to-day business of running a plantation was conceived in new ways – as the performance of management through time management, the regulation of slave lifestyles and surveillance. Estate landscapes enacted improvement as the 'various wheels, turning in different directions' described by Martin constituted the larger 'machine'. Thus, the heterogeneous elements of the estate were 'improved' together, including not only the agricultural and technological elements described above but also natural, animal and human slave components.

Planters aimed to ensure and improve the productivity of all elements of this assemblage. Thus, the 'situation' of an estate, in relation to geology, wind and soil for instance, was emphasised (Roughley 1823, 188). Planters and overseers concerned themselves with the nutrition of slaves by encouraging 'provision grounds' (Ward 1988, 109-11). As seen above, Scottish doctors, imported medicines and medical handbooks were deployed to 'improve' contributed to the health of slaves (Sheridan 1974, 372; 1985), as part of broad efforts to optimise agricultural production through science. Janet Schaw, visiting Samuel Martin's Greencastle Estate in 1774, described how the planter effectively reared both slaves and animals through his careful management

> Cultivated to the height by a large troop of healthy Negroes, who cheerfully perform the labour imposed on them by a kind and beneficent Master, not a harsh and unreasonable Tyrant. Well fed, well supported, they appear the subjects of a good prince, not the slaves of a planter. The effect of this kindness is a daily increase of riches by the slaves born to him on his own plantation. He told me that he had not bought in a slave for upwards of twenty years, and that he had the morning of our arrival got the return of the state of his plantations, on which there were then no less than fifty two wenches who were pregnant. These slaves, born on the spot and used to the Climate, are by far the most valuable, and seldom take these disorders, by which such numbers are lost that many hundreds are forced yearly to be brought into the Island… By turning many of the plantations into grass he…is able to rear cattle which he has done with great success. I never saw finer cows, nor more thriving calves, than I saw feeding in his lawns, and his waggons are already being drawn by oxen of his own rearing (Andrews and Andrews 1939, 104-6).

The point can be illustrated by considering James Grainger's poem, which was mentioned above. The new estate management literature was influenced by the increased interest in Virgil's *Georgics* during the mid 18th century (Watts 1987, 384 ff; Goodwin 1987, 163). In 1764, soon after his return St Kitts (where he would die two years later), the poet James Grainger, mentioned above, published his 'didactic poem' *The Sugar Cane!* It described, in highly laboured georgic diction, sugar cultivation in St Kitts, presenting 'some part of the science of husbandry put into a pleasing dress' (Sandiford 2000, 69; Gilmore 2000, 27-8, 63). Grainger described the Wingfield River, and Romney:

> The brawling Naiads for the planters toil.
> Howe'er unworthy; and, through solemn scenes,
> Romantic, cool, with rocks and woods between,
> Enchant the senses! but, among thy swains,
> Sweet Liamuiga! Who such bliss can boast?
> Yes, Romney, thou may'st boast' of British heart,
> Of courtly manners, join'd to antient worth.
> (Grainger 2000 [1764], 135 (Book III, 284-290).

In Grainger's vision, the Wingfield River 'enchanted the senses'. St Kitts was known by its native Carib name – Liamuiga, or 'Fertile Island'. Slaves were 'swains', and Romney's pedigree, 'join'd to antient worth'. Sitting in the shade of a tree by the river, Grainger described a picturesque landscape

> Then should I scarce regret the banks of Thames
> All as we sat beneath that sand-box shade;
> Whence the delighted eye expatiates wide
> O'er the fair landscape; where in loveliest forms,
> Green cultivation hath array'd the land.
> See! there, what mills, like giants raise their arms,
> To quell the speeding gale! what smoke ascends
> From every boiling house! What structures rise,
> Neat tho' not lofty, pervious to the breeze;
> With galleries, porches or piazzas grac'd!
> Nor not delightful are those reed-built huts,
> On yonder hill, that front the rising sun;
> With plantanes, with banana's bosom'd deep,
> That flutter in the wind: where frolick goats,
> Butt the young Negroes, while their swarthy sires,
> With ardent gladness wield the bill; and hark,
> The crop is finish'd, how they rend the sky!
> (Grainger 2000 [1764], 141 (Book III, 521-537).

It is not simply that the rural idylls of improvement obscured or masked slavery and inequality. Rather, the enactment of the material geographies of the estate landscape, like the theatrical poetic diction, served to animate these assemblages, creating aesthetic and active fields of people and things. As Elizabeth Bohls has argued, this 'planter picturesque' was characterised by a certain 'staginess' (2002, 63; cf. Bohls 1999). Improvement served not only to 'obfuscate' tensions or inequalities (Seymour 2002, 209-11), but to bring about new intersections between people and things. Through the material performance or enactment of the idea of improvement in plantation estates, complex choreographies of maps and plans, soils, slaves, animals, kin relations, crushing machines, letters, rivers, bricks, verandas, teacups, the wind and rain, were achieved. Productivity emerged from climate, geology artefacts, people and animals. In these entangled relations, material engagements lay at the heart of improvement – bringing human and nonhuman actors together in the agrarian 'theatres' of plantation estates. And as these performances continued, the complexities and inequalities, the violence and the horror of racial slavery were disguised. Through the ideology of improvement, people appeared as objects and animals, bought, sold, reared, put to work as slaves. And through the enactment of improvement, incoherences and inequalities, and the distinctions between people and things, appeared evened out and blurred.

The Material Geographies of Improvement

As well as the performative dimensions of improvement, ideas of improvement brought about new approaches to geography among the planter elite. A good point of departure here is the literature in historical studies over 'absenteeism'. For one tradition of West Indian history, since Pitman (1917) and Ragatz (1928), the period explored in this chapter was one of increasing economic decline, central to which was the wide-spread nature of absentee landlordism. While this model of decline has been widely critiqued (e.g. Drescher 1977), and while Ragatz himself admitted that the picture was a very varied one: and some estates, and some islands, saw no 'decline' even in the face of absentee ownership, a reassessment of the economically negative impact of 'absenteeism' is overdue. While such reassessment is beyond the scope of the present study, the importance of moving beyond the deployment of anecdotal evidence of poor management by disinterested British inheritors of plantations – who, choosing not to travel to the West Indies, expected profits to flow from their mismanaging West Indian agents (Mason 1993) – can be noted. Indeed, the development of concerns about post-emancipation absentee plantation ownership in the Colonial Office is the most probable origin for the anti-absentee model: this then being projected back into the 18th century in models such as that of Pitman and Ragatz.

An alternative is to view Windward expansion and 'absenteeism' as part of the emerging geographies of 'improvement' among the Caribbean planter class of the 18th century. Processes such as the confident development of the sugar estate at Balenbouche from the 1770s or the leasing of Wingfield from 1713 demonstrate quite the opposite of economic decline, and indicate no connection between absentee ownership and poor economic performance (Ward 1988, 264). In many respects, in this period the absences of what historian David Hancock (1995) has called these 'citizens of the world' were not economically detrimental for them or their estates, but were a part of the engagement of the planter elite on a new scale and in new ways in an increasingly integrated Atlantic arena (compare Hall 1964; Sheridan 1961, 385-7; Goveia 1965; Brathwaite 1971). As David Hancock has argued, 18th-century merchants such as William Freeman of St Kitts and London had 'a world of business to do': 'the most critical asset a merchant could deploy in the first century of empire was acquaintance in the colonies' (Hancock 2000, 29).

The expansion of estates in the Leewards and the new plantations in the Windwards were thus part of a more general expansion of commercial interests, as Atlantic merchants and planters developed complex portfolios of commercial investments. 'Absenteeism' can thus be understood as a result of new elite ideas of prestige and improvement based on material engagements in the Atlantic world. By relocating 'absenteeism' as part of a new elite desire to be engaged internationally, an insight into elite systems of power and prestige, in which the material enactment of the improving impulse was an important part, in the eastern Caribbean is provided.

The character of such 'improving' geographical engagements was related closely to ideas of landscape – social, natural and material. The relationships between absenteeism and landscape were, as was noted at the start of this chapter, particularly visible in the development of maps and plans. These bundles of paper and cloth, fair copies and embellished plans, were a central part of a new geographical imaginary among improving planters. Such observations may be extended by considering how in the performance of Atlantic cosmopolitanism, the material construction and management of estate landscapes in both the Caribbean and Britain came to be increasingly important during the 18th century. For example, Charles Tudway, after inheriting the Parham Hill Estate in Antigua in 1748 commissioned Thomas Paty in 1758 to build The Cedars in Wells, North Somerset, and combined absentee plantation ownership with a position as MP for Bristol from 1754 (Higham 1921, 217; Tudway Quilter 1985, cf. Tudway Mss). Similarly, Susanne Seymour, Stephen Daniels and Charles Watkins have studied the close relationships between the development of Sir George Cornewall's Moccas estate in Herefordshire and his La Taste estate in Grenada (1771-1819). By 'examining landed estates and their owners in an imperial context', Seymour *et al.* (1998, 341) demonstrate a series of 'overlapping concerns…especially in terms of the management of land, labour and finance' at the two sites. Such geographies folded together a number of different scales, including transatlantic connections as well as the immediate physical landscape. They raise important issues of how we write histories of improvement in Britain, as well as in colonial situations, in the present.

The 18th-century designed plantations in the eastern Caribbean discussed above came to be similar in form to English landscape parks (Seymour *et al.* 1998, 333). Indeed, during the 1820s one visitor to the Leewards described how

> the tall and moving windmills, the houses of the proprietors, the works and palm-thatched cottages of the negros embosomed in plantains, present the appearance, as indeed they are the substance, of so many country villages in England. (Coleridge 1826, 216)

Moreover, just as the new plantation landscapes were open rather than enclosed, so the large-scale geographical expansion of planters' interests to the Windward Islands in the second half of the 18th century was in an important sense outward-looking. What we may term the 'material geographies' of improvement in the eastern Caribbean were, then, bound up with broader Atlantic geographies. More specifically, the ideas of improvement that developed in colonial contexts – as they have been studied by historians (Hancock 1995, 281-5) and historical geographers (Daniels and Seymour 1990, Briggs 1963) – were bound up with the emergence of these ideas in Europe.

In their studies of British agrarian landscapes, historical geographers have emphasised the significance of the notion of 'improvement' during the post-medieval period, whether between the 1780s and 1860s (Briggs 1963) or between 1730 and 1914 (Daniels and Seymour 1990). In their classic statement on 'landscape design and the idea of improvement', Stephen Daniels and Susanne Seymour described how from the 1730s 'improvement' related to new elite landscape designs 'on a large scale and with great attention to detail', and hence to the management of parks and estates, and beyond:

> Landscape in Georgian England was not just a matter of conventions of taste; it was a highly complicated discourse in which a whole range of issues, which we might now discriminate as 'economic', 'political', 'social' and 'cultural' were encoded and negotiated... The concept of improvement was integral to these negotiations. Initially used to denote profitable operations in connection with land, notably aristocratic enclosure, by the end of the eighteenth century 'improvement' referred not just to a variety of progressive farming practices but to a broad range of activities from music to manufacturing, with a series of overlapping resonances – financial, pragmatic, moral, educational, aesthetic. A central issue of eighteenth century polite culture, at least from a conservative point of view, was the relation between improvement in various spheres of life; the discourse of landscape provided a way of both diagnosing disharmony between these spheres and brining them into balance (Daniels and Seymour 1990: 488).

Daniels and Seymour, following Duckworth (1971) and Raymond Williams (1976: 132-3), suggest that the 'key word' of improvement was itinerant and locally nuanced. Raymond Williams sketched how between the sixteenth and eighteenth centuries the idea of 'improving' in England shifted from describing 'profitable operations in connection with land' to a 'wider meaning of "making something better" ...often in direct overlap with economic operations', and then to 'the characteristic "improve oneself"', whereupon 'such phrases as "improving reading" followed':

> Jane Austen was aware of the sometimes contradictory senses of improvement, where economic operations for profit might lead to, or might hinder, social and moral refinement. In *Persuasion* (1818, Chapter V), a landowning family was described as 'in a state of alteration, perhaps of improvement'. The separation of the general meaning from the economic meaning is thereafter normal, but the complex underlying connection between 'making something better' and 'making a profit out of something' is significant when the social and economic history during which the word developed in these ways is remembered (Williams 1976: 133).

Williams suggested that the 'agricultural revolution' was in reality 'no revolution, but the consolidation, the improvement, the expansion of an existing social class'. Improvement shifted across 'soil, stock, yields, in a

working agriculture' to 'the improvement of houses, parks, artificial landscapes', and into polite social life –

> Cultivation has the same ambiguity as improvement: there is increased growth, and this is converted into rents; and then the rents are converted into what is seen as a cultivated society. What the 'revolution is for, then, is this: the apparently attainable quality of life (R. Williams 1985 [1973], 115-6).

This itinerancy can be explored still further. Sarah Tarlow (2003) has extended the temporal dimensions of 'improvement', noting its appearance in literary sources from the early 17th century as well as clearly continuing in currency and importance into the 20th century, but her explorations have remained geographically restricted. It is the mobilities of 'improvement', however, sometimes moving across the mercantile and estate landscapes of the British Atlantic world (Hancock 1995, 281-5) that are perhaps most striking. Richard Drayton (2000, 55-9) has observed how the notion of improvement was central to English colonial activities from the early 17th century, representing a distinctive blend of agricultural, economic and political interests. The colonial contexts of 'improvement' range from at Kew gardens through the geographical networks of plant science (Drayton 2000), across the Scottish highlands (Womack 1989), and Ireland (Busteed 2002). For the cultivation of sugar cane, Griggs (2004) has recently traced the improving activities of the Colonial Sugar Refining Company in New South Wales, Australia, between 1864 and 1915: including the introduction of ploughing, fertiliser use, land drainage and new paddock design.

The implications of acknowledging the material geographies of British colonial improvement are considerable. This was not simply a case of metropolitan ideas being played out in new, colonial landscapes, the study of which might provide new perspectives on our understanding of these ideas 'at home', but a situation in which it is probable that colonial landscapes 'might actually have contributed' to 'supposedly metropolitan' developments (Bohls 2002: 63). The vast open fields of sugar estates in St Kitts did, after all, precede Capability Brown's turfed landscapes in England, in which from the 1760s mansions stood in a 'boundless sea of turf' (Williamson 1995: 2), by more than a generation.

In this context, British post-medieval archaeology – perspective from which the present study is written – appears provincial, inward-looking and mortgaged to nationalist historiographies. For example, the 'improving' impulses of agricultural enclosure (Johnson 1996, 61-69) and polite landscapes (Williamson 1995) have been examined as part of the emerging ideology of capitalism, producing compelling and revealing analyses of the significance of the 'physical processes' of landscape change (Johnson 1996, 71). Such work will be extended by Sarah Tarlow (2007) in her forthcoming study of 'the archaeology of improvement in Britain, AD 1750-1850' in a range of agricultural and urban situations. But while such work contributes much to the development of archaeologies of the modern world in Britain, archaeological studies of improvement that are conducted in isolation from its broader colonial histories are inadequate. Two British archaeologists have more successfully used the idea of 'improvement' as a way of examining elite landscape changes in Scotland during the 18th and 19th centuries (Symonds 1999, Dalglish 2003). Chris Dalglish's study of improvement in the southern Scottish highlands traces a radical shift from nucleated townships (*bailtean*) and shielings to new patterns of dispersed settlement and isolated farmsteads. In his comparison of Kintyre and Kilfinan, Dalglish acknowledges that 'improvement' was adopted in different ways in different places (Dalglish 2003, 205), and emphasises the relationships between improvement, elite and national identity. Similarly, in his examination of 'improvements' in South Uist in the Outer Hebrides, Symonds has suggested that

> Rather than trying to impose an "ideological confidence trick"…upon a mass of the population, the actions of the elite were in many ways geared to reaffirming their own social positioning, and to validating their own belief in the ideology of "improvement" through material expressions (Symonds 1999, 118).

The work of Dalglish and Symonds provides insights upon the diversity of improvement: its contextual variation, itinerancy, the local contingencies of its performance, and the attendant changing conceptions of landscape. Nevertheless, the question of how ideas such as improvement can contribute to the development of 'archaeologies of the British' is raised (Hicks 2004a) – a question which will be explored further in the next chapter.

Conclusions

This chapter has documented the shift from early enclosed sugar works to sugar monoculture during the 18th century, and has identified the idea of improvement as an important organising principle through which the emerging planter elite brought together material and social concerns. The creation of new, open estate landscapes was a central part of the enactment of improvement. In many ways these new estates removed earlier landscapes, but the role of designed landscapes as places for the production and consumption of material culture persisted. 'Improved' sugar landscapes were places at which broader Atlantic worlds were imagined and brought about by a new elite planter class. Through the performative dimensions of improvement, which centred upon classical imagery of villas and slaves that contrasted with earlier feudalisms, new ideas relating to control over natural and material environments were worked out – ideas that were closely bound up with the ideology of racial slavery.

The transatlantic engagements of 18th-century merchants and planters – described so vividly by historians such as David Harvey (1995) – bring into question the limits and boundaries of archaeological research into sugar landscapes in this period. In this chapter, I have explored this question by considering alternative studies of 'improvement' in Britain and in colonial contexts. In the final chapter, this crucial issue of the geographies of archaeology of British colonialism will be considered further, in relation to the crucial issue of 'legacies'.

CHAPTER 5

ATLANTIC LEGACIES (FROM *C.* AD 1838, AND IN THE PRESENT)

The processes of landscape change documented in Chapter 4 ended with slave emancipation (effected in AD 1838). However, this was not the end of the life histories of these sugar landscapes: the legacies of the human and material landscapes transformed in the 17th and 18th centuries continued to shape the histories of the eastern Caribbean during the 19th and 20th centuries. And today in 2007, at the bicentenary of the abolition of the slave trade, these legacies continue to shape social life in postcolonial situations in both the Old and New Worlds. In this brief concluding chapter, I want to return to consider the 'afterlives' of the plantation landscapes of Wingfield and Balenbouche, and then to explore some aspects of how archaeology can understand the material legacies of Atlantic slavery. By doing so, I want in conclusion to indicate how the scope and research agendas of 'British' post-medieval archaeologies might be reconsidered and relocated, and the prospects and challenges for historical archaeology in the eastern Caribbean in the future.

Post-Emanciptation Landscapes

The history of eastern Caribbean sugar landscapes after emancipation is one of different ways in which the material remains of the massive landscape changes wrought in previous decades were negotiated – whether re-used, re-modelled, or abandoned. Standard accounts portray the post-emancipation period as one in which the British West Indies became colonial backwaters. Such a view was even part of Seymour Drescher's (1977) critique of Lowell Ragatz's (1928) model of the earlier (18th-century) decline of the plantation economy. But such a picture obscures how some islands at some times saw confident and highly profitable investments in the sugar industry, while there was retraction on others (Green 1976 Adamson 1972)[27]. The vagaries of the fate of the sugar industry were reflected in the different trajectories taken by each island's post-emancipation settlement patterns (Bolland 1981, Hall 1978), and by patterns of inter-island migration (Richardson 1983, 79-107).

Slavery legally ended on 1st August 1834, with a four-year apprenticeship period until emancipation was effected on 1st August 1838, with British planters receiving £20 million in compensation from the British government (Ragatz 1928, Chapter XII; Drescher 1977;

Ward 1988, Green 1976, 119). In contrast with peaceful transitions elsewhere, in St Kitts the enforcement of the Emancipation Act on 1 August 1834, and the beginning of the 4-year period of apprenticeship, was met with widespread work refusals. Martial law was enforced, and a naval force was sent from English Harbour in Antigua (Hall 1971, 24). Despite these large payments, unlike the compensation of 1666 or 1706 in St Kitts, this capital was not invested in the Caribbean region. Many planters instead invested in industrial and commercial ventures in the Britain, although the history of the investment of these payments remains unstudied.

Indentured opportunities were offered to workers by agents from Demerara and Trinidad, and thousands emigrated there from St Kitts and Nevis in the 20 years after emancipation (see Caddy 1837, Day 1852, Watkins 1924, Iles 1871, Watts 1973). A St Kitts planter complained to the Select Committee in 1842 that 'emigration is our greatest evil' (Hall 1971, 33; Minutes of Evidence and Report of the Select Committee on the West India Colonies, 1842). In the mid 1840s, the St Kitts Assembly and Legislature made efforts to encourage immigration: chiefly of white workers from Britain, Ireland, Portugal and Madeira. Portuguese-speaking indentured labourers were also brought from the Azores and Malta. However, as early as 1842, migrant Nevisians began to return from Trinidad and other locations: a process which accelerated during the late 1840s in tandem with the advent of new indentured labour from East India. A complex sequence of inter-island labour movements developed.

After emancipation, plantation labour requirements were variously met by wage-labour and share-cropping (*metayage* or *metairie*) systems. Under the share-cropping system in St Kitts and Nevis, workers were given 2 acres to cultivate in sugar, and would receive between a third and half of the crops as wages (Marshall 1980; Hall 1971, 113-4). The system was adopted very widely on Nevis, and metayage was also adopted across the Windward Islands (Marshall 1965, 1980, 1993; Davy 1854, 284). Wage labour enjoyed some success and continued as most common in St Kitts, where ploughing and steam power had reduced the amount of labour required: although the reduction in wages during the late 1840s caused some tensions. As the Trinidadian and Guianan agents widened their search for labour, the eastern Caribbean sugar industry was radicalised by the importation of several hundred thousand East Indian indentured labourers from the late 1850s. In

---

[27] For accounts of St Lucia at this time see Jeremie 1832, Sturge and Harvey 1838, Breen 1972 [1844], Morris 1891, Yorke 1931, Peter 1933.

Nevis, 315 East Indians arrived on 30 March 1874: some of whom reportedly broke their contracts and quickly left for Trinidad, while others remained, buying land or shops on the expiration of their contracts.[28]

The changes brought about by emancipation in the plantation system saw, in the 1840s, various attempts by plantation owners across the eastern Caribbean to create a dependent labour force through tenancy arrangements For instance in St Kitts, the tenancy arrangements of the apprenticeship period continue for plantation labourers. Labourers continued to live in the former slave villages, and to grow food in the provision grounds. The threat of ejection of labourers from their houses was used by planters to secure a permanent resident labour force: making a sham of labourers' new free status (Louis 1982, 168). In reaction, many St Kitts wage labourers began to rent houses and agricultural land, or to rent land on which to build their own houses (Hall 1971, 49). Encouraged by the colonial administration, owners of large areas of land – usually former estates – rented small lots to workers. This shift radically altered the landscape of St Kitts, as new Independent Villages developed. After the renting out of land at Challengers (1841), villages at Leighs, St Pauls, Parsons, Sadlers and Tabernacle developed (Merrill 1958, 95). Even where plantation work continued, slave accommodation was abandoned: on Nevis, Davy described in 1854 how

> the old villages on the estates have been nearly abandoned, and dwellings of a better description have supplied their place, either near the old ones or on detached spots. (Davy 1854, 462-3)

These new villages were developed as a new generation who had never experienced slavery themselves grew up and an increasing unwillingness to work in the cane fields developed. While some previous commentators have seen this as 'choos[ing] idleness in preference to toilsome penury', these changes are more accurately characterised as part of a wider rejection of the former slave ways of life.

From the 1840s, sugar works and cane fields were managed and developed speculatively – for short-term profit with as little infrastructural investment as possible. The dramatic landscape changes made possible by enslaved labour no longer took place. A description of the Olivees estate house in St Kitts in 1854 describes vividly the material legacies of sugar and slavery

> It stands on a well raised stone terrace, paved with marble, and in its best days, it is now out of repair, has spacious open galleries and verandahs. One large finely proportioned room extends the whole length of the

front, with a handsome deep cornice, and ample doors, both of dark mahogany, and if I recollect rightly, a half wainscot of the same material. It was in the bygone and convivial times, the great reception and dining room…the gentleman then residing there said that the whole might be purchased for £3000 – a less sum than the original cost of the house (Davy 1854, 462-3).

The sugar plantation literature discussed in Chapter 4 evolved during the 1840s into practical handbooks or manuals: designed to provide potential investors or local overseers with a standardised approach to sugar manufacturing (Evans 1847, Wray 1848; Scoffern 1849; Burgh 1863). Many speculative investors bought up large amounts of West Indian land, giving rise to deep concerns in the Colonial Office about the social implications of absentee ownership. Hall (1971, 106) gives the example of Benjamin Buck Greene, a merchant and ship-owner who had acquired 8 estates by 1848, and was consignee of the sugar of several others. The purchase of estates was made easier by the Incumbered Estates Acts (1854-1892), which provided special courts for owners to sell any estates 'incumbered' by debts. The Act was brought into operation in St Kitts in March 1860 (Breen 1972 [1844], 317-318). The first such system – the 'Vacant Successions' legislation – had operated in St Lucia from 1833 (National Archives CO 253/134). In both cases, the purchase price was used to pay off the outstanding debts (Cust 1865)[29].

Plantation owners and colonial officials alike sought solutions to the post-emancipation labour problems in investment in new technology. In the 1840s, a civil engineer was employed, at a salary of £500 per year, by the St Kitts government for three years to 'promot[e] any improvements in machinery that he might suggest' (Hall 1971, 108). Changes in sugar processing technology at this time included the introduction of vacuum pans to make the boiling process more efficient – not only by speeding it up but also by reducing the heat damage to the sugar (Hall 1971, 110) – and steam-powered centrifugal driers to speed up the curing process, separating out the molasses very quickly. The use of the plough became widespread on the flatter islands of the eastern Caribbean such as St Kitts and Antigua, and there was widespread investment in mills powered by steam engines (Hall 1971, 54, 109; Davy 1854,

---

[28] Adamson 1972; Roberts and Byrne 1966; Engerman 1982, 1983, 1984; Laurence 1971; Saunders 1984; Tinker 1974; Richardson 1983, 96; Olwig 1993, 111 note 6.

[29] The records of the incumbered estates commission are held at the National Archives at Kew (CO 441). For St Kitts it holds CO 441/5/8 (Lomax and Byam, Hermitage 1863-1892); CO 441/6/16 (Plumer (deceased), Goat Hill alias Belvidere, 1866-1892); CO 441/8/1 (Wilson, Greenhill, 1777-1892); CO 441/9/12 (Gordon, Canada. 1870-1876); CO 441/10/6 (Cavan and others, Helden's alias Negroe's Nest, 1834-1888); CO 441/10/10 (Pogson, Goodwin's alias Godwin's, 1873-1892); CO 441/11/5 (Faile, Cunningham, 1854-1892); CO 441/13/11 (Murray, Stone Fort, 1876-1881); CO 441/14/5 (Sinclair, Belle Vue and Pogson's, 1877-1892); CO 441/15/16 (Berkeley and Berkeley, Con Phipps, Shadwell and La Guerite 1885); CO 441/17/4 (Napier, Milliken 1884-1892); CO 441/21/1 (Berkeley and others, Fountain, 1881-1892); CO 441/21/2 (Berkeley, Profit and Mercers, 1885-1892); CO 441/22/1 (Berkeley, Pond etc., 1883-1893). For Nevis it holds: CO 441/11/1 (Huggins, Clark's etc. 1861-1892); CO 441/24/1 (Blake, Kades Bay and Pot Work, and Clifton, 1876-1889); CO 441/24/2-3 (Wilkin, Clay Gut, etc, Hick's, 1875-1892).

446). Such investment was alongside the continued use of earlier plantation infrastructure. In Nevis around 1850

> a cattle mill [was still] employed, and it was apparently of an antique and rude construction…. [It] consisted of three perpendicular rollers of small size, worked by six mules, three abreast, driven by two boys (Davy 1854, 455, note).

There were only four steam engines on Nevis in the 1830s, three of which were 'out of repair' (Coleridge 1832, 183). In contrast, by 1846, 33 engines were recorded on the island:

> A start ha[d] been made…in substituting the steam engine in many instances for the windmill (Davy 1854, 453-4).

In 1859, a single investor from Barbados, T. Graham Briggs, purchased some 15 estates – Hamilton's, Stony Grove, Tower Hill, Round Hill, Old Windward, Shaw's, New River and Coconut Walk, Golden Rock, Fothergill's, Australia, Old Manor, Indian Castle, Morgans and Douglas – and installed steam-powered mills on all of them (Olwig 1993, 96; Nevis Blue Books; Hall 1971, 126, note 72). There were 73 steam-powered mills in St Kitts by 1878, and 35 in Antigua (Hall 1971, 112). In parallel with the increased use of steam engines, a new trade in the importation of coal developed, in which Basseterre, St Kitts and Castries, St Lucia were important markets

From the 1870s West Indian sugar production experienced its first genuine competition from a new source: as beet-sugar extraction was perfected in northern Europe, and the new beet industry spread. Sugar beet, often subsidised by European governments, swamped the British market. The solution of the colonial administration to this crisis was a bureaucratic rationalisation of sugar production through central sugar factories ('centrals') which made use of railways, the new invention of the triple expansion steam engine, and developments in vacuum pan technology. The idea of establishing central factories in the British sugar islands had first been suggested in the 1840s (Biggs 1849), but it was not until 1874 that the first such British factories were established in Trinidad and St Lucia, inspired by the recent success of similar schemes in Martinique and Guyana (Beachey 1957, 84-86; Renard nd; Harmsen 1999, 55; B. Richardson 1983, 136; Louis 1982, 238). In St Lucia, the first 'Centrals' were at Cul de Sac (1874), Vieux Fort (1882), and soon afterwards at Roseau and Dennery. These factories were designed to rely mainly on peasant share-cropping: the cane being brought to the factory by a new system of tramways and by water in steam-powered 'bugs' and 'lighters' (Louis 1982, 243-4). The success of the Lucian Centrals led to a new sugar boom: many labourers abandoned the cultivation of traditional staples, cultivating only sugar (Louis 1982, 249). The 1897 West India Committee Report recommended that further centrals should be established elsewhere in the British Caribbean (Emeruwa 1973). This led to the establishment in 1911 of the St Kitts Central Factory at Golden Rock, and to two similar factories in Antigua.

The cultivation of sugar in St Lucia and Nevis was greatly reduced during the early 20th century, and the last Nevisian sugar crop was harvested in 1969 (Richardson 1983, 165). In contrast, in St Kitts the sugar industry was continued by the government, which effected a compulsory purchase of cane land in 1975 (Richardson *ibid*, 168). The decision to shift out of sugar by the St Kitts Government 2001, and its implementation in 2005, represents a watershed in the history of the eastern Caribbean sugar industry – the end of the only remaining landscape of sugar cane fields in the eastern Caribbean.

Wingfield and Balenbouche

The complex histories of the post-emancipation sugar industry, including sporadic and opportunistic investments and periods of abandonment and decline, is clear from the results of archaeological and documentary research at both Wingfield, St Kitts and Balenbouche, St Lucia.

At Wingfield, the changes to the landscape depicted on the 1828 McMahon map (**Figure 15**) were described in Chapter 4. The lease arrangement with Romney ended in 1819. After this date the Jeaffresons leased the works at Wingfield, with one John Tyson as overseer of Wingfield. After arguments over mismanagement, in 1822 Wingfield Estate passed from John Tyson to the guarantors of his lease, Dennistoun of Glasgow. Wingfield was the object of considerable investment in the post-emancipation period, creating a very large works. The 1848 survey of St Kitts by HMS Thunder (Hydrographic Office L6601) shows Wingfield as 'Romney', with no works marked at Romney. The Romney works appears to have gone out of use after emancipation: and with the Wingfield works serving a large area. The post-emancipation investment appears to have occurred in two distinct phases identified during building recording. In the first phase, steam power was introduced to power the crushing: alongside (rather than replacing) water power. The provision of two crushers dramatically increased the efficiency of the works. Cane was brought into two separate crushing areas at the north of the works. The new steam-powered crushing area consisted of a large stone platform with battered walls, on which rested a horizontal rolling mill for crushing and a small horizontal steam engine, supplied with steam from the boiler. The fly wheel pit and ties for the steam engine survive. In a second phase of post-emancipation development – associated with the provision of a new brick chimney with a date-stone of 1871 – a new steam system was provided in the boiling house. New flues were served by a Lancaster boiler, fired from the west side rather than the east. The perimeter wall was removed, and new tanks to store molasses were provided.

The scale of these late investments is considerable, and suggests the possibility that the works served a wide area. The possibility that the mill returned to its late 17th-century role, processing cane from other planters' land, seems very probable. By July 1879, when Wingfield was leased, it was a great size, described as

> all that Estate or Sugar Plantation situate in the Island of St Christopher in the West Indies forming four contiguous Estates, or Sugar Plantations, and known by the general description of Verchilds Estate, Williams and Crab Hole Estates, Romneys Estate and Wingfield Manor Estate. All which four several estates or Sugar Plantations have long since been thrown into and cultivated as one Estate or Sugar Plantation and are now commonly called or known as the Wingfield Manor Estate. Together with all messuages or tenements thereon and all appurtenances thereto and all fixed and unfixed machinery and live and dead stock... (Bristol University Library (Special Collections), UK. DM 1104)

The transnational links of Kittitian planters at this time are underlined by this lease, from James Philip and Mrs Eliza Philip (of 84 Richmond Road, Bayswater, Middlesex, England) to five parties – Margaret Ann Roger (of 16 Westmoreland Place, Bayswater), Charles Roger (Foxwood, Dumfries), Archibald Roger (a magistrate on St Kitts), Elizabeth Roger (of Deer Park, Ontario, Canada) and Charles William Paterson (of Aurora, Canada).

In 1911, the national railway line for St Kitts' new central factory was completed, running past Wingfield. After this date – as occurred with all Kittitian sugar estates – the works were abandoned and become overgrown. A small wooden house was erected within the walls of the old curing house during the 1920s, and was lived in by the overseer of the cane field gangs (Campbell Evelyn *pers. comm.*). Meanwhile the estate houses continued to be occupied by an estate overseer, managing the cultivation of the cane fields. Two historic photographs of the Sugar Works were identified in the archives of the St Christopher Heritage Society (**Figures 22 & 23**). These appear to date from the first decades of the 20th century, and show the works in partial ruin, although with the iron water wheel surviving. A final use of the water, first exploited in 1680, was for a turbine, with piped water from the aqueduct, which may first have been used to power machinery,

FIGURE 22. WINGFIELD IN THE EARLY 20TH-CENTURY, FROM VERANDA LOOKING EAST
(ST CHRISTOPHER HERITAGE SOCIETY ARCHIVE)

FIGURE 23. WINGFIELD IN THE EARLY 20TH-CENTURY, LOOKING EAST (ST CHRISTOPHER HERITAGE SOCIETY ARCHIVE)

but was later used to generate electricity for the house at Romney, which was by then owned by the Boon family. Inter-island labour migration was important in the running of Wingfield in the 1930s: when the seasonal arrival of the 'Antiguan cutters' boosted labour when cane was being harvested (Campbell Evelyn *pers. comm.*). A range of later shacks, using galvanised corrugated iron, were erected during the late 20th century within the Wingfield works area.

Just as in St Kitts, the fortunes of the sugar industry in St Lucia were varied. The new concerns with respectability in St Lucian society were demonstrated by the establishment by three sisters of the Alexander family at River Dorée estate, to the west of Balenbouche, of a small Protestant community, with a popular school. The Protestant church and school survive today. The Stipendiary Magistrate's report of 1846 reported that

> these talented and devoted ladies devote themselves entirely to the inhabitants of the estate, who, formerly the slaves of the property, with few exceptions, since emancipation have never quitted the locality; and having been instructed by the family in the Protestant faith, form but an increasing congregation of 182 souls. (National

Archives CO 258/16 Stipendiary Magistrate's Report 1846, quoted by Louis 1982, 158).

By 1847, the proprietor of Balenbouche was Gaillard de Laubenque, who was cultivating 120 acres (Rennard nd; Detaille and Jamet 1847). The establishment of the centrals in the 1870s did not see the end of the sugar works at Balenbouche: due to its isolated location. Indeed, as at Wingfield around the same time, the scale of Balenbouche suggests that it provided sugar processing facilities for a wide area. Balenbouche was the only non-central factory in St Lucia to make use of East Indian indentured labourers: and a community of St Lucians of East Indian descent lives today in the nearby Balca area (Harmsen 1999).

During the 1850s-60s, the boiling and curing houses were newly fitted out. Concrete was extensively used to alter the fabric of the buildings, and a new water wheel and crushing machine, supplied by Fletcher of London, were provided.[30]

---

[30] The Fletcher company was established in London in the late 18th century, and grew to become one of the world's leading manufacturers of sugar machinery. The company relocated to Derby between 1862 and 1864 (Bradley 1972). Later water wheels manufactured by the London are marked 'Fletcher London and Derby'.

This considerable investment appears to be associated with the new use of East Indian indentured labour in the 1860s. During the 20th century, as the metayage system persisted in St Lucia, the Sugar Company provided workers with land, seed-cane and the funds for cultivation, and claiming one third of the harvest, and buying the remaining two-thirds. Yet while the centrals continued, the works at Balenbouche appear to have gone out of use in the early 20th century, although some structures were altered for cassava processing at a later date. The 1946 air photograph of Balenbouche (**Figure 17**) clearly shows the majority of the estate under intensive coconut cultivation for the export of copra.

Today, the Caribbean economy is driven by tourism. Balenbouche is a guest house (http://www.balenbouche. com), Romney houses a batik shop, Caribelle Batik, and the landscaped botanical gardens of both sites make use of the built heritage of the plantations.

Conclusions

This study has traced presented a sequence of landscape change from the ditched, palisaded or walled enclosures of Carib and English settlements in the early 17th century to enclosed sugar works that were viewed as 'manors' with tenant and servants, and then to the open and larger landscapes of sugar monoculture, with the villas, plantations and slaves modelled on a classical style and through which ideas of 'improvement' were performed. Throughout this sequence, it has been suggested that designed landscapes in the eastern Caribbean were crucial sites at which broader transatlantic landscapes were imagined and brought about – through the movement of human beings (both free, indentured and unfree), and the trade and exchange of tropical staples and European industrial manufactures across the Atlantic. In this concluding section, I want to reflect in more general terms upon the question of what British archaeologies bring to the study of the sugar landscapes of the eastern Caribbean. I want briefly to highlight two ways in which this study has tried to answer this question, and then to consider the prospects for the future development of historical archaeology in the Caribbean region.

Colonial Legacies and 'British' Archaeologies
My first answer is that British archaeology represents a distinctive place from which to engage with the legacies of colonialism – one that brings particular challenges and particular perspectives. In this respect, my work in the Caribbean aimed to start to rethink 'British' archaeology. Central here is the issue of choice: decision-making processes of researchers choosing to conduct research on one particular theme, or on another. As Michel-Rolph Trouillot has argued, the production of history is an active process of 'mentions' and 'silences':

> The presences and absences embodied in sources (artefacts and bodies that turn an event into fact) or

archives (facts collected thematized and processed as documents or monuments) are neither neutral or natural. They are created. As such, they are not mere presences or absences, but mentions or silences of various kinds and degrees. By silence, I mean an active and transitive process: one 'silences' a fact or an individual as a silencer silences a gun (Trouillot 1995, 48).

As a British archaeologist, my choices of how to study the post-medieval period have been similarly active. Like all archaeological practices, my choice to study the landscapes of British colonialism in the eastern Caribbean was contemporary, and inevitably political – revealing some stories and silencing others. The legacies of colonialism and racial slavery are often forgotten in Britain, and are often excluded from national historiographies and debates over British heritage. Writing a PhD in the Atlantic port city of Bristol, this study was an attempt to interrogate the geographical and thematic limits of 'British' archaeology in the modern world.

The idea of studying colonial contexts to inform the study of British social history 'at home' has, of course, been explored in other fields. Most famously, in literary studies Edward Said's examination of the exclusion of references to Sir Thomas Bertram's Antiguan sugar plantations from his fictional rural elite landscape *Mansfield Park* (Austen 1814) has inspired 'postcolonial' studies that acknowledge the influence of imperial worlds upon highly 'English' cultural situations (Said 1993, 95-116). Here, my discussion of the idea of improvement (Chapter 4 above) can serve to highlight my point. Said observed how Austen described social life in the households and landscapes of the elite as 'implicated in the rationale for imperialist expansion':

> The "attainable quality of life", in money and property acquired, moral discriminations made, the right choices put in place, the correct "improvements" implemented, the finely nuanced language affirmed and classified (Said 1993, 100).

Bertram's Antiguan estate landscapes were 'held in a precise place within Austen's moral geography' of improvement, as she connected 'the actualities of British power overseas to the domestic imbroglio within the Bertram estate' (*ibid*: 112, 114, cf. Johnson 1996, 210). Similar impulses are visible in historical studies of the colonial Atlantic have seen the emergence of what David Armitage has termed 'cis-Atlantic' accounts, aiming to provide a counterpoint to national historiographies written in the Victorian period and the early 20th century by writing the history of particular locations in wider Atlantic perspective (Armitage 2002, 23-28). By seeking to define the uniqueness of a particular situation 'as the result of the interaction between local particularity and a wider web of connections', such historical studies bring 'methodological pluralism and expanded horizons' (*ibid*: 23, 29). Such perspectives are keeping with the motivations for interest in improvement in historical geography as

> usefully reposition[ing] enlightened culture, away from the prime focus on the metropolitan, libertarian world of London to the more regulated rural world of the landed estate (Daniels *et al.* 1999, 346).

Such research directions, across literary, geographical and historical studies, are united by an awareness of the entanglements of empire and metropole. In the study of Caribbean sugar plantations, such perspectives are indebted to the legacy of Trinidadian historian Eric Williams 1944 study, *Capitalism and Slavery*. The 'Williams Thesis' argued that the development of British industrial society was closely bound up with the cultural and economic capital produced by the sugar islands of the eastern Caribbean (E. Williams 1944). Similarly, in his classic examination of the relationships between urban and rural situations, *The Country and the City*, the other Williams discussed here – Raymond Williams – acknowledged the 'larger context' of the British empire, and its profound effects upon British imagination and landscape from the late 19th century (R. Williams 1985[1973]): perspectives that can be applied before the 19th century as well (Said 1993, 98). Inspired by both Eric and Raymond Williams' examinations of estate landscapes, in both Britain and the Caribbean, we can examine the estate landscapes in St Kitts and St Lucia during the later 18th century in relation to improvement as an elite, transatlantic phenomenon of the Georgian Atlantic.

It is not simply that British archaeology has not adequately acknowledged colonial legacies, and must add such material to its canon. More radically, in writing insular, national archaeologies of modern Britain the field has failed to develop studies that move beyond illustrating the narratives of secondary social histories, and produce work that uses material culture to the undocumented, diverse and multicultural dimensions of early modern British history. The challenge for British archaeologies of 'improvement' (Tarlow 2003, 2007) is to acknowledge the politics and complex geographies of such ideas – how they were, for instance, by bringing new conceptions of the agency of humans, material things and landscape entangled with the ideology of racial slavery in the manner that I have described above. The risk for British archaeology is it finds in ideas such as improvement a kind of 'surrogate capitalism' (Hicks 2004b) – replacing one grand, evolutionary process with another by missing out the situations (such as colonial or marginal British locations) where ideas such as 'improvement' were adopted and used in different ways.

Materiality and Landscape

The second aspect of the study that I want to highlight is its focus upon materiality and landscape, a theme that relates to the nature of the archaeological contribution to the study of colonialism. Recent work has highlighted the potential

of understanding European colonialism as a fundamentally material process (Gosden 2004, Lawrence and Shepherd 2006). My interest here has been to contribute a sustained and situated case study in methodology to such important theoretical understandings of the colonial archaeology.

The study has made use of the 'empirical tradition' of British landscape archaeology. As I observed in Chapter 1, this is an unfashionable choice. It is difficult to think beyond understandings of landscapes as concerned with meaning and ideology, especially because of the strength of the research in historical geography such as the studies of improvement discussed in Chapter 4. Such approaches form part of a more general approach to designed landscapes, set out by Stephen Daniels and Denis Cosgrove most clearly in the opening lines of their seminal statement on 'the iconography of landscape':

> A landscape is a cultural image, a pictorial way of representing, structuring or symbolising surroundings. This is not to say that landscapes are immaterial. They may be represented in a variety of materials and on many surfaces – in paint on canvas, in writing on paper, in earth, stone, water and vegetation on the ground. A landscape park is more palpable but no more real, not less imaginary, than a landscape painting or poem. Indeed the meanings of verbal, visual and built landscapes have a complex interwoven history. To understand a built landscape, say an eighteenth-century English park, it is usually necessary to understand written and verbal representations of it, not as 'illustrations', images standing outside it, but as constituent images of its meaning or meanings. And of course every study of a landscape further transforms it meaning, depositing yet another layer of cultural representation. In human geography, the interpretation of landscape and culture has a tendency to reify landscape as an object of empiricist investigation, but often its practitioners do gesture towards landscape as a cultural symbol or image, notably when likening landscape to a text and its interpretation to 'reading' (Daniels and Cosgrove 1993, 1)

However, in such an approach the material dimensions of landscapes tend to be reduced to the 'image', 'symbol' or text. As Tim Ingold famously argued, Daniels and Cosgrove risk dividing mind from matter, meaning from substance (Ingold 1993, 152-4). In contrast with meaning and reading, archaeology can explore the landscapes of improvement through their materiality and performance. Here, Matthew Johnson's (2005, 2006) comments on landscape archaeology, in which he presents a critique of a certain provincialism in British landscape archaeology, can be stood upon their heads. As described in Chapter 1, the empirical focus of landscape archaeology (e.g. Aston 1985) was critiqued by 'interpretive' approaches to landscape in archaeology during the 1980s and 1990s. In contrast, I have here been concerned with the potential for using these techniques to document material detail and material change. While the attempt by the interpretive critique to move beyond dry description is well taken, the risk is that such complexities are lost through an emphasis upon ideational landscapes, meaning, social context and 'reading' landscape.

The archaeological contribution to the study of European colonialism relates, as Chris Gosden and others have rightly observed, to the field's abilities to explore the material dimensions of colonialism. In this context, the techniques of landscape archaeology – documenting earthworks, standing buildings and other landscape features and combining them with a distinctive use of documents and historic maps (which are read for their empirical content) to present a sequence of landscape change – represent a significant disciplinary resource that can be put to use. As I have argued with Laura McAtackney elsewhere (Hicks and McAtackney forthcoming), there is significant potential in the methods and practices of landscape archaeology to make use of what Alison Wylie (2002, 177) has described as archaeology's 'mitigated objectivism', in order to negotiate

> the tensions created by a commitment to use the tools of systematic empirical enquiry to rigorously question the authority and presuppositions of scientific enquiry, to turn science and history against themselves when they serve as tools of oppression, and to reclaim their emancipatory potential (Wylie 1995, 272).

In this case, the production of a regional sequence has been able to expose how landscapes were altered, persisted and were remodelled. The influence of Carib enclosures upon the form of British plantation landscapes, and the continuing role of designed landscapes as places for the production and consumption of material culture, are among the narratives that emerge from such a perspective – examining the material contingencies of previous landscapes influenced how new ideas and impulses were worked out in the landscape. Such an approach does not deny the important observations of 'interpretive' approaches (e.g. Hodder 1986, 61-70) that designed landscapes were understood in different ways by different people, rather than 'duping' subaltern populations into compliance or false consciousness. But it allows better calibrated and more finely detailed accounts of how colonial impulses were worked out in particular situations, facilitating the thick description of landscape change and the weaving together of documentary and archaeological data

Closing Thoughts

This book has sought to explore research directions that are similar to those taken by many of the contributions to Susan Lawrence's edited collection of 'Archaeologies of the British' (2003). Inspired specifically by Matthew Johnson's (1996, 210) call for modern world archaeologies to explore the complexities of global contexts, I have sought to use the techniques of landscape archaeology to combine a sense of the complex materialities of British

colonialism with the contemporary political need for British archaeologists to highlight the histories and legacies of colonialism. Through this combination I have aimed to produce an extended case study in how archaeology might provide distinctive and situated perspectives upon the histories, geographies and legacies of European colonialism. A second volume (Hicks forthcoming) will explore in more detail how a critical awareness of the Atlantic contexts of the material culture of the modern world can serve to relocate and reorient the limits and agendas of British historical archaeology. But in these closing thoughts, I want to consider some of the future possibilities and challenges for historical archaeology in the eastern Caribbean.

Archaeologies of the modern eastern Caribbean must be more than the illustration of global historical processes through local contemporary engagements. Colonial and postcolonial histories must, as Anne Stoler (2001) has observed, acknowledge contradictions, complexities and the nuances of 'tense and tender ties' as well as grand narratives. My choice to explore the status of the landscapes of the region as part of 'British' archaeology is just one story that can be told about the recent past in the region. It is a story that has tried to highlight the oppression of and violence against Indigenous and African Caribbean people, to explore the origins and complexities of the ideology of racial slavery and the legacies of colonialism, and to contribute to broader impulses in historical archaeology to document the material conditions of oppression (e.g. Leone 2005). But at the same time, this focus has meant that in this study I have been much less effective in writing histories of African Caribbean people and other undocumented stories. This is a question that cannot be entirely removed from questions of methodology: as I have noted, landscape archaeology involves a range of attitudes to landscape and field practices that are closely related to the history of British colonialism.

The principal challenge for Caribbean historical archaeology in the next decade is to promote diversity in theory and practice – encouraging the generation of many accounts, from many perspectives, of the histories of the region. To achieve this, it will be important for the impulses in some Americanist literature towards unified 'world historical archaeologies' (e.g. Orser 1996) to be resisted. Such approaches risk reducing archaeologies of the Caribbean region to the role of illustrating grand, Eurocentric narratives of domination and resistance – stories that because they are approached as being the same everywhere lose any sense of the contemporary power – both political and affective – of the heritage of the recent past. Rather than flattening out the rich and diverse histories of the Caribbean region, archaeologists must work to achieve and to celebrate the kind of diversity that I am describing. As Mary Beaudry has put it, historical archaeology is at its best not when aiming to 'contribute…to our understanding of sweeping and amorphous cultural processes', but when striving 'to inform us of the intimate and unheralded details of day-to-day life' (1996: 496).

Caribbean historical archaeology is much more than an archaeology of the British. The development of African Caribbean, African Diaspora and Indigenous archaeologies represent some of the most exciting aspects of the development of world archaeology over the past two decades. The study of other identities – the colonial histories of French, Dutch and other European nations in the eastern Caribbean, and the many minority religious, ethnic and other populations in the region – is also a crucial field in which further work needs to be developed. One major current obstacle is the unhelpful division between prehistoric and historical archaeology in the region, and efforts to work across these boundaries are desperately needed. The neglect of 19th- and 20th-century archaeological remains also serve to limit the potential of archaeologies of the recent past in the region. The development of trained Caribbean-based archaeologists and the proper funding of national archaeological and heritage organisations are also of great importance. While the present study has focused on the British in order to begin to recognise the international and multicultural dimensions of postcolonial 'British' archaeologies of the recent past, and to start to think through how archaeology can study the influence of colonial history upon the metropole (following Williams 1944), archaeologies in the eastern Caribbean must explore diverse materials of local and contemporary significance and value – alternative legacies from which to tell untold stories about the past for the future.

APPENDICES

Appendix 1

Jeaffreson's Description of the Hurricane on 27th August 1681

Saturday the 27th of August, about one or two in the morning, the winde blew very hard at north-east, which did some small damage. Before day, the weather broke up with the appearance of fair weather; but before nine of the clocke, it was overcast and proved a rayney, blustery day. About eight or nine o'clock at night the wind, veering more to the north and from the north to the north-west, increased until midnight; at which tyme it blew so vehemently hard, and so continued with small rayne and frequent lightnings, until lesse than an hour of daybreake (when the storm began to cease), that I had not a house standing upon my plantation, in which I could shelter myself from the weather.

It was a little after midnight when a great part of the roof of my dwelling-house began to fly away; severall of my out-houses being already downe. Then I thought it time to shift myselfe; which I did. Turning my people out before (who had been driven into my house by the insufficiency of their out houses), I locked the door, and took the key in my pocket. I could not goe against the winde; and with no small difficulty could I goe with it, for feare of beeing driven away by it. At last we got (all but one of our company) to a little hut, which, we had agreed upon before, to make our rendezvous in. Which sheltered vs from the violence of the storme, but not of the raine, the thatch being partly blown away. But to be wet was then no news to vs.

We were in continual feare oue little cottage should have been blown away; which rocked like a cradle. As soone as the storme began to cease, I went up to my house which I found miserably torne, and flat with the ground. My sugar-worke, in like manner, and all my buildings. I walked downe to my new sugar worke, which I had built not long before, about a quarter of a mile or more from my house, towards the sea, to make my tenants' sugar canes; to whom I had leased fifty acres of land, and had newly begun to make sugar at it, and was then boiling at it, when the storme began. I found that likewise flatt with the ground – the stone wall overturned, and the timber scattered in divers places, farre distant from the house ...

... It was a deplorable sight to see the spoyle that was done in the canes and provisions, in comparison of which the losse of all our houses and workes is as nothing.

That day, although Sunday, I got up a little house, in which to secure myselfe and the best of my goods from the wet; and I used all diligence to get up a couple of roomes, and one of my sugar workes, and to put some Indian provisions in the ground, having thirty two negroes, besides whites, to feed every day (for which I bless God).'

(Jeaffreson to Madam Brett 25 October 1681. Jeaffreson 1878, Vol. 1, 274-80)

Appendix 2

Extracts from 'Old Accounts of the Manor of Wingfield, 1685' (Jeaffreson Collection M79: h)

Appendix 2a. An Inventory of the Estate of Capt. Christopher Jeaffreson taken by Ltt. Zachariah Rice and Ltt. Francis Kerie the 29th July 1685 by virtue of a Commission from the hono'ble the Governor to that effect unto us directed beareing date the 17th of this July

[illegible]s	One man serv't named Wm. Boddingfield
	One woman serv't named Cath. Bull
Bulls:	Chattin, Morrean, Ranger, Dick a Bull kept to ½ wth Srgt. Wm. Maugh
Steers:	Rodger, Guia, Ranger, Ponzy, Stuart[illegible], Two young steers [illegible]
Cows	Young Rose, Old Cherry, young Cherry

Heifers: Bald Face, Betty

Two young heifers, tow young bulls, two heifer calves

Negro Men

Thom	Ned
Pelor	Sam
Athello	Matthew
George	Kitt
Tophott	James
Wingfeild	Alexander
Tom Tinker	David
Periot	Daniell
John	Bajazott

Negro Women

Grande Maria	Candas & Child
Little Maria	Johanna
Catherin	Christianna
Franeh	Agnes
Bridgett	Debora
Grace	Celia
Peggy	Maria Arrada
Nanny	

Negro Children

Primrose, Franeh and Sarah

a cassada mill
Two Paire of New Wheels
Two Carts
Two Paire of Truck Wheels
One waterworke vizt.
A Cassada mill
a boyling house
eight coppers
Three skimmers
One ladle
One Scoupe
One Iron Crow
Two Sledges
One sett Ffam

One greate paire of Styllyards[31]
One Paire of Iron Crooks
One Whip Saw
One Cross cut saw
One Copp'r Cooler
Two wooden coolers
One large wooden trough
Three lamps
Two stills wth heads wormes and wormes Caske[32]

Skiming Caske
Eight Cipes
Three Punchions[33]

One dwelling house wth 3 roomes
Six leather chaires
One Gable and Fframe
A Beneh
One Hamacca
One Cargo Chest
a Bedsted
a feather bed & Boulsters
a Square Gable and Fframe
Two Score skin trunkes
Two Fuzes[34]
Four Pewter Dishes
Seaven Pewter Plates
One Porringer
One Pewter Quart Pott
One Pewter Pint pott
Two Pewter Candlesticks worne out
One brass candlestick
One Pestle & Mortar
one small Paire of Stilliards[35]
One iron box
one brass skillet – worne out[36]
one frying pan
three iron potts
three musquetoons[37]
One fflizoo[38]
One Musquett
One paire of Brass Scales wth weights

One Iron Spitt
One Grindstone
House Posts, Bridge beam and Capistan[39]

---

[31] = Steelyard, a weighing device: 'A balance consisting of a lever with unequal arms, which moves on a fulcrum; the article to be weighed is suspended from the shorter arm, and a counterpoise is caused to slide upon the longer arm until equilibrium is produced, its place on this arm (which is notched or graduated) showing a weight' (OED).

[32] = worm. OED 16.i 'a long spiral or coiled tube connected with the head of a still, in which the vapour is condensed.'

[33] Large cask for liquids of fixed volume.

[34] = fusees. 'A light musket or firelock' (OED).

[35] = Steelyard. See note 31 above.

[36] skillet = cooking pot or stew-pot, usually with feet.

[37] = musketoon. A short musket with large bore (OED).

[38] Unknown word. Possibly a woodworking tool, hence 17th century use of 'Flizz: a splinter' (OED).

[39] Unclear. Possibly = Capstan (a lifting mechanism).

A Cook Roome wth Steward roome
A Chest
An Ovall Gable and frame
A Boyling house shingled

Zachariah Rice, Francis Kerie

Appendix 2b. An Account of what is – of the Estate of Capt. Xpher Jeaffreson since the last Accot. Sent him by Ensign Edward Thorne taken this 27th day of August 1685 by Ltt Zachariah Rice and Ltt Francis Kerie

One negro man named Calabar	dead
One negro woman named Nelle	dead
One Bull brought of Willm Long	dead
One Ditto bought of Srgt Wm Maugh	dead
One Darke Iron Gray horse	dead
One young Black horse	dead
One ladle worne out	worne out
One Hammacca	worne out
One Suite of old curtains & Vallens[40]	worne out
One flock[41] bed and Bolster	worne out
Two looking glasses broaken	broaken
One Pewter Chamber pott lost	lost
Five pewter plates	lost & worne out
Eight pewter Spoones	lost & broaken
One Porringer	lost & broaken
One Bason	worne out
One Case of Black handled knives	lost & broaken
One Ginn dripping Pan[42]	worne out
One Earthen Leamonade Pott	broaken
One hanging Cupboard	
Two musquetts	sold
One Iron Spitt	Lost
One Grid Iron[43]	Lost
One small Brass Ladle	Lost
One Paire of Iron Crooks	Lost
One Old Trunk	Broaken
Two Saddles and Bridle	worne out
One fyle and sett and one pair compasses	lost
One yoake and Iron Bows	lost
One Cas'a mill & appur'ts	Sold
Three Iron hoopes for the Rollers – wooden in the middle [not legible]	
One Iron Gudgeon[44]	used in ditto

Two Dowlass[45] Table Cloaths	
Two Diaper[46] Ditto	
10 Dyaper napkins	worne out and stolen
One paire fine sheets	
One paire Course ditto	

---

[40] prob. = vallances (short curtains).
[41] presumably a wool- or cotton-stuffed mattress.
[42] Obscure, but presumably a receptacle to catch sugar juice or similar from a crushing machine (='gin').
[43] a cooking utensil of parallel bars of iron.
[44] A metal pivot on which a wheel turns or a bell swings.
[45] = dowlas, a coarse linen.
[46] = diaper, a fine linen or cotton fabric.

| 28 yards of Canvas | used |
| 35 yards of Osnabriggs[47] | used |

Zachariah Rice
Francis Kerie

Capt. Christopher Jeaffreson[48]

1685

July 10	3 Gallons of Brandy at	0210
	To Sugr Paid John Gremaine[illegible] for his order	0291
	To Ditto Carryed home wth him	3687
	To Mr John London for sundrys and	1152
	44 for soape at 574	
	2 Bottles of Oyle 50	
	128 of ffish at 128	
	6 hh'ds of Lyme from Nevis 400	
	For Mr Rich'd Tippott and Comp. For sundrys and	3462
	29 yards Blew Linnen at 290	
	100 of 10" nailes at 10	
	54 of Rope at 216	
	60 yards of Canvas at 20	
	1 browne thread & a bottle of oyle 70	
	26 nutmeggs & 200 cloves 47	
	For 500 6" nailes 25	
	one stock cock[49] 30	
	one bottle of Oyle 30	
	2 Bushall of Pease 128	
	1 Bar'l Of Beefe 320	
	1 hhd. Of Cod fish at 756	
	one barrell of mackerell 250	
	46 foot of Deale Boarde[50] at 69	
	one barrell of Oyle 500	
August 2nd	To Peter Kolly for fitting a roller	0048
	To Cath paid for takeing up Bajazett[51]	0096
	To Mr Bolinger for one Bushell of Pease	0064
	To Mr Thomas Westeott for Sundries &	2626
	24 heads at 44 Sugar per head 330	
	25 0/4 yards of Osenbrigg 300	
	2 hhd of Indian corne 850	
	6 p[illegible]s 24	
	30 soap at 360	
	9 yards of osenbrigg 100	
	240 hoopes 360	
	one sword for his serv't 200	
	6 Norway Diales[52] At 96	
		£11635

---

[47] = Osnaburg, a coarse linen.

[48] This table lists items bought and services received by Jeaffreson.

[49] presumably = stop-cock: 'a tap or short pipe furnished with a valve operated from the outside by turning a key or handle, for the purpose of stopping or permitting as required the passage of liquid, air, steam, gas or the like.'

[50] = deal board: a thin board of fir or pine.

[51] This is unclear. Bajazott is listed as a 'Negro man' above. Possible meanings would include obtaining him as a slave, hiring him as a servant, overseeing him, or training him.

[52] presumably compasses which point north rather than timepieces.

from ye other side	£11635
To Thomas Carrell for makeing a Receiver	0160
To ditto Carroll for Sawing &c.	1719
To Morris Spoolane for Ditto	0924
To Gilbert Avide for Ditto	0634
To Ralph Speneson for one cow & calfe	1250
To Guilliamme a fr. Coop'r for worke done	0200
a new sett of Rollers	1200
To [illegible] George Carpenter for worke done as per acco't	6338
wording Your Lt of Attorney one Action [illegible]	0090
2 Ticketts For Nevis	0028
an Answer to Heny Kings Declared	0050
drawing articles of agreement wth – George	0120
45 of Bacon	0183
To Andrew Eliot for 36 of fish and 6 qrts of Oyle	0960
To John Gannott for 2 Barl's of Beefe	
To [illegible] Peterson Melot Smith for worke done	0750
To Henry Fonds Ditto for worke done	4300
makeing Collors and Whips	0078
8 yards Perpetuana[53] for your Boyes	0160
To Gov [illegible] Taylor for worke done	1050
One paire for Cart wheeles	1400
one paire ditto	0760
6 pound of Beefe bought at Nevis	1640
makeing 3 cart wheeles and mending 3 ditto	1240
3 Bushalls of Beanes	0120
To Mr [illegible] Vickers and comp. For sundrys and c.:	208
fr't your goods from Nevis 400	
one peew[54] of Timber 882	
200 of 30" nailes 50	
1000 of Ditto Nailes 250	
freight carrying 40 [illegible] Sugar on board 400	
one empty hhd 100	
	39005

---

[53] Perpetuana = woollen cloth.

[54] Unclear. Possibly – 'pew: a pointed stake, a large stick shod with iron' (OED), but OED quotes no usage before 1861.

from ye other side	39005
fr't of one Sheet of Lead from Nevis	0100
new Stocking a Gunn and fixing others	0200
To Dearmon Murphy for looking after cattle	0208
To Mr Bolinger for 1164 feet of Board	1164
To David a Lawyer for 1 month's Wages	0100
To Peter Kelly for a sloop load of lime stones	0600
To Lt. Gen. Munday for 2 Bulls and a sloop load of limestones	3500
To Rich'd Bryan for one Months wages	0300
To Thomas Fox for one load of mackerell	0200
To Ditto for 1 hhd of fish qt. Nt. 736 at	0552
3 Leavies to the church 1175:720:595	2490
To John Steele for 15 months 22 days wadges	5900
To John Rodgers for worke done	0300
To John Shalton for looking after ye flock	1000
To Capt. Wm. Marys for a young Bull	0850
To Capt. John Pogson for Sundrys &c.	3264
1 [illegible] of Oyle 100	
3 wedges 050	
6 hoopes at 600	
6 hhds lyme 1152	
50 dayes worke of his Mason 1250	
To Symon Froners For 2 Barrells of Beefe	0600
Cutting 25½ Coard Of wood	0540
To Mr Lord for one Barrl of Same	0300
To Duagg Free Negro for 12 m's service	1000
To Edw'd Browne for 4 Barl of Beefe	1000
To John Jolly carpenter for 1½ mo. Wadges	0390
To Doct'r Hobbs for looking after the plant'n	3000
To ye country for a Leavy	1640
To Doc'r Wanhalmaioll for looking after ye plant'n	3177
	71380

from ye other side	71380
[illegible] hotts and cassada sifters	0040
[illegible] Barke axes[illegible] at severall times	0050
To Lt Munday for 1 Sloope load limestones	0800
To Capt Loveraigne for one sloop load ditto	0800
One barr'l of Beefe	0300
To Capt Wimple for 17 [illegible] of Timber	1484
One Barrell of Mackerell	0200
One Barrell of Beefe	0300
To Wm Grace Mason for 2 mo. Wadges	0700
To Wm Woodrop for 230 of Iron & c.	0575
To Wm Long for a young Bull	0900
To Petr Jolly Carpenter for worke done	6650
To Alexander Merrefeild Mason for 37 days worke	0700
To Edwd Lea Ditto for worke done	0408
To [illegible] Moloone Ditto for worke done	0408
To [illegible] Lawrence Ditto for 3 days worke	0048
3 lotts of Iron -reaks and Nailes	1972
To Major Crisce for one Band of Same	0300
For 15 Dayes worke of John Dawson Mason	0100
To Capt Perry for 441 of Peters [illegible]	0661
To Joseph Mose Lawyer for worke done	0338
To Mr Fox for 24 of [illegible]	0048
A Barr'l of Frame Oyle	0500
One hhd of fish	0780
4 Barrl of Mackererll	0600
A Barrell of Beefe	0300
To Capt Sharples for 12 Barr. Of Ditto	2600
One Negrowoman of Appraisement	3000
3 sloopes load of limestones	1784
To Capt Phipps for 12 Barrl of Beefe	2880
Pipes and Punchzuns[55]	0780
To John Garkon for 12 Mo. Sallery [illegible]	3400
To Richd Collway for wadges	1050
	107765

---

[55] Presumably pipes for the boiling/stilling processes rather than tobacco pipes.

from ye other side	107765
To John Ellis for Six weeks Boyling	0480
To a Ffrenchman for boyling	0048
To Nicholas Leech for Ditto	0930
A Barrell of Beefe	0300
A sett of Rowlers	4400
A paire of womans shoes for Cate your Servt	0036
A Dozz. Of Spoones	0060
A Barrel of Beefe of Mr Woodrex	0360
To Cate Paid for takeing up James and Athello[56]	0096
To Jonathan Walker for worke done	0370
To Mr Soley for one hhd of fish	0633
To Mr Seampion Cooper for worke done	1918
To Wm Wotten Mason for worke done	0474
To Wme for Cate when she was sick	0024
To Mr Holecroft	0629
4 Thread	0160
180 yards for Canvas	2232
39 yards of white Osnebriggs	0351
2693 Cassadas Bought at severall times	2693
21½ yards of Blew Linnen	0172
32 yards browne Ozzenbriggs	0288
My passage and Expenses to Nevis	0160
20 Candles for the boyling house	0100
To Mr Murphy for Cassadoe	0116
3 Axes – and 51 of Lignum Vitae barke	0163
To Mr Barry's Acco't.	0426
To Walter Branen for 2 Barr'l of Mackerell 360	0703
To Ditto for 343 of Fish 343	
4 stock cocks	0048
Thomas Carney	0091
To Thomas Downes for a Bar'l of Oyle	0300
To Mr Roe for 5 Barr'l of Beefe	1250
135¼ yards Canvas	1039
30 soap at	0300
To Mr Spamores for wadges as Overseer	1233
	127348

---

[56] See footnote 51 above.

from ye other side	127348
[illegible] Barr'l of Lyme	0040
To Daniell Sullivan for Cassadoe	0188
To James Bond for 813 feet of Board	0915
9 paire womans & mens shoes dor your srv't Cate	0316
37½ yards of blew Linnen	0300
To Capt Elijha Bennet for Nailes	0250
18 Barrells of Beefe at 210 per barrell	3780
A Tickett for Wm the Mason	0024
A hhd for Sugar lost of Lt Ke-es Bay	1319
To Morgan Orwonny for looking after Stephen Bumsted a Convict	0200
To Wme to driving the Cattle	0150
A Paire of hindges for the Pew	0012
A hammaco	0200
To Mr Monthus ffarrier[57]	0204
To Cax. Chiss for 1 Gallon of Rum	0024
To 300 of 10" nailes	0024
One Iron Pott	0200
A Barrell of Beefe & freight from Nevis	0320
4 Barrl of Lyme	0160
One Gallon of Rume	0024
One Barrell of Beefe	0260
One hhd of Lyme	0200
One quart of Rume	0006
To Cate paid for makeing shirts & c. for ye serv'ts	0064
To Mr Moore for one Axe	0025
To Ocum To mind ye Spouts[58]	0048
6 yards of blew Cloath for Cate	0120
To [illegible] paid to Sundry persons upon his acco't as follows Vizt	1203
To Sergt John Domuse 340	
To Henry Jones 7835	
To Jonathan Walker 80	
	137924

---

[57] Possibly an individual tending to horses and other animals (closer to a vet: a sense traditionally associated with military contexts) rather than simply making horseshoes.

[58] Presumably the spouts refer to stilling.

from ye other side	137924
To William Ravlon	0433
To William Grace	0217
To Dennis Murphy	2000
To Morgan Olivery	0308
To John Peterson Moleat Smith	2350
To Mr McArthur	2079
To John George	0600
To Thomas Cazney	0091
To Mr Nouvie	0320
To Mr Mathers	0205
To Mr Bigot	0197
To Gullo Royly	0200
To Lt [illegible] Munday	0679
To Thomas Pelham	1441
To Thomas Westcott	8786
To Mr London	14629
To Mich. Gippott & Comp'y	28832
To Mr Craznly	0381
To Henry Carpenter and Comp.	28832
To Matthew Vanhalman	0504
To Ens. Matthew Gohagan	5700
To Mordecay Rogers	440
To David Cuzzons	764
To Peter Kelly	1470
To Thomas Bolsenger	800
To Capt. [illegible] Parry	3383
To Henry George	300
To Mr John Addy	9920
Sug'r Shipped you by Capt Shippard	12547
10 hhd at 500 sugr per tonn	1250
Ye Duty of 4½ per cent	542
Sug'r shipped by Capt Gouznell	8843
7 hhds at 450 per tonn	787
Ye Duty of 4½ percent	398
	262031

brought from ye other side	262031
Sugr shipped him by Capt Morley	21685
16 hhds at 400 per tonn	1600
Ye Duty of 4½ percent	1008
My comission of Two hundred forty three thousand eight hundred twenty and seaven pounds of Sugar at 10 percent	21348
My comission of sales and receipts of forty two thousand six hundred forty and nine pounds of sugar at 10 percent	4265
To my comission of receipts of twenty thousand six hundred and sixty pounds from several at 5 percent	1033
To Thomas Casill	620
My comission for receipts of severall [illegible]s at 5 [illegible] [illegible] the whole sume received being fourteen thousand two hundred sixty three pounds of sugr	710
To Louis a Free Negro for a weeks boyling	100
	314461

Errors and Omissions excepted this 27th of Aug't 1685, St Xphers, Edward Thorne

Per Contra – Credit

Henry King	570
Thomas Poince	350
Daniell Sullevan	115
Capt Robt Smith	150
John Clunn	327
Joseph Moore	2300
[illegible] [illegible]	650
John Dixon	156
John Stoole	628
Wm Woodrop	279
[illegible] [illegible]	40
Morgan Oswenny	350
the sales merchandizes of Capt Holmes by the sales 50 paire of plaine shoes at	1200
By the sales 22 paire of falls[59] Ditto	1100
The sale of one Sword	1000
The sales 96 yards wt. Ozzenbriggs	1251
The sales four hoes [illegible] [illegible]	100
The sales of 1 Box of Medicines	1850
The sales 32 yards of Canvas	492
The sales of 23 2/4 yards of Brown Ozzenbriggs	250
The sales of Brown thread	200
The sales of 95¼ Blew linnen	1091
The plantacon and sundrys as appeared by the Debteside amount	3203
83 of Tobacco	186
11 yards of Ozzenbriggs	132
10 S[illegible]ds of Thredd	10
612 of fish	892
2 Gunns to the country	400
By Mr Murphy Rent	1477
By Ralph Jonsons Ditto	2183
	22932

---

59 This appears to be a reference to the bands or collars worn around the neck which were fashionable during the 17th century.

[by amount of the other side]	22932
By Ditto for Pasturing Cowes	120
By William Long	218
By Ditto for Pasturing Cattle	65
By Henry King for Rent	93
By Garret Dorey for Ditto	288
By Srgt Wm Mango For Ditto	288
By Ditto for Rattan, Cotton & c.	70
By Morgan Sheenny for rent	384
By John Ellis for Ditto	384
By Daniel W[illegible] for Ditto	240
By [illegible] [illegible] for Ditto	240
By Wm Murphy for Ditto	240
By [illegible] [illegible] [illegible]	40
By Buckaneere [illegible]	790
61 of Beefe	185
Morris Spelane for Rent	1200
Ditto for Pasture [illegible] December next	200
Lt. Paine for Lott of Cases and Rowlers	10000
Your Negro Peters worke at ye Church	418
7 of Beefe	21
One Bar'l of Mackerell	200
5 Bar'l of Beefe	1432
Capt James Phipps for 3 – sold him	7500
Capt John Munday for a [illegible] sold him	2200
Lt Francis Rosie[illegible] For	8000
Capt James Phipps	600
Thomas Cavell	231
Thomas Pogson	100
Dorothy Cla [illegible]	450
John Murphy	1642
Ralph Johnson	924
	70208

[by amount of the other side]	70208
Wm Long	1374
Garat Darcy	1344
Honozah Shaw	90
2 p wheeles sold Ens. Mathew	576
300 peews of Reading [illegible]	300

An Acco't of ye sugar made to ye halfes
Garrard Darcy 11454
Henry King 16428
Wm Long 5376
John Murphy 1104
Ralph Tomson 2378
John Murphy and Comp. 44977
Capt Wm Maugh 162110

By his moiety of the sugar made to the halfe being one hundred twenty one thousand nine hundred * eighteen pounds the whole two hundred forty three thousand eight hundred & twenty pounds	121918
Sugar made of the Plantation	91563
262 Gallons of Molasses	1048
260 Gallons of Rum	6023
An overcharge on a Sloop loade of Limestone of Lt John Munday	800
9 of Soder to Ens. Mathew	81
	295115
	19346
	314461

By Balance Due this 27th Aug't 1685
Errors and Omissions Excepted this 27th of August in St Xphers 1685 Edward Thorne

Aug't 27	The Balance of the Account	19346

Per Contra – Creditor

By two [illegible] of the three [illegible]ifyed in the award of us to Mr Nicholas Tippett [illegible] hee finds that the estate aught to have creditt for those of the Mill to – Paine and the Mare [illegible] To Capt Phipps his comission amounting to one [illegible] and [illegible] [illegible] and fifty pounds of sugar	01750
Ballance due to Thorne this 27th of Aug't 1685	17596
	19346

Examined and sworne before us Zachariah Rice Francis Kerie.

A true coppy from the Originall comission by [illegible] John Fox Sec'ry

Appendix 3

List of Payments by Christopher Jeaffreson, 13 December 1682
(Jeaffreson Archive M71, 13/12/1682)

Four coppers	34-13-01
A Still of copper	10-01-03
A Worme Tubb Iron Bound wth cost wth hangeing [illegible]	01-06-06
5 white leather skins at 3	00-15-00
1 Copper ladle & scummer wth socket handles	00-14-08
1 worme of pewter 70¾ at 13	03-16-00
1 pewter swansneck still head 46¼ at 22	04-00-00
1 silver hilted sword wth false scabbard cappe etc.	03-07-06
Payd Custome Duties, Portridge Cartidge Wharfeige Waters and wateridge charges	04-00-00
Payd Freight and Primeage	05—2-06
	153-10-00

Appendix 4

Copy (*c.*1823) of Inventory of Wingfield Estate from 30th July 1713 (Jeaffreson Archive M71)

An Inventory and Appraisement taken and made the 30th day of July 1713 of the Negroes and other matters and things belonging to & being upon the Plantation and Lands within mentioned by John Panton and George Milward Esq'rs Appraisers indifferently chosen for that purpose as follows vizt

Negroe Men
Bragadah	£15
Jaik	£40
Johnno	£36
Winfield (not fit for any service)	–
	£91

Negroe Women
Frankey	£36
Catto	£36
Betty Congo	£20
Conduit	£20
Old Frank	£15
Katy	£25
Old Kate (NB she has but one hand)	£5
	£157

Negroe Girls
Molly	£12
Peggy	£5
	£17

An Old Boiling House and Walls estimated at	£10
Four Mill Posts and one Bridge Tree of the Island Wood	(no value)
One Main roller of Ban wood with one case and two half Gudgeons estimated at	£10

One deal Water spout rotten & of no value

Four Cocoa nut trees

No Canes Plant or Ratoon or Provision of any kind upon the s. Plantation nor are there any buildings thereon save only a few negro houses

Memorandum that the above Negroes Matters and things were valued and appraised by us

Signed J. Panton Geo. Milward

APPENDIX 5

REGISTER OF PLANTATION SLAVES, BALLEMBOUCHE ESTATE. 13TH DECEMBER 1815 (NATIONAL ARCHIVES T71/379)

General List of Slaves

Name	Occupation	Age	Sex	Country of Birth
Paul Livre	charpentiere	50	M	Saint Lucia
Petit Charles Mouche	charpentiere	45	M	Saint Lucia
Frederick Laronde	charpentiere	24	M	Saint Lucia
Urbain Jourme	charpentiere	24	M	Saint Lucia
Jean Francois Registe	charpentiere	22	M	Saint Lucia
Jean Pointe	tonnelier	54	M	Saint Lucia
Jean Cadet	charpentiere	30	M	Saint Lucia
Vital Bonda	tonnelier	30	M	Congo
Alexis Aeougua	macon	45	M	Saint Lucia
Edward Jaffia	cuisinier	40	M	Mandingo
Jean Francois Grand Laguin	rumier	28	M	Congo
Smart Fig	guardian	26	M	Congo
Giles Gilo	culivateur	26	M	Congo
Pierre Langaide	culivateur	34	M	Congo
Jasmime Sampson	culivateur	34	M	Mayombe
Michel Andre	rumier	32	M	Saint Lucia
Antoine Laurent	culivateur	41	M	Saint Lucia
Inocent Lamie	culivateur	26	M	Saint Lucia
Melville Banon	culivateur	26	M	Saint Lucia
S. Louis Julien	culivateur	26	M	Dominique
Jean Presse Negre	culivateur	32	M	Saint Lucia
St Amour Love	culivateur	26	M	Saint Lucia
Marcil Mask	culivateur	18	M	Saint Lucia
Manuel Lefort	culivateur	20	M	Saint Lucia
Louisson Bon	culivateur	20	M	Saint Lucia
Purie Pitiful	culivateur	30	M	Saint Lucia
James Jones	matelot	32	M	Guadeloupe
Laguesse Falballa	matelot	36	M	Arada
Uzeb Baneoche	commandeur	45	M	Moeo
John Charles Hilaire	commandeur	30	M	Saint Lucia
Vieux Charles Figue	point	80	M	Ibo
Augustine Couteau	point	92	M	Moeo
Levsville Agupa	guardien	60	M	Mine
John Pierre Yeux Blanc	guardien	40	M	Ibo
Uzebe Sappotee	culivateur	17	M	Saint Lucia
Jacque Aboukina	culivateur	68	M	Mandingo
Glaude Crab	culivateur	68	M	Moeo
Gabriel Gorge	guardien	58	M	Ibo
Honore Pinsl	infirme	34	M	Saint Lucia
Postilon Voleur	infirme	36	M	Mandingo
Registe Jambe Coupé	guardien	30	M	Saint Lucia
John Baptiste Tortue	pecheur	65	M	Ibo
Eustache Potaleau	cultivateur	17	M	Saint Lucia
Jean Bart Gouga	domestique	12	M	Saint Lucia
Leon Pesealier	matelot	14	M	Saint Lucia
Jose Pecteur	matelot	44	M	Senegal
Ellenne Rouge	guardien	14	M	Saint Lucia
Jean Charles Aypea	cultivateur	23	M	Saint Lucia

Edmund Lazarre	cultivateur	10		M		Saint Lucia
Louis Pene	cultivateur	34		M		Saint Lucia
Sophie Sorrowful	cultivateur	26		F		Saint Lucia
Toineste Poison	cultivateur	50		F		Saint Lucia
Victoire Agathe	cultivateur	44		F		Saint Lucia
Jeane Poule	cultivateur	13		F		Saint Lucia
Rosine Mouche	cultivateur	26		F		Saint Lucia
Janekine Barie	cultivateur	33		F		Saint Lucia
Adelaide Micoud	cultivateur	46		F		Saint Lucia
Therese Ravine	cultivateur	36		F		Congo
Webiane Rance	cultivateur	44		F		Ibo
Marianne Congo	cultivateur	48		F		Ibo
Angel Praslin	cultivateur	48		F		Congo
Charlotte Dangolle	cultivateur	19		F		Saint Lucia
Charlotte Creole	cultivateur	17		F		Saint Lucia
Mari. Jeanne Youthe	domestique	20		F		Saint Lucia
Mia Rat	cultivateur	41		F		Saint Lucia
Nanon Canal	cultivateur	17		F		Saint Lucia
Dorothe Dirty	cultivateur	40		F		Ibo
Marie Calhassie Aeajou	cultivateur	26		F		Saint Lucia
Lisette Cromonisse	cultivateur	26		F		Saint Lucia
Adilaide Chique	cultivateur	34		F		Saint Lucia
Francoise Yaya	cultivateur	32		F		Saint Lucia
Marie Victoise Gros Peid	cultivateur	26		F		Saint Lucia
Genieve Aradax	cultivateur	30		F		Saint Lucia
Jemerance Caposse	cultivateur	29		F		Saint Lucia
Rose Sansnem	cultivateur	17		F		Saint Lucia
Desirée Beauté	cultivateur	20		F		Saint Lucia
Lucille Cayanne	cultivateur	39		F		Sossos
Doncé Campecke	cultivateur	56		F		Saint Lucia
Dame Bishop	cultivateur	15		F		Ibo
Luce Negresse	cultivateur	15		F		Saint Lucia
Ann Rave	cultivateur	47		F		Saint Lucia
Justine Justice	cultivateur	56		F		Saint Lucia
Adee Femelle	cultivateur	24		F		Saint Lucia
Catherine Catiche	hospitalisse	69		F		Saint Lucia
Petronille Yamannde	point	9		F		Saint Lucia
Madelaine Dinde	point	7		F		Saint Lucia
Marie Ursul Pigeon	point	9		F		Saint Lucia
Marie Louise Canarde	point	89		F		Saint Lucia
Grande Liselle Codendre	point	49		F		Saint Lucia
Julie Ibo	point	52		F		Saint Lucia
Catherine Lala	domestique	33		F		Martinique
Louise Civante	domestique	33		F		Saint Lucia
Camille Gros Bois	domestique	18		F		Saint Lucia
Caroline Geulle Rouge	domestique	16		F		Saint Lucia
Judith Pentarde	domestique	60		F		Montserrat
Victoire Ogurz	domestique	41		F		Moco
Euphrozine Canelle	petit atelier	53		F		Ibo
Julie Aguax	petit atelier	57		F		Mine
Marie Mare Diguz	petit ateler	57		F		Saint Lucia

Slave Families
Cleronne

Charles Clèronne	cultivateur	43		Father	Saint Lucia
Henriette Cleronne	cultivateur	35		Mother	Saint Lucia
Louise Cleronne	cultivateur	15		Daughter	Saint Lucia
André Cleronne	cultivateur	13		Son	Saint Lucia
Agathe Cleronne	cultivateur	6		Daughter	Saint Lucia
Lucienne Cleronne	cultivateur	4		Daughter	Saint Lucia
Jean Francois Cleronne	cultivateur	1		Son	Saint Lucia

Cooper

Jacque Cooper	tonnelier	37	Father	Saint Lucia
Rosiette Cooper	cultivateur	33	Mother	Saint Lucia
Silvain Cooper	cultivateur	13	Son	Saint Lucia
Theresine Cooper	point	8	Daughter	Saint Lucia
St Rose Cooper	point	3	Daughter	Saint Lucia
Florentine Cooper	point	1	Daughter	Saint Lucia

Yoyo

Joseph Yoyo	macon	28	Father	Saint Lucia
Glorianne Yoyo	cultivateur	28	Mother	Saint Lucia
Aimee Yoyo	cultivateur	3	Daughter	Saint Lucia
Pouline Yoyo	point	1	Daughter	Saint Lucia

Calebasse

Louis Calebasse	cultivateur	33	Father	Saint Lucia
Venus Calebasse	cultivateur	33	Mother	Congo
Andre Calebasse	point	1½	Son	Saint Lucia

Bouteille

Marcel Boutielle	cultivateur	42	Father	Saint Lucia
Marthe Boutielle	cultivateur	28	Mother	Saint Lucia
Eugine Boutielle	point	1½	Daughter	Saint Lucia

Pauban

Dominique Pauban	rafineur	28	Father	Saint Lucia
Jeanette Pauban	cultivateur	34	Mother	Saint Lucia
Marie Claire Pauban	guardien	13	Daughter	Saint Lucia
Cecil Pauban	point	4	Daughter	Saint Lucia

Tobacco

Jenny Tobacco	cultivateur	45	Mother	Saint Lucia
Catherine Tobacco	cultivateur	24	Daughter	Saint Lucia

Tierney

Jacqueline Tierney	hospitalisse	54	Grandmother	Grenada
Victorie Tierney	cultivateur	43	Mother	Saint Lucia
Susanne Tierney	cultivateur	16	Daughter	Saint Lucia
Jeanne Rose Tierney	cultivateur	14	Daughter	Saint Lucia
Prosper Tierney	guardien	12	Son	Saint Lucia
Rose Tierney	point	3	Daughter	Saint Lucia
Lisette Tierney	domestique	5	Daughter	Saint Lucia

Bolte

Serephin Bolte	cultivateur	28	Brother	Saint Lucia
Susanne Bolte	cultivateur	23	Sister	Saint Lucia

Soulier

Martine Soulier	cultivateur	46	Mother	Ibo
Laureneine Soulier	cultivateur	28	Daughter	Saint Lucia

Cravatte

Rosette Cravatte	cultivateur	40	Mother	Ibo
Joseph Cravatte	domestique	14	Son	Saint Lucia
Elienne Cravatte	guardien	13	Son	Saint Lucia
Augustine Cravatte	point	3	Son	Saint Lucia
Marie Jean Cravatte	point	5	Daughter	Saint Lucia

Rivier

Gertrude Rivier	cultivateur	37		Mother	Saint Lucia
Pelage Rivier	guardien	10		Daughter	Saint Lucia

Banane

Felieste Banane	infirme	54		Mother	Saint Lucia
Charles Banane	cultivateur	17		Daughter	Saint Lucia

D'Orange

Jeanne Rose d'Orange	point	9		Brother	Saint Lucia
Paul d'Orange	point	1½		Brother	Saint Lucia

Mango

Fatma Mango	cultivateur	50		Mother	Mandingo
Julie Mango	cultivateur	14		Daughter	Saint Lucia

Akanna

Georgette Akanna	cultivateur	56		Mother	Ibo
Auguste Akanna	cultivateur	22		Son	Saint Lucia

Corosolle

Lucette Corosolle	cultivateur	44		Mother	Ibo
Jean Piere Corosolle	cultivateur	16		Son	Saint Lucia
Noel Corosolle	cultivateur	11		Son	Saint Lucia
Marshal Corosolle	cultivateur	8		Son	Saint Lucia
Sabine Corosolle	cultivateur	13		Daughter	Saint Lucia

Chapeau

Madalaine Chapeau	cultivateur	41		Mother	Ibo
Eloise Chapeau	cultivateur	11		Daughter	Saint Lucia
Zabeth Chapeau	cultivateur	9		Daughter	Saint Lucia
Elieste Chapeau	point	7		Daughter	Saint Lucia

Wilberforce

Louise Wilberforce	cultivateur	42		Mother	Ibo
Charlotte Wilberforce	domestique	13		Daughter	Saint Lucia

Punch

Marie Paul Punch	cultivateur	30		Mother	Saint Lucia
Joachim Punch	cultivateur	10		Son	Saint Lucia
Rosanne Punch	point	7		Daughter	Saint Lucia

Erielie

Monique Erielie	petit atelier	46		Mother	Ibo
Adeé Erielie	point	10		Daughter	Saint Lucia

Muton

Agoumou Muton	cultivateur	54		Mother	Ibo
Antoine Muton	cultivateur	10		Son	Saint Lucia

Gommier

Gertrude Gommier	cultivateur	33		Mother	Saint Lucia
Jn. Baptiste Gommier	point	8		Son	Saint Lucia

Micoua

Mariette Micoua	domestique	56		Grandmother	Martinique
Rose Micoua	domestique	30		Mother	Saint Lucia
Lucile Micoua	point	12		Daughter	Saint Lucia

Cajouca

Julienne Cajouca	cultivateur	12	Sister	Saint Lucia
Renette Cajouca	cultivateur	22	Sister	Saint Lucia
Xavier Cajouca	cultivateur	8	Brother	Saint Lucia
Cerille Cajouca	point	4	Brother	Saint Lucia
Laureneia Cajouca	point	2	Brother	Saint Lucia

Agoutz

Marie Joseph Agoutz	cultivateur	28	Mother	Saint Lucia
Cile Agoutz	cultivateur	9	Daughter	Saint Lucia
Rosalie Agoutz	point	4	Daughter	Saint Lucia

Manioc

Flose Manioc	cultivateur	72	Mother	Saint Lucia
Marie Madelaine Manioc	cultivateur	33	Daughter	Saint Lucia
Jeanette Manioc	cultivateur	28	Daughter	Saint Lucia
Nelson Manioc	cultivateur	9	Son	Saint Lucia

Regonne

Zabeth Regonne	cultivateur	50	Mother	Saint Lucia
Monlouis Regonne	cultivateur	34	Daughter	Saint Lucia
Raymond Regonne	cultivateur	21	Son	Saint Lucia
Francois Regonne	cultivateur	9	Son	Saint Lucia

Stoe

Zabeth Stoe	cultivateur	72	Mother	Ibo
Margaritte Stoe	cultivateur	33	Daughter	Saint Lucia
Jn Philip Stoe	macon	27	Son	Saint Lucia
Charles Stoe	mousse	10	Son	Saint Lucia
Rosalie Stoe	point	8	Daughter	Saint Lucia

Trotto

Rosiette Trotto	cultivateur	26	Mother	Saint Lucia
Marthe Trotto	point	3½	Daughter	Saint Lucia

Dangolle

Luce Dangolle	cultivateur	60	Mother	Ibo
Francois Dangolle	cultivateur	19	Son	Saint Lucia
Laurieneine Dangolle	cultivateur	17	Daughter	Saint Lucia

Primary Archive Sources

Letterbook of Christopher Jeaffreson, 1675-1686

Special collections, Library Services, University College, London. MS Add70

Jeaffreson MSS, Beinecke Lesser Antilles Collection, Hamilton College, Clinton, New York

Jeaff. UCC Mss. Room

Romney MSS, Centre for Kentish Studies, Maidstone, Kent

Accounts, inventories and plans, 1760-1834

Pinney MSS, Special Collections, University of Bristol

The Godwin

Letterbooks, accounts and other papers: John Pinney (Mountravers Estate, Nevis)

National Archives, Kew

CO 28:16 V 36 William Gordon July 14 1720 Advantages and Disadvantages of Settling St Lucia

CO 441 incumbered estates commission

T71 *Registers of Plantation Slaves*

St Lucia National Archives, Castries

Uncatalogued plan of the Quartier de l'Islet a Caret, 1770

Lefort De Latour 1787. Description general et particuliere de l'ille de St Lucie pur servir a l''intelligence…. (Ms held by St Lucia National Archives; also translated as 'Map of St Lucia 1787…Together with a General description of the Island' London 1883)

Tudway MSS, Somerset Record Office, Taunton. DD/TD.

Parham Plantation, Antigua: accounts, letters and maps

Aarons, G.A. 1983. 'Archaeological Sites in the Hellshire Area'. *Jamaica Journal* 16, 76-88

Aarons, G.A. 1989. 'Port Royal: An Archaeological Adventure'. *Jamaica Journal* 22, 32-40

Adamson, A.H. 1972. *Sugar Without Slaves: The Political Economy of British Guiana 1838-1904*. New Haven: Yale University Press

Agorsah, E.K. 1991a. 'Evidence and Interpretation in the Archaeology of Jamaica'. *Proceedings of the 13th International Congress for Caribbean Archaeology*, Curaçao, pp. 2-14

Agorsah, E.K. 1991b. 'Recent developments in archaeological research in Jamaica'. *Proceedings of the 14th International Congress for Caribbean Archaeology*, Barbados, pp. 416-424

Agorsah, E.K. 1992. Jamaica and Caribbean Archaeology. Archaeology Jamaica 6, 1-14

Agorsah, E.K. 1993. 'Archaeology and Resistance History in the Caribbean'. *African Archaeological Review* 11, 175-96

Agorsah, E.K. (ed.) 1994. *Maroon Heritage: Archaeological, Ethnographic and Historical Perspectives*. Kingston: Canoe Press

Agorsah, E.K. 1996. 'The Archaeology of the African Diaspora'. *African Archaeological Review* 13(4), 221-224

Agorsah, E.K. 1999. 'Ethnoarchaeological consideration of the social relationship and settlement patterning. Among Africans in the Caribbean diaspora'. In Haviser (ed.), pp. 38-64

Ahlman, T. 1997. *Archaeological Evidence of African Slave Occupation at Brimstone Hill Fortress National Park, St Kitts*. Brimstone Hill Archaeological Project Report No. 2

Ahlman, T. and G.F. Schroedl 1997 *Artifacts Recovered during Archaeological Investigations at the Brimstone Hill Fortress National Park, St Kitts, West Indies, July 1996*. Brimstone Hill Archaeological Project Report No. 3

Ahlman, T., G.F. Schroedl, E. Howard, and A. McKeown 1997. *Artifact Inventory from the July 1996 Excavations at the Brimstone Hill Fortress National Park, St Kitts, West Indies*. Brimstone Hill Archaeological Project Report No. 4

Alegría, R.E. 1983. *Ball Courts and Ceremonial Plazas in the West Indies*. New Haven: Yale University Press (Publications in Anthropology 79)

Allaire, L. 1974. 'An archaeological reconnaissance of St Kitts, Leeward Islands'. *Proceedings of the 5th International Congress for Caribbean Archaeology, Antigua*, pp. 158-161

Allaire, L. 1980. 'On the historicity of Carib migrations in the Lesser Antilles'. *American Antiquity* 45(2): 238-245

Allaire, L. 1997. 'The Lesser Antilles before Columbus'. In Wilson (ed.) *The indigenous people of the Caribbean*. Gainesville: University Press of Florida: The Ripley P. Bullen series, pp. 20-28

Allaire, L. 2003. 'Agricultural Societies in the Caribbean: The Lesser Antilles'. In J. Sued-Badillo (ed.) *General History of the Caribbean, Volume 1 – Autochthonous Societies*. Paris: UNESCO, pp. 195-227

Andrews, E.W. and C.M. Andrews (eds) 1939. *Journal of a Lady of Quality: being the narrative of a journey from Scotland to the West Indies, North Carolina and Portugal in the years 1774 to 1776*. New Haven [= diary of Janet Schaw; 1774-6]

Andrews, K.R. 1978. 'The English in the Caribbean 1560-1620'. In K.R. Andrews *et al.* (eds), pp. 103-123

Andrews, K.R., N.R. Canny and P.E.H. Hair (eds) 1978. *The Westward Enterprise. English Activities in Ireland, the Atlantic and America 1480-1650*. Liverpool: Liverpool University Press

Anon. 1638. *News and strange newes from St Christophers of a tempestuous Spirit, which is called by the Indians a Hurrin-cano or whirlewind*. London

Anon 1965. *Report on certain historic buildings, monuments and sites on St Lucia*. Castries: Office of the Chief Minister

Armitage, D. 2002. 'Three concepts of Atlantic history'. In D. Armitage and M.J. Braddick (eds) *The British Atlantic World, 1500-1800*. New York: Macmillan, pp. 11-27

Armstrong, D.V. 1982. 'The "Old Village" at Drax Hall: An Archaeological Progress Report'. *Journal of New World Archaeology* 5(2), 87-103

Armstrong, D.V. 1983a. 'The Old Village at Drax Hall'. In *Proceedings of the Ninth International Congress for the Study of Pre-Columbian Cultures of the Lesser Antilles, Santo Domingo, Dominican Republic, August 1981*. Montreal: Centre de Recherches Caraïbes, Université de Montreal, pp. 431-442

Armstrong, D.V. 1983b. *The Old Village at Drax Hall Plantation: An Archaeological Examination of an Afro-Jamaican Settlement*. Unpublished Ph.D. dissertation, University of California, Los Angeles

Armstrong, D.V. 1985. 'An Afro-Jamaican Slave Settlement: Archaeological Investigations at Drax Hall'. In T. Singleton (ed.), pp. 261-287

Armstrong, D.V. 1990a. *The Old Village and the Great House: An Archaeological and Historical Examination of Drax Hall Plantation, St Ann's Bay, Jamaica*. Urbana: University of Illinois Press

Armstrong, D.V. 1990b. 'Research at Seville Plantation: A Progress report'. *Archaeology Jamaica* 1(2), 7-8

Armstrong, D.V. 1991a. 'The Afro-Jamaican House Yard: An Archaeological and Ethnohistorical Perspective'. *Florida Journal of Anthropology Special Publication* 7, 51-63

Armstrong, D.V. 1991b. 'Recovering an early 18th-century Afro-Jamaican community: Archaeology of the slave village at Seville, Jamaica'. *Proceedings of the 13th International Congress for Caribbean Archaeology*, Curaçao, pp. 344-362

Armstrong, D.V. 1992. 'African-Jamaican Housing at Seville. A Study in Spatial Transformation'. *Archaeology Jamaica* (NS) 6, 51-63

Armstrong, D.V. 1999. 'Archaeology and Ethnohistory of the Caribbean Plantation'. In T. Singleton (ed.), pp. 173-192

Armstrong, D.V. 2001. 'A Venue for Autonomy: Archaeology of a changing cultural landscape, the East End Community, St John, Virgin Islands'. In Farnsworth (ed.), 142-164

Armstrong, D.V. *Creole Transformation from Slavery to Freedom: Historical Archaeology of the East End Community, St John, Virgin Islands*. Gainesville: University Press of Florida

Armstrong, D.V. And Fleischman, M. 1993. *Seville African Jamaican Project. Summary Report: Analysis of Four House Area Burials from the African Jamaican Settlement of Seville.* Syracuse University Archaeological Report 6

Armstrong, D.V. and K. Kelly 2000. 'Settlement Patterns and the Origins of Jamaican Society: Seville Plantation, St Ann's Bay, Jamaica'. *Ethnohistory* 47(2), 369-397

Aston, M. 1985. *Interpreting the Landscape*. London: Batsford

Attema, Y. 1976. *St Eustatius: A Short History of the Island and its Monuments*. Holland: De Walburg Pers Zutphen

Axtell, J. 1978. 'The Ethnohistory of Early America: a review essay'. *William and Mary Quarterly* 35(1), 110-144

Bailyn, B. 1986. *The Peopling of British North America*. New York: Vintage

Barbotin, F.M. 1970. 'Les sites archéologiques de Marie-Galante (Guadeloupe)'. *Proceedings of the 3rd International Congress for Caribbean Archaeology*, St Georges, Grenada, pp. 27-44

Barbotin, F.M. 1978. 'Dècouverte de crânes, fémurs et autres os'. *Bulletin de la Société d'Histoire de la Guadeloupe* 38, 3-37

Barka, N.F. 1985. 'Archaeology of St Eustatius, Netherlands Antilles: An Interim Report on the 1981-1984 Seasons'. *St Eustatius Archaeological Research Series No. 1*. Department of Anthropology, College of William and Mary

Barka, N.F. 1986. 'Archaeology of the Government Guest House, St Eustatius, Netherlands Antilles: An Interim Report'. *St Eustatius Archaeological Research Series No. 2*. Department of Anthropology, College of William and Mary

Barka, N.F. 1987. 'Archaeological Investigations of the Princess Estate, St Eustatius, Netherlands Antilles: An Interim Report on the Supposed Jewish Mikve'. *St Eustatius Archaeological Research Series No. 3*. Department of Anthropology, College of William and Mary

Barka, N.F. 1988a. 'Archaeology of the Jewish Synagogue Honen Dalim, St Eustatius, Netherlands Antilles'. *St Eustatius Archaeological Research Series No. 4*. Department of Anthropology, College of William and Mary

Barka, N.F. 1988b. 'The 1988 second season of archaeological investigations of the Government Guest House, St Eustatius'. *St Eustatius Archaeological Research Series, No. 5*. Department of Anthropology, College of William and Mary

Barka, N.F. 1988c. 'The Simon Doncker House: archaeological exploration of the yard'. *St Eustatius Archaeological Research Series, No. 6*. Department of Anthropology, College of William and Mary

Barka, N.F. 1989. 'A Progress Report on the Structural Aspects of the Government Guest House Complex, St Eustatius, Netherlands Antilles'. *St Eustatius Archaeological Research Series No. 5*. Department of Anthropology, College of William and Mary

Barka, N.F. 1990a. 'Archaeological Investigations of Structure 4, Government Guest House Complex, St Eustatius, Netherlands Antilles'. *St Eustatius Archaeological Research Series No. 6*. Department of Anthropology, College of William and Mary

Barka, N.F. 1990b. 'The potential for historical archaeological research in the Netherlands Antilles'. *Proceedings of the 11th International Congress for Caribbean Archaeology*, San Juan, pp. 393-399

Barka, N.F. 1991a. 'The merchants of St Eustatius: An archaeological and historical analysis'. *Proceedings of the 13th International Congress for Caribbean Archaeology*, Curaçao, pp. 384-392

Barka, N.F. 1991b. 'Ebenezer Plantation, A Preliminary Archaeological Survey, Sint Maarten, Netherlands Antilles'. *St Maarten Archaeological Research Series No. 2*. Department of Anthropology, College of William and Mary

Barka, N.F. 1991c. 'Archaeological Investigations of Battery Concordia, St Eustatius, Netherlands Antilles'. *St Eustatius Archaeological Research Series No. 7*. Department of Anthropology, College of William and Mary

Barka, N.F. 1993. 'Archaeological Survey of Sites and Buildings, St Maarten, Netherlands Antilles: I'. *St Maarten Archaeological Research Series No. 3*. Department of Anthropology, College of William and Mary

Barka, N.F. 1996a. 'Archaeology of the Dutch Elite: The Country Estate of Johannes de Graff at Concordia, St Eustatius, Netherlands Antilles'. *St Eustatius Archaeological Research Series No. 9*. Department of Anthropology, College of William and Mary

Barka, N.F. 1996b. 'Citizens of St Eustatius 1781: An Archaeological and Historical Study'. In R.L. Paquette and S.L. Engerman (eds) *The Lesser Antilles in the Age of European Expansion*. Gainesville: University Press of Florida, pp. 223-238

Barka, N.F. 2001. 'Time Lines: Changing Settlement patterns on St Eustatius'. In P. Farnsworth (ed.), pp. 103-141

Barka, N.F. And Sanders, S. 1990. 'A Preliminary Study of Welgeleegen, St Maarten, Netherlands Antilles'. *St Maarten Archaeological Research Series No. 1.* Department of Anthropology, College of William and Mary

Barker, D. and T. Majewski 2006. 'Ceramic Studies in Historical Archaeology'. In D. Hicks and M.C. Beaudry (eds) *The Cambridge Companion to Historical Archaeology*. Cambridge: Cambridge University Press, pp. 205-231

Barrett, J. 1999. 'Chronologies of Landscape'. In P. Ucko and R. Layton (eds) *The Archaeology and Anthropology of Landscape*. London: Routledge (One World Archaeology), pp. 21-30

Barrett, W. 1965. 'Caribbean Sugar Production Standards in the Seventeenth and Eighteenth Centuries'. In J. Parker (ed.) *Merchants and Scholars*. Minneapolis: University of Minnesota Press, pp. 148-168

Batie, R.C. 1976. 'Why Sugar? Economic Cycles and the Changing of Staples on the English and French Antilles, 1624-1654'. *Journal of Caribbean History* 8-9, 1-41

Bayly, C.A. 1989. *Imperial Meridian. The British Empire and the World 1780-1830*. London: Longman

Beachey, R.W. 1957. *The British West Indies Sugar Industry in the late 19th century*. Oxford: Blackwell

Beaudry, M.C. 1996. 'Reinventing Historical Archaeology'. In L. De Cunzo and B.L. Herman (eds) *Historical Archaeology and the Study of American Culture*. Winterthur, DE: Henry Francis Du Pont Winterthur Museum, pp. 473-497

Beckford, W. 1790. *A descriptive account of the island of Jamaica: with remarks upon the cultivation of the sugar cane... also observations and reflections upon what would possibly be the consequences of an abolition of the slave trade, and of the emancipation of the slaves* (2 vols). London: T. and J. Egerton

Beckles, H. 1990. 'A "riotous and unruly lot": Irish indentured Servants and Freemen in the English West Indies'. *William and Mary Quarterly* 47(4), 503-522

Bellin, J.N. 1758 *Description géographique des isles Antilles possédées par les Anglais*. Paris

Benn, D.M. 1974. 'The Theory of Plantation Economy and Society: A Methodological Critique'. *Journal of Commonwealth and Comparative Politics* 12, 249-260

Bennett, J.H. 1967. 'The English Caribbees, 1642-1646'. *William and Mary Quarterly* 24, 367-373

Bequette, K.E. 1991. 'Shipwrecks of St Eustatius: A preliminary study'. *Proceedings of the 13th International Congress for Caribbean Archaeology*, Curaçao, pp. 787-800

Berkhofer, R.F. 1978. *The White Man's Indian: Images of the American Indian from Columbus to the Present.* New York: Alfred Knopf

Berlin, I. and P.D. Morgan (eds) 1991. *The Slaves' Economy: Independent Production by Slaves in the Americas*. London: Frank Cass

Biggs, J. 1849 'On the Establishment of Central Sugar Works in the British Sugar Colonies'. *The Colonial Magazine* 12

Blades, B.S. 1986. 'English Plantations in the Londonderry plantation'. *Post-Medieval Archaeology* 20, 257-269

Bohls, E.A. 1999. 'The Gentleman Planter and the Metropole: Long's History of Jamaica' (1774). In G. MacLean, D. Landry and J.P. Ward (eds) *The Country and the City Revisited: England and the Politics of Culture, 1550-1850*. Cambridge: Cambridge University Press, pp. 180-96

Bohls, E.A. 2002. 'The Planter Picturesque: Matthew Lewis' Journal of a West India Proprietor'. *European Romantic Review* 13, 63-76

Bolland, O.N. 1981. 'Systems of Domination after Slavery: The control of land and labour in the British West Indies after 1838'. *Comparative Studies in Society and History* 23 (4), 591-619

Boucher, P.P. 1992. *Cannibal Encounters: Europeans and Island Caribs 1492-1763*. Baltimore: Johns Hopkins University Press

Boxer. C.R. 1957. *The Dutch in Brazil*. Oxford: Oxford University Press

Bradley, D. 1972. *Fletcher and Stewart: a business history, with special reference to the firm's role in the world sugar industry*. Unpublished M. Phil. thesis, University of Nottingham

Brannon, N. 1999. 'Archives and Archaeology: The Ulster Plantations in the Landscape', In G. Egan and R.L. Michael (eds), pp. 97-105

Brathwaite, E.K. 1971. *The Development of Creole Society in Jamaica*. Oxford: Clarendon

Breen, H.H. 1972 [1844]. *St Lucia Historical Statistical and Descriptive*. London: Frank Cass

Breton, R. 1958 [1665]. *Carib-French Dictionary*. New Haven

Brewer, J. and R. Porter (eds) 1984. *Consumption and the World of Goods*. London: Routledge

Bridenbaugh, C. and R. Bridenbaugh. 1972. *No Peace Beyond the Line: The English in the Caribbean 1624-1690*. Oxford: Oxford University Press

Bridges-Lee, J. 1892. *On Indigo Manufacture: A Practical and Theoretical Guide to the Production of the Dye.* Calcutta

Briggs, A. 1963. *The Age of Improvement, 1787-1867*. London: Longman

Bruneau-Latouche, E. and R. Bruneau-Latouche 1989. *Sainte-Lucie: Fille de la Martinique*. Paris: private printing

Bullbrook, J.A. 1960. *The Archaeology of Tobago*. Ms. on file, Archaeology Centre, University of the West Indies, St Augustine, Trinidad

Bullen, R.P. 1966a. 'The first English settlement on St Lucia'. *Caribbean Quarterly* 12(2), 29-35

Bullen, R.P. 1966b. 'Barbados and the archaeology of the Caribbean'. *Journal of the Barbados Museum and Historical Society* 32, 16-19

Burgh, N.P. 1863. *A Treatise on Sugar Manufacturing*. London

Burns, A. 1954. *A History of the British West Indies*. London: Allen and Unwin

Buxton, L., J. Trevor and A. Julien 1938. 'Skeletal Remains from the Virgin Islands'. *Man* 38(47), 49-517

Caddy, J.H. 1837. *Scenery of the Windward and Leeward Islands*. London: Ackerman

Cain, P.J. and A.G. Hopkins 1986. 'Gentlemanly Capitalism and British Expansion Overseas, I: The Old Colonial System, 1688-1850'. *Economic History Review* 39, 501-525

Campbell, J. 1763. *Candid and impartial considerations on the nature of the sugar trade: the comparative importance of the British and French islands in the West Indies. With the value and consequences of St Lucia and Grenada truly stated*. London: R. Baldwin

Canny, N.P. 1973. 'The Ideology of English Colonisation: From Ireland to America'. *William and Mary Quarterly* 30, 575-598

Casid, J.H. 2005. *Sowing empire: Landscape and colonization*. Minneapolis: University of Minnesota Press

Chiarelli, J.A. 1998. *Coconut Walk Estate Project, Nevis – Project Summary for Earthwatch Europe*. Unpublished ms for Earthwatch

Clarke, C.G. 1975. *Kingston, Jamaica: urban growth and social change 1692-1962*. Berkeley: University of California Press

Clarke, C.G. and A.G. Hodgkiss. 1974. *Jamaica in Maps*. London: Hodder and Stoughton

Clement, C.O. 1994. 'The Tobago Archaeological Program: Developing a comprehensive historic preservation program for Tobago'. *Public Archaeology Review* 2(2), 14-19

Clement, C.O. 1995. *Landscapes and Plantations on Tobago: A regional perspective*. Unpublished Ph.D. dissertation, Department of Anthropology, University of Florida, Gainesville, FL

Clement, C.O. 1997. 'Settlement patterning on the British Caribbean island of Tobago'. *Historical Archaeology* 31(2), 93-106

Clement, C.O. 2000. 'Remnant Amerindian Groups on Eighteenth Century Tobago, West Indies? A Comparison of Coarse Earthenwares from Four Sites'. *Florida Anthropologist* 53(1), 12-25

Coke, T. 1808-11. *A History of the West Indies, containing the Natural, Civil and Ecclesiastical History of Each Island*. (3 volumes). Liverpool: Nuttall, Fisher and Dixon

Coleridge, H.N. 1826. *Six Months in the West Indies in 1825*. London: John Murray

Colt, H. 1925 [1631]. 'The Voyage of Sr. Henry Colt Knight to ye Illands of ye Antilles in ye Shipp called ye Alexander whereof William Burch was Captayne & Robert Shapton Master accompanied with divers Captaynes and Gentlemen of Note'. In V.T. Harlow (ed.) *Colonising Expeditions to the West Indies and Guiana, 1623-1667*. London: Haklyut Society (Haklyut Society Publications Series 2, Volume 56)

Cooper, F. 2005. *Colonialism in Question: Theory, Knowledge, History*. Berkeley: University of California Press

Corruccini, R.S. and J.S. Handler. 1980. 'Tempromandibular Joint Size Decrease in American Blacks: Evidence from Barbados'. *Journal of Dental Research* 59(9), 1528

Corruccini, RS, A.C. Aufderheide, J.S. Handler and L.E. Wittmers, Jr 1987. 'Patterning of Skeletal Lead Content in Barbados Slaves'. *Archaeometry* 29, 233-39

Corruccini, R.S., J.S. Handler and K. P. Jacobi 1985. 'Chronological Distribution of Enamel Hypoplasias and Weaning in a Caribbean Slave Population'. *Human Biology* 57, 699-711

Corruccini, R.S., J.S. Handler, R.J. Mutaw and F.W. Lange. 1982. 'Osteology of a Slave Burial Population from Barbados, West Indies'. *American Journal of Physical Anthropology* 59, 443-459

Cotter, C.S. 1970. Sevilla Nueva: 'The Story of An Excavation'. *Jamaica Journal* 4(2), 15-22

Courtaud, P., A. Delpuech and T. Romon 1999. 'Archaeological investigations at colonial cemeteries on Guadeloupe: African slave burial sites or not?' In J. Haviser (ed.), pp. 277-290

Cox, E.L. 1984. *Free Coloureds in the Slave Societies of St Kitts and Grenada, 1763-1833*. Knoxville: University of Tennessee Press

Cox, E.L. 1988. 'Free Coloureds and Slave Emancipation in the British West Indies: The case of St Kitts and Grenada'. *Journal of Caribbean History* 22, 68-87

Craton, M. 1978. *Searching for the Invisible Man: Slaves and Plantation Life in Jamaica*. Cambridge, MA: Harvard University Press.

Craton, M. 1982. *Testing the Chains: Resistance to Slavery in the British West Indies*. Ithaca: Cornell University Press

Craton, M. 1997. *Empire, Enslavement and Freedom in the Caribbean*. Kingston: Ian Randle Publishers

Craton, M. & Walvin, J. 1970. *A Jamaican Plantation: The history of Worthy Park, 1670-1970*. Toronto: University of Toronto Press

Crouse, N. M. 1940. *French Pioneers in the West Indies 1624-1664*. New York: Colombia University Press

Cruxent, J.M. and I. Rouse 1958-9. *An Archaeological Chronology of Venezuela* (two volumes). Washington, DC: Pan American Union (Social Science Monograph 6)

Curet, L.A. 2004. 'Island Archaeology and Units of Analysis in the Study of Ancient Caribbean Societies'. In S.M. Fitzpatrick (ed.) *Voyages of Discovery: the archaeology of islands*. Westport: Praeger, pp. 187-202

Cust, R.J. 1865. *A Treatise on the West Indian Encumbered Estates Acts* (Second Edition). London

Dalglish, C. 2003. *Rural Society in the Age of Reason: an archaeology of the emergence of modern life in the southern Scottish highlands*. New York: Kluwer/Plenum

Daniels, S. and D. Cosgrove (eds) 1988. *The Iconography of Landscape: Essays on the Symbolic Representation, Design and Use of Past Environments*. Cambridge: Cambridge University Press

Daniels, S. And S. Seymour 1990. 'Landscape Design and the Idea of Improvement 1730-1900'. In R.A. Dodgshon and R.A. Butlin (eds) *An Historical Geography of England and Wales*. London: Academic Press, pp. 487-520

Daniels, S., S. Seymour and C. Watkins 1999. 'Enlightenment, Improvement and the Geographies of Horticulture in Later Georgian England'. In D.N. Livingstone and C.W.J. Withers (eds) *Geography and Enlightenment*. Chicago: University of Chicago Press, pp. 345-371

Dash, J.S. 1965. 'The windmills and copper walls of Barbados'. *Barbados Museum and Historical Society Journal* 31, 43-60

Davies, K.G. 1957. *The Royal African Company*. London: Longmans

Davies, J. 1666. *A History of the Caribbee-Islands...* London: Dring and Starkey. [Translation of C. de Rochefort 1658 Histoire naturelle et morale des Antilles de l'Amerique...Avec une vocabulaire Caraibe. Rotterdam]

Davis, D.B. 1966. *The Problem of Slavery in Western Culture*. Ithaca: Cornell University Press

Davis, D.D. and R.C. Goodwin 1990. 'Island Carib Origins: Evidence and Nonevidence'. *American Antiquity* 55, 37-48

Davy, J. 1854. *The West Indies, before and since slave emancipation, comprising the Windward and Leeward Islands military command...* London: W. and F.G. Cash

Dawud, A.H.T.A. 1971. 'Archaeological and Historical Sites in Antigua'. *Caribbean Conservation Association Environmental Newsletter* 2(1), 29-39

Day, C. W. 1852. *Five Year's Residence in the West Indies*. London

De Latour, L. 1787. *Description general et particuliere de l'ille de St Lucie pur servir a l''intelligence....* (Ms held by St Lucia National Archives; also translated as 'Map of St Lucia 1787...Together with a General description of the Island' London 1883)

Deagan, K. 1982. 'Avenues of Inquiry in Historical Archaeology'. In M.B. Schiffer (ed.) *Advances in Archaeological Method and Theory* Volume 5. New York: Academic Press, pp. 151-177

Deagan, K. 1987. *Artifacts of the Spanish Colonies of Florida and the Caribbean: 1500-1800. Vol. I, Ceramics, Glassware, and Beads*. Washington DC: Smithsonian Institution Press

Deagan, K. 1996. 'Colonial Transformation: Euro-American Cultural Genesis in the early Spanish-American colonies'. *Journal of Anthropological Research* 52(2), 135-158

De Corse, C.R. 1991. 'West African Archaeology and the Atlantic Slave Trade'. *Slavery and Abolition* 12(2), 92-96

De Corse, C.R. 1992. 'Culture Contact, Continuity and Change on the Gold Coast, AD 1400-1900'. *African Archaeological Review* 10, 163-96

DeCorse, C.R. 1996. 'Historical archaeology'. *African Archaeological Review* 13, 18-21

DeCorse, C.R. 1999. 'Oceans Apart: Africanist Perspectives of Diaspora Archaeology'. In T.A. Singleton (ed.) *I Too Am America: Archaeological Studies of African-American Life*. Charlottesville and London: University Press of Virginia Press, pp. 132-155

Deerr, N. 1943. 'The evolution of the sugar cane mill'. *Transactions of the Newcomen Society* 21, 1-10

Deerr, N. 1949. *The History of Sugar*. Volume 1. London: Chapman and Hall

Deerr, N. 1950. *The History of Sugar*. Volume 2. London: Chapman and Hall

Deerr, N. And A. Brooks 1943. 'The early use of steam power in the cane sugar industry'. *Transactions of the Newcomen Society* 21, 11-21

Deerr, N. And A. Brooks 1946. 'Development of the Practice of Evaporation with special reference to the sugar industry'. *Transactions of the Newcomen Society* 22, 1-19

Deetz, J. 1991. 'Introduction: Archaeological Evidence of sixteenth and seventeenth century encounters'. In L. Falk (ed.) *Historical Archaeology in Global Perspective*. London: Smithsonian Institution Press, pp. 1-9

Deetz, J. 1993. *Flowerdew Hundred. The Archaeology of a Virginia Plantation*. Charlottesville: University of Virginia Press

Delle, J.A. 1989. *A Spatial Analysis of Sugar Plantations on St Eustatius, Netherlands Antilles*. Unpublished MA Thesis, Department of Anthropology, College of William and Mary

Delle, J.A. 1994. 'A Spatial Analysis of Sugar Plantations on St Eustatius, Netherlands Antilles'. In D.W. Linebaugh and G.G. Robinson (eds) *Spatial Patterning in Historical Archaeology: Selected Studies of Settlement*. Williamsburg: King and Queen Press. pp. 33-62

Delle, J.A. 1996. *An archaeology of crisis: The manipulation of social spaces in the Blue Mountain coffee plantation complex of Jamaica, 1790-1865*. Ph. D. thesis: University of Massachusetts

Delle, J.A. 1998. *An Archaeology of Social Space. Analysing Coffee Plantations in Jamaica's Blue Mountains*. London: Plenum Press

Delle, J.A. 1999. 'Extending Europe's Grasp: An archaeological comparison of colonial spatial processes in Ireland and Jamaica'. In G. Egan and R.L. Michael (eds), pp. 106-116

Delle, J.A. 2000. 'The Material and Cognitive Dimensions of Creolization in Nineteenth Century Jamaica'. *Historical Archaeology* 34(3), 56-72

Delpuech, A. 2001. 'Historical Archaeology in the French West Indies: Recent research in Guadeloupe'. In P. Farnsworth (ed.), pp. 21-59

Dethlefsen, E. 1982. 'The historical archaeology of St Eustatius'. *Journal of New World Archaeology* 5(2), 73-86

Dethlefsen, E., S. Gluckman, D.R. Mathewson and N.F. Barka. 1979. *A Preliminary Report on the Historical Archaeology and Cultural Resources of St Eustatius, Netherlands Antilles*. Williamsburg, VA: Department of Anthropology, College of William and Mary

Dethlefsen, E., S. Gluckman, D.R. Mathewson and N.F. Barka. 1982. 'Archaeology on St Eustatius: Pompeii of the New World'. *Archaeology* 35(2), 8-17

Devaux, R. L. 1975. *Historical and Archaeological Sites on St Lucia*. Castries: St Lucia National Trust

Dijkshoorn, S. 1986. *Belvedere, een plantagahuis op St Maarten*. Philipsburg

Drayton, R. 2000. *Nature's government: Science, imperial Britain and the 'improvement' of the world*. New Haven and London: Yale University Press

Drescher, S. 1977. *Econocide: British Slavery in the Era of Abolition*. Pittsburgh: University of Pittsburgh Press

Drewitt, P.L. 1990. *Prehistoric Barbados*. London: Institute of Achaeology

Drewett, P.L. and M.H. Harris. 1991. 'The archaeological survey of Barbados; 1985-87'. *Proceedings of the 12th International Congress for Caribbean Archaeology*, Martinique, pp. 175-202

Drewett, P.L., M.H. Harris and C.R. Cartwright. 1987. 'Archaeological Survey of Barbados: First Interim Report'. *Journal of the Barbados Museum and Historical Society* 38, 44-80

Driver, F. 2002. 'Geography, Enlightenment and Improvement'. *The Historical Journal* 45 (1), 229-33

Du Tertre, J.B. 1654. *Histoire Générale des Isles de St Christophe, se la Guadaloupe, de la Martinique, et autres dans l'Amerique*. Paris

Du Tertre, J.B. 1667-71. *Histoire Générale des Antilles habitées par les Francais*. Paris. (Four volumes)

Duckworth, A. 1971. *The Improvement of the Estate: A Study of Jane Austen's Novels*. Baltimore

Dunn, R.S. 1972. *Sugar and Slaves: The Rise of the Planter Class in the English West Indies, 1624-1713*. Chapel Hill: University of North Carolina Press

Earle, K.W. 1922. *Reports on the geology of St Kitts-Nevis and Anguilla*. London: Crown agents for the colonies

Eastman, J.A. 1996. *An Archaeological Assessment of St Eustatius, Netherlands Antilles*. Unpublished MA Thesis, Department of Anthropology, College of William and Mary.

Edwards, B. 1819. *The History, Civil and Commercial of the British Colonies in North America*. London: Stockdale. Third edition [first edition 1796] (5 volumes)

Egan, G, and R.L. Michael (eds) 1999. *Old and New Worlds. Historical/Post Medieval Archaeology Papers from the Societies' joint conferences at Williamsburg and London 1997 to mark thirty years of work and achievement*. Oxford: Oxbow Books (Society for Post Medieval Archaeology/ Society for Historical Archaeology Monograph)

Emerson Smith, A. 1947. *Colonists in Bondage*. Chapel Hill: University of Carolina Press

Emeruwa, L.E. 1973. *The British West Indies, 1897-1902, with special reference to the implementation of the 1897 Royal Commission Report*. Unpublished M. Phil. thesis, University of London

Engerman, S.L. 1982. 'Economic Adjustments to Emancipation in the United States and the British West Indies'. *Journal of Interdisciplinary History* 13, 191-220

Engerman, S.L. 1983. 'Contract Labor, Sugar and Technology in the Late Nineteenth Century'. *Journal of Economic History* 43, 635-659

Engerman, S.L. 1984. 'Servants to Slaves to Servants: Contract Labor and European Expansion'. In E. van der Boogaart and P.C. Emmer (eds) *Colonialism and Migration: Indentured Labour before and after Slavery*. The Hague, pp. 263-94

England, S. 1986. *An Archaeological perspective on settlement patterns on British West Indian sugar estates*. Unpublished MPhil thesis, Department of Archaeology, University of Cambridge

England, S. 1991. 'An Archaeological perspective on settlement patterns on British West Indian sugar estates'. *Caribena* 1, 107-122

Epperson, T.W. 1999. 'Beyond Biological Reductionism, Ethnicity and Vulgar Anti-Essentialism: Critical Perspectives on Race and the Practice of African-American Archaeology'. *African-American Archaeology* 24, 2-5, 8

Eubanks, T.H. 1992. *Sugar, Slavery and Emancipation: The Industrial Archaeology of the West Indian Island of Tobago*. Unpublished Ph. D. dissertation, University of Florida, Gainesville

Evans, W.J. 1847. *The Sugar Planter's Manual*. London: Longman, Brown, Green and Longmans

Ewen, C.R. 2001. 'Historical Archaeology in the Colonial Spanish Caribbean'. In Farnsworth (ed.), pp. 3-20

Farnsworth, P. 1982. *Geophysical surveys at Drax Hall, Jamaica*. Unpublished MA thesis, Archaeology Program, UCLA

Farnsworth, P. 1993. 'Archaeological Excavations at Wade's Green Plantation, North Caicos'. *Journal of the Bahamas Historical Society*. 15(1), 2-10

Farnsworth, P. 1994. 'Archaeological Excavations at Promised Land Plantation, New Providence'. *Journal of the Bahamas Historical Society*. 16(1) 21-29

Farnsworth, P. 1996. 'The Influence of Trade on Bahamian Slave Culture'. *Historical Archaeology* 30(4), 1-23

Farnsworth, P. 1999. 'From the Past to the Present: An exploration of the formation of African-Bahamian Identity during Enslavement'. In J. Haviser (ed.), pp. 94-130

Farnsworth, P. (ed.) 2001. *Island Lives. Historical Archaeologies of the Caribbean*. Tuscaloosa and London: University of Alabama Press

Ferguson, L. 1992. *Uncommon Ground: Archaeology and Early African America 1650-1800*. Washington DC: Smithsonian Institution Press

Flieschman, M. and D.V. Armstrong. 1990. *Preliminary Report: Analysis of burial SAJ-B1 recovered from house-area 16, Seville Afro-Jamaican settlement*. Kingston, Jamaica: Syracuse University Report 6

Flory, R. and D.G. Smith 1978. 'Bahian merchants and planters in the seventeenth and early eighteenth century'. *Hispanic American Historical Review* 58, 571-584

France, L.G. 1984. *Sugar Manufacturing in the West Indies: A Study of Innovation and Variation*. Unpublished MA Thesis, Department of Anthropology, College of William and Mary

Fremmer, R. 1973. 'Dishes in Colonial Graves: Evidence'. from Jamaica. Historical Archaeology 7, 58-62

Funari, P.P.A. 1999. Maroon, race and gender: Palmeres material culture and social relations in a runaway settlement. In P. Funari *et al.* (eds), pp. 308-327

Funari, P.P.A., M. Hall and S. Jones (eds) 1999. Historical Archaeology: Back from the Edge. London: Routledge

Fussell, G.E. 1931. John Wynn Baker: An 'Improver' in Eighteenth Century Ireland. Agricultural History 5(4), 151-161

Galenson, D. 1981a. White Servitude in Colonial America. Cambridge: Cambridge University Press

Galenson, D. 1981b. White Servitude and the Growth of Black Slavery in Colonial America. Journal of Economic History 41, 39-47

Games, A. 1999. Migration and the Origins of the English Atlantic World. Cambridge, MA: Harvard University Press

Gartley, R.T. 1979. Afro-Cruzan Pottery: A New Style of Colonial Earthenware from St Croix. Journal of the Virgin Islands Archaeological Society 8, 47-61

Gay, E.F. 1928. Letters from a Sugar Plantation in Nevis, 1723-1732. Journal of Economic and Business History 1, 149-173

Gell, A. 1992. Inter-tribal commodity barter and reproductive gift-exchange in old Melanasia. In C. Humphrey and S. Hugh-Jones (eds) Barter, Exchange and Value: An Ethnographic Approach. Cambridge: Cambridge University Press, pp. 142-168

Gerace, K. 1982. Three Loyalist Plantations on San Salvador Island, Bahamas. Florida Anthropologist 35(4), 216-222

Gerace, K. 1987. Early Nineteenth Century Plantations on San Salvador, Bahamas: Archaeological Record. Journal of the Bahamas Historical Society 9, 14-21

Gilmore, J. (ed.) 2000. The Poetics of Empire. A Study of James Grainger's The Sugar Cane (1764). London and New Brunswick: Athlone Press

Goggin, J.M. 1968. Spanish Majolica in the New World, Types of the Sixteenth to Eighteenth Centuries. New Haven: Yale University Publications in Anthropology No. 72

Goodman, J. 1993. Tobacco in History. The Cultures of Dependence. London: Routledge

Goodwin, C.M. 1982. Archaeology on the Galways Plantation. Florida Archaeologist 34(4), 251-53

Goodwin, C.M. 1987. Sugar, Time and Englishmen: A study of management strategies on Caribbean plantations. Unpublished Ph. D. dissertation, Dept of Anthropology, Boston University

Goodwin, C.M. 1994. Betty's Hope Windmill: An Unexpected Problem. Historical Archaeology 28(1), 99-110

Goodwin, R.C. 1979. The prehistoric cultural ecology of St Kitts, West Indies. A Case Study in Island Archaeology. Ann Arbor: University Microfilms

Gordon, W. 1720. Advantages and Disadvantages of Settling St Lucia. National Archives, Kew. CO 28:16 V 36 (July 14 1720)

Gosden, C. 2004. Archaeology and Colonialism. Cambridge: Cambridge University Press.

Goucher, C.K. 1990. John Reeder's Foundry: a study of eighteenth-century African-Caribbean technology. Jamaica Journal 23 (1), 39-43

Goucher, C. 1999. African-caribbean Metal Technology: Forging Cultural Survivals in the Atlantic World. In Haviser (ed.), pp. 143-156

Goveia, E.V. 1965. Slave Society in the British Leeward Islands at the End of the Eighteenth Century. New Haven: Yale University Press

Graecocke, R. 1752 [1623] Untitled account. In A. Churchill and J. Churchill (eds) A Collection of Voyages and Travels (8 volumes). London: Thomas Osborne. Volume 2, p. 343

Grainger, J. 2000 [1764] The Sugar Cane: A Poem in Four Books. In J. Gilmore (ed.), pp. 86-198

Green, W.A. 1976. British Slave Emancipation: The Sugar Colonies and the Great Experiment, 1830-1865. Oxford: Clarendon

Griggs, P. 2004. Improving Agricultural Practices: Science and the Australian Sugarcane Grower, 1864-1915. Agricultural History 78(1), 1-33

Guarch-Delmonte, J.M. 2003. The First Caribbean People: Part 1, The Palaeoindians in Cuba and the Circum-Caribbean. In J. Sued-Badillo (ed.) General History of the Caribbean, Volume 1 – Autochthonous Societies. Paris: UNESCO, pp. 93-118

Gundaker, G. 1998. Signs of Diaspora, Diaspora of Signs: Literacies, Creolization and Vernacular Practice in African America. Oxford: Oxford University Press

Hakluyt, R. (ed.) 1904 [1598-1600]. The Principal navigations, voyages, traffiques and discoveries of the English Nation. Twelve Volumes. Glasgow: Everyman's Library

Hall, D.G. 1964. Absentee-proprietorship in the British West Indies to about 1850. Jamaican Historical Review 4, 15-35

Hall, D.G. 1971. Five of the Leewards, 1834-1870: The Major Problems of the Post-Emancipation Period in Antigua, Barbuda, Montserrat, Nevis and St Kitts. Barbados: Caribbean Universities Press

Hall, D.G. 1978. The Flight from the Estates Reconsidered: The British West Indies 1838-1842. Journal of Caribbean History 10-11, 7-24

Hancock, D. 1995. Citizens of the World: London Merchants and the Integration of the British Atlantic Community, 1735-1785. Cambridge: Cambridge University Press

Hancock, D. 2000. "A World of Business to Do": William Freeman and the Foundations of England's Commercial Empire, 145-1707. William and Mary Quarterly 57, 3-34

Handler, J.S. 1963a. A Historical Sketch of Pottery Manufacture in Barbados. Journal of the Barbados Museum and Historical Society 30(3), 129-153

Handler, J.S. 1963b. Pottery making in Rural Barbados. Southwestern Journal of Anthropology. 19, 314-34

109

Handler, J.S. 1964. Notes on Pottery-making in Antigua. *Man* 183-184:150-151. Antigua

Handler, J.S. 1972. 'An Archaeological Investigation of the Domestic Life of Plantation Slaves in Barbados'. *Journal of the Barbados Museum and Historical Society* 34(2), 64-72

Handler, J.S. 1974. *The Unappropriated People: Freedmen in Slave Societies of Barbados*. Baltimore: Johns Hopkins University Press

Handler, J.S. 1982. 'A Ghanaian Pipe from a slave cemetery in Barbados, West Indies'. *West African Journal of Archaeology* 11, 93-99

Handler, J.S. 1983. 'An African Pipe from a slave cemetery in Barbados, West Indies'. In P. Davey (ed.) *The Archaeology of the clay tobacco pipe; America.* Oxford: British Archaeological Reports (International Series 175), pp. 245-254

Handler, J.S. 1994. 'Determining African Birth from Skeletal Remains: A Note on Tooth Mutilation'. *Historical Archaeology* 28(3), 113-119

Handler, J.S. 1995. 'An African-type burial, Newton Plantation, Barbados'. *African-American Archaeology* 15(1), 5-6

Handler, J.S. 1996. 'A Prone Burial from a Plantation Slave Cemetery in Barbados, West Indies: Possible Evidence for an African-type Witch or Other Negatively-Viewed Person'. *Historical Archaeology* 30(3), 76-86

Handler, J.S. 1997. 'An African-type Healer/Deviner and his Grave Goods: A burial from a plantation slave cemetery in Barbados, West Indies'. *International Journal of Historical Archaeology* 1(2), 91-130

Handler, J.S. and F.W. Lange 1990. *An Ethnoarchaeological Study of the Cisterns of Oranjestad, St Eustatius, Netherlands Antilles.* Unpublished MA Thesis, Department of Anthropology, College of William and Mary

Handler, J.S. and R.C. Corruccini 1983. 'Plantation slave life in Barbados: a physical anthropological analysis'. *Journal of Interdisciplinary History* 14, 65-90

Handler, J.S. and R.C. Corruccini 1986. 'Weaning Among West Indian Slaves: Historical and Bioanthropological Evidence From Barbados'. *William and Mary Quarterly* 43, 111-117

Handler, J.S. and F.W. Lange 1978. *Plantation Slavery in Barbados – An Archaeological and Historical Investigation.* Harvard University Press

Handler, J.S. and F.W. Lange 1979. 'Plantation Slavery on Barbados'. *Archaeology* 32(4), 45-52

Handler, J.S., A.C. Aufderheide, R.C. Corruccini, E.M. Brandon and L.E. Wittmers 1986. 'Lead Contact and Poisoning in Barbados Slaves: Historical, Chemical, and Biological Evidence'. *Social Science History* 10(4), 399-425

Handler, J.S, M.D. Conner, and K.P. Jacobi. 1989. *Searching for a slave cemetery in Barbados, West Indies.: A bioarchaeological and ethnohistorical investigation.* (Centre for archaeological investigations, Carbondale: Research Paper 59 (South Illinois University)

Handler, J.S., R.C. Corruccini and R.J. Mutaw. 1982. 'Tooth Mutilation in the Caribbean. Evidence from a slave burial population in Barbados'. *Journal of Human Evolution.* 11, 297-313

Handler, J.S., F. Lange and C.E. Orser. 1979. 'Carnelian Beads in necklaces from a slave cemetery in Barbados, West Indies'. *Ornament* 4(2), 15-18

Handler, R. and E. Gable 1997. *The New History in the Old Museum: Creating the Past at Colonial Williamsburg.* Durham, NC: Duke University Press

Harlow, V.T. (ed.) 1925. *Colonising Expeditions to the West Indies and Guiana, 1632-1667.* London: The Hakluyt Society

Harmsen, J. 1999. *Sugar, Slavery and Settlement. A Social History of Vieux Fort, St Lucia, from the Amerindians to the present.* Castries: St Lucia National Trust

Hauser, M. (ed.) forthcoming. 'Scales of Analysis in Caribbean Archaeology. Special Issue of International'. *Journal of Historical Archaeology*

Hauser, M. and D.V. Armstrong. 1999. 'Embedded Identities: Piecing together relationships through compositional analysis of low-fired earthenwares'. In J. Haviser (ed.), pp. 65-93

Hauser, M. and C.R. DeCorse 2003. 'Low-fired earthenwares in the African diaspora: problems and prospects'. *International Journal of Historical Archaeology* 7(1), 67-98

Hauser, M. and D. Hicks forthcoming. 'Colonialism and Landscape: Power, Materiality and Scales of Analysis in Caribbean Historical Archaeology'. In D. Hicks, G. Fairclough and L. McAtackney (eds) *Envisioning Landscapes: Situations and Standpoints in Archaeology and Heritage.* Walnut Creek, CA: Left Coast Press (One World Archaeology)

Haviser, J.B. 1988. *An Archaeological Survey of St Martin – St Maarten.* Reports of the Institute of Archaeology and Anthropology of the Netherlands Antilles, No. 7, Netherlands Antilles

Haviser, J.B. 1991. 'Preliminary results of test excavations at the Hope Estate site (SM-026), St Martin'. *Proceedings of the 13th International Congress for Caribbean Archaeology*, Curaçao, pp. 647-666

Haviser, J.B. 1999a. 'Identifying a post-emancipation (1863-1940) African-Curaçaoan material culture assemblage'. In J. Haviser (ed.), pp. 221-263

Haviser, J.B. (ed.). 1999b. *African Sites Archaeology in the Caribbean.* Kingston: Ian Randle Publishers

Haviser, J.B. 2001. 'Historical Archaeology in the Netherlands Antilles and Aruba'. In P. Farnsworth (ed.), pp. 60-81

Haviser, J.B. and N. Simmons-Brito. 1995. 'Excavations at the Zuurzak site: a possible 17th century Dutch slave camp on Curaçao, Netherlands Antilles'. *Proceedings of the 15th International Congress for Caribbean Archaeology*, San Juan, pp. 71-82

Heath, B.J. 1988. *Afro-Caribbean Ware: A Study of Ethnicity on St Eustatius.* Ph. D. dissertation, Department of American Civilization, University of Pennsylvania, Philadelphia

Heath, B.J. 1991a. 'Afro-Caribbean Ware on St Eustatius: A preliminary typology'. In E. Ayubi and J. Haviser (eds) *Proceedings of the 13th International Congress for Caribbean Archaeology*, Curaçao, pp. 338-343

Heath, B.J. 1991b. 'Pots of Earth; Forms and Functions of Afro-Caribbean ceramics'. *Florida Journal of Anthropology* 7(16), 33-49

Heath, B.J. 1999. 'Yabbas, Monkeys, Jugs and Jars: An Historical Context for African-Caribbean Pottery on St Eustatius'. In J. Haviser (ed.), pp. 196-220

Hicks, D. 2000. 'Race, Ethnicity and the Archaeology of the Atlantic Slave Trade. Assemblage 5'. http://www.shef. ac. uk/~assem/5/hicks.html

Hicks, D. 2003. 'Archaeology Unfolding: Diversity and the Loss of Isolation'. *Oxford Journal of Archaeology* 22(3):315-329

Hicks, D. 2004a. 'Historical Archaeology and the British'. *Cambridge Archaeological Journal* 14(1), 101-6

Hicks, D. 2004b. 'From the 'Questions that Count' to the Stories that 'Matter' in Historical Archaeology'. *Antiquity* 78, 934-939

Hicks, D. 2005. '"Places for Thinking" from Annapolis to Bristol: situations and symmetries in "world historical archaeology"'. *World Archaeology* 37(3), 373-391

Hicks, D. in prep. *A Material Atlantic*. Manuscript in preparation.

Hicks, D. and M.C. Beaudry 2006. 'Introduction: The Place of Historical Archaeology'. In D. Hicks and M.C. Beaudry (eds) *The Cambridge Companion to Historical Archaeology*. Cambridge: Cambridge University Press, pp. 1-9

Hicks, D. And M.C. Horton 2001a. *Landscape Survey and Excavations at Balenbouche, St Lucia: Winter 2000-2001 Season*. Bristol: Bristol University Department of Archaeology (typescript report)

Hicks, D. And M.C. Horton 2001b. *Landscape Survey and Excavations at Wingfield Estate, St Kitts: Summer 2001 Season*. Bristol: Bristol University Department of Archaeology (typescript report)

Hicks, D. and L. McAtackney forthcoming. 'Landscapes as Standpoints'. In D. Hicks, G. Fairclough and L. McAtackney (eds) *Envisioning Landscapes: Situations and Standpoints in Archaeology and Heritage*. Walnut Creek, CA: Left Coast Press (One World Archaeology)

Higham, C.S.S. 1921. *The development of the Leeward Islands under the restoration 1660-1688*. Cambridge: Cambridge University Press

Higman, B.W. 1974. 'A report on excavations at Montpelier and Roehampton'. *Jamaica Journal* 8(1-2), 40-45

Higman, B.W. 1975. *Report on excavations at New Montpelier, St James, Jamaica, 22-24 March and 3-18 August, 1975*. MS, History Department, University of West Indies, Mona, Jamaica.

Higman, B.W. 1976. *Report on excavations at New Montpelier, St James, Jamaica, 28 December 1975 to 10 January 1976*. MS, History Department, University of West Indies, Mona, Jamaica.

Higman, B.W. 1984. *Slave Populations of the British Caribbean 1807-1834*. Baltimore; John Hopkins University Press

Higman, B.W. 1986. *Jamaican Coffee Plantations 1780-1860: A Cartographic Analysis*. Caribbean Geography 2, 73-91

Higman, B.W. 1987. 'The spatial economy of Jamaican Sugar Plantations: Cartographic evidence from the 18th and 19th centuries'. *Journal of Historical Geography* 13(1), 17-19

Higman, B.W. 1988. *Jamaica Surveyed: Plantation maps and plans of the 18th and 19th centuries*. Jamaica, Institute of Jamaican Publishers

Higman, B.W. 1996. 'Economic and Social Development of the British West Indies'. In *The Cambridge Economic History of the United States*. Volume 1: The Colonial Era. Cambridge

Higman, B.W. 1999a. 'The British West Indies'. In R.W. Winks (ed.) *The Oxford History of the British Empire*. Volume 5: Historiography. Oxford: Oxford University Press, pp. 134-145

Higman, B.W. 1999b. *Writing West Indian Histories*. London: Macmillan Heinemann

Higman, B.W. and G. Aarons. 1978. *A Report on Archaeological Work Carried out at the Slave Village site, New Montpelier, St James*. Report on file, History Department, University of the West Indies, Mona, Jamaica.

Higman, C.S.S. 1921. *The Development of the Leeward Islands under the Restoration, 1660-1688*. Cambridge: Cambridge University Press.

Hilton, J. 1925 [1675]. *Revelation of the first settlement of St Christopher and Nevis by John Hilton, Storekeeper and First Gunner of Nevis* (Egerton Mss, British Library; reprinted by Hakluyt Society, London)

Hodder, I. 1986. *Reading the Past*. Cambridge: Cambridge University Press

Houghton, J. (ed.) 1681. *Collection of Letters for the Improvement of Husbandry and Trade* (volume 1). London: John Gain

Howard, B. 1991. *Fortifications of St Eustatius: An Archaeological and Historical Study of Defense in the Caribbean*. MA Thesis, Department of Anthropology, College of William and Mary

Howard, R.R. 1965. 'New Perspectives on Jamaican Archaeology'. *American Antiquity* 31(2), 250-55

Hudson, L., Y. Renard and G. Romulus. 1992. *A System of Protected Areas for St Lucia*. Castries: St Lucia National Trust

Hulme, P. 1986. *Colonial Encounters: Europe and the native Caribbean 1492-1797*. New York: Methuen

Hulme, P. and N.L. Whitehead. 1992. *Wild Majesty: Encounters with Caribs from Columbus to the Present Day*. Oxford: Clarendon Press

Iles, J.A.B. 1871. *An Account Descriptive of the Island of Nevis, West Indies*. Norwich: Fletcher and Son

Ingold, T. 1993. 'The Temporality of Landscape'. *World Archaeology* 25, 152-74

Ives, V.A. 1984. *The Rich Papers. Letters from Bermuda 1615-1646. Eyewitness Accounts Sent by the Early Colonists to Sir Nathaniel Rich.* Toronto: University of Toronto Press for Bermuda National Trust

Jacobs, J. 1996. *Edge of Empire: Postcolonialism and the City.* London: Routledge

James, C.L.R. 1938. *The Black Jacobins: Toussaint L'Ouverture and the San Domingo Revolution.* New York: Vintage Books

Jane, C. (ed. & trans.) 1930. *Select Documents illustrating the Four Voyages of Columbus (Two Volumes). Volume One: The First and Second Voyages.* London: Hakluyt Society

Jeaffreson, J.C. (ed.) 1878. *A Young Squire of the 17th century, from the papers (AD 1676-1686) of Christopher Jeaffreson* (2 vols). London: Hurst and Blackett

Jeffreys, T. 1780. *The West India Atlas, or a Compendius Description of the West Indies; illustrated with forty correct charts and maps taken from actual surveys, together with an Historical Account of the several Countries and Islands which comprise that part of the World.* London: R. Sayer and J. Bennett. Held at National Archives CO 700/West Indies 21

Jeremie, J. 1832. *Four essays on colonial slavery.* London: J. Hatchard

Jesse, C. 1952. 'Rock-cut basins on St Lucia'. *American Antiquity* 2, 166-168

Jesse, C. 1964. *Outlines of St Lucia's History* (second edition). Castries: St Lucia Archaeological and Historical Society

Jesse, C. 1969. *Early Days, 1493-1763.* Castries: St Lucia Archaeological and Historical Society (St Lucia Miscellany 2)

Johnson, J.R.V. 1966. 'The Stapleton Sugar Plantations in the Leeward Islands'. *Bulletin of the John Rylands Library* 48, 175-206

Johnson, M.H. 1991. 'Enclosure and Capitalism: The History of a Process'. In R. Preucel (ed.) *Processual and Postprocessual Archaeologies: Multiple ways of knowing the past.* Carbondale: Centre for Archaeological Investigations, pp. 159-167

Johnson, M.H. 1996. *An Archaeology of Capitalism.* Oxford: Blackwell.

Johnson, M.H. 2005. 'On the Particularism of English Landscape Archaeology'. *International Journal of Historical Archaeology* 9(2), 111-122

Johnson, M.H. 2006a. 'Acknowledgements'. In M. Hall and S.W. Silliman (eds) *Historical Archaeology.* Oxford: Blackwell (Blackwell Studies in Global Archaeology), pp. xvi-xvii

Johnson, M.H. 2006b. 'The Tide Reversed: Prospects and Potentials for a Postcolonial Archaeology of Europe'. In M. Hall and S.W. Silliman (eds) *Historical Archaeology.* Oxford: Blackwell (Blackwell Studies in Global Archaeology), pp. 313-331

Johnson, M.H. 2007. *Ideas of Landscape.* Oxford: Blackwell

Keegan, W.F. 1994. 'West Indian Archaeology 1. Overview and Foragers'. *Journal of Archaeological Research* 2(3), 255-284

Keegan, W.F. 1996. 'West Indian Archaeology 2. After Columbus'. *Journal of Archaeological Research* 4(4), 265-294

Keegan, W.F. 2000. 'West Indian Archaeology 3. Ceramic Age'. *Journal of Archaeological Research* 8(2), 135-167

Keeler, M.F. (ed.) 1981. *Sir Francis Drake's West Indian Voyage* 1585-6. London: Hakluyt Society

Kelly, K.G. 1989. *Historic Archaeology of Jamaican Tenant-Manager Relationships: A Case Study from Drax Hall and Seville Estates, St Ann, Jamaica.* Unpublished MA thesis, Department of Anthropology, College of William and Mary

Kelly, K.G. 2004. 'Historical Archaeology in the French Caribbean: An Introduction to a Special Issue of the Journal of Caribbean Archaeology'. *Journal of Caribbean Archaeology Special Publication* 1, 1-10

Kelly, K.G. and D.V. Armstrong. 1991. 'Archaeological investigations of a 19th century free laborer house, Seville Estate, St Ann's, Jamaica'. *Proceedings of the 13th International Congress for Caribbean Archaeology,* Curaçao, pp. 429-435

Kelso, W.M. and R. Most (eds) 1990. *Earth Patterns: Essays in Landscape Archaeology.* Charlottesville: University Press of Virginia

Keymis, L. 1904 [1596] 'The second voyage to Guiana performed and written in the year 1596'. In R. Hakluyt (ed.) *The Principal Navigations, Voyages, Traffiques and Discoveries of the English Nation* (series 1, volume 10). Glasgow: Hakluyt Society, pp. 452-489

Khudabux, M. R. 1999. 'Effects of Life Conditions on the health of a Negro slave community in Suriname'. In J. Haviser (ed.), pp. 291-312

Klippel, W. 1997. *Faunal Remains from the 1996 Excavations at Brimstone Hill, St Kitts, West Indies.* Brimstone Hill Archaeological Project Report No. 6

Klippel, W. 1998. *Faunal Remains from the 1997 Excavations at Brimstone Hill Fortress, St Kitts, West Indies.* Brimstone Hill Archaeological Project Report No. 10

Klippel, W. 2000. *Sugar Monoculture, Bovid Skeletal Parts Frequencies, and Stable Carbon Isotopes: Interpreting Enslaved African Diet at Brimstone Hill, St Kitts, West Indies.* Brimstone Hill Archaeological Project Report No. 16

Klippel, W. E. and G.F. Schroedl. 1999. *African slave craftsmen and single-hole bone discs from Brimstone Hill, St Kitts, West Indies.* Post-Medieval Archaeology 33, 222-232

Lacy, B. 1979. 'The Archaeology of British Colonization in Ulster and America: A comparative approach'. *Irish-American Review* 1, 1-5

Labat, J.B. 1722. *Nouveau voyage aux isles de l'Amerique.* 6 volumes. Paris (New edition 1724, The Hague; new edition 1742 (8 volumes), Paris; new edition 1972, Fort-de-France)

Lange, F.W. and F.B. Carlson. 1985. 'Distribution of European earthenwares on plantations on Barbados, West Indies'. In T.A. Singleton (ed.) *The Archaeology of Slavery and Plantation Life*. New York: Academic Press, pp. 97-120

Lange, F.W. and J.S. Handler. 1985. 'The Ethnohistorical approach to Slavery'. In T.A. Singleton (ed.) *The Archaeology of Slavery and Plantation Life*. New York: Academic Press, pp. 15-32.

Laurence, K.O. 1971. *Immigration into the West Indies in the 19th century*. St Lawrence, Barbados

Lawrence, S. 2003. 'Introduction'. In S. Lawrence (ed.) *Archaeologies of the British: Explorations of identity in Great Britain and its colonies, 1600-1945*. London: Routledge (One World Archaeology 46), pp. 1-13

Lawrence, S. and N. Shepherd. 2006. 'Historical Archaeology and Colonialism'. In D. Hicks and M.C. Beaudry (eds) *The Cambridge Companion to Historical Archaeology*. Cambridge: Cambridge University Press, pp. 69-86

Leone, M.P. 1984. 'Interpreting Ideology in Historical Archaeology: Using the Rules of Perspective in the William Paca Garden in Annapolis, Maryland'. In D. Miller and C. Tilley (eds) *Ideology, Power and Prehistory*. Cambridge: Cambridge University Press, pp. 25-35

Leone, M.P. 2005. *The Archaeology of Liberty in an American Capital: Excavations in Annapolis*. Berkeley: University of California Press

Lightfoot, K. 1995. 'Culture Contact Studies: Redefining the relationship between prehistoric and historical archaeology'. *American Antiquity* 60, 199-217

Ligon, R. 1657. *A True and Exact history of the island of Barbados*. London

Littleton, T. 1908 [1629] 'Littleton Vs. Glover – Bill of Complaint'. In W.V. Oliver (ed.) Volume 1, pp. 2-3

Loftfield, T. C. 1991. 'The Bendeshe/Byde Mill sugar factory in Barbados: the ceramic Barbados evidence'. In A. Cummins and P. King (eds) *Proceedings of the Fourteenth International Congress for Caribbean Archaeology*, Barbados, pp. 408-415

Loftfield, T. C. 1994. 'Afro-European Archaeology in Barbados'. *African-American Archaeology* 12(6). http://www.diaspora.uiuc.edu/A-AAnewsletter/Winter1994.html (consulted 1 August 2006)

Loftfield. T.C. 2001. 'Creolization in Seventeenth Century Barbados'. In P. Farnsworth (ed.), pp. 207-233

Lorimer, J. 1977. 'Ralegh's First Reconnaissance of Guiana? An English Survey of the Orinoco in 1587'. *Terrae Incognitae* 9, 7-21

Lorimer, J. 1978. 'The English Contraband Tobacco Trade in Trinidad and Guiana 1590-1617'. In K.R. Andrews *et al.* (eds), pp. 124-150

Lorimer, J. 1993. 'The Failure of the English Guiana Ventures 1595-1667 and James I's Foreign Policy'. *Journal of Imperial and Commonwealth History* 21: 1-30

Louis, M. 1982. *An Equal Right to the Soil. The Rise of a peasantry in St Lucia 1838-1900*. PhD thesis, Johns Hopkins University

Manchester, K.D. 1971. *Historic Heritage of St Kitts, Nevis, Anguilla*. Port-of-Spain: Syncreators

Mandle, J. R. 1973. *The Plantation Economy: Population and Economic Change in Guyana, 1838-1960*. Philadelphia: Temple University Press.

Mann, R.W., L. Meadows, W. M. Bass and D. R. Watters. 1987. 'Description of Skeletal Remains from a Black Slave Cemetery From Montserrat, West Indies'. *Annals of Carnegie Museum* 56(19), 319-336.

Margry, P. 1863. *Origines Transatlantiques: Belain d'Esnambuc et les Normands aux Antilles d'après des documents nouvellement retrouvés*. Paris: A. Faure

Marshall, W.K. 1965. 'Metayage in the Sugar Industry of the British Windward Islands, 1838-1865'. *Jamaican Historical Review* 5, 28-55

Marshall, W.K. 1980. *Metayage in the Sugar Industry of the British Windward Islands, 1838-1865*. Mona: University of the West Indies Department of History

Marshall, W.K. 1993. 'Provision Ground and Plantation Labor in Four Windward Islands; Competition for Resources during Slavery'. In Berlin, I. and P.D. Morgan (eds) *Cultivation and Culture. Labor and the Shaping of Slave Life in the Americas*. Charlottesville: University Press of Virginia, pp. 203-220

Martin, S. 1750. *An Essay upon Plantership, humbly inscrib'd to all the planters of the British sugar-colonies in America, the second edition, corrected and enlarged, by an old planter*. Antigua: T. Smith

Martin-Kaye, P.H.A. 1959. *Geology of the Leeward and British Virgin Islands*. Castries, St Lucia: The Voice Publishing Co. Ltd

Martin-Kaye, P.H.A. 1969. 'A Summary of the Geology of the Lesser Antilles'. *Overseas Geology and Mineral Resources* 10(2), 172-206

Marx, R.F. 1967. *Pirate Port: The Story of the Sunken City of Port Royal*. Cleveland: World Publishing

Marx, R.F. 1968a. 'Divers of Port Royal'. *Jamaica Journal* 2(1), 15-33

Marx, R.F. 1968b. 'Excavating the Sunken City of Port Royal'. *Jamaica Journal* 2(2), 12-18

Marx, R.F. 1968c. 'Discovery of Two Ships of Columbus'. *Jamaica Journal* 2(4), 13-17

Marx, R.F. 1968d. *Excavation of the Sunken City of Port Royal, January, 1967-March, 1968: A Preliminary Report*. National Trust Commission, Kingston, Jamaica.

Marx, R.F. 1969a. 'Port Royal'. *Oceans Magazine* 1(5), 66-77

Marx, R.F. 1969b. *Glass Bottles Recovered from the Sunken City of Port Royal, Jamaica, May 1, 1966-March 31, 1968*. Caribbean Research Institute, College of the Virgin Islands, St Thomas, V.I.

Marx, R.F. 1973. *Port Royal Rediscovered*. Garden City, NY: Doubleday

Mason, K. 1993. 'The world an absentee planter and his slaves made: Sir William Stapleton and his Nevis Sugar Estate, 1722-1740'. *Bulletin of the John Rylands University Library of Manchester* 75, 103-131

Massachusetts Historical Society (ed.) 1944. *The Winthrop Papers. Volume V (1645-1649)*. Boston: Massachusetts Historical Society

Mathewson, R. D. 1972a. 'History from the Earth: Archaeological Excavations at Old King's House'. *Jamaica Journal* 6(1), 3-11

Mathewson, R. D. 1972b. 'Jamaican Ceramics: An Introduction to 18th-century Folk Pottery in a West African Tradition'. *Jamaica Journal* 6(2), 54-56

Mathewson, R. D. 1973. 'Archaeological Analysis of Material Culture as a Reflection of Sub-Cultural Differentiation in 18th-century Jamaica'. *Jamaica Journal* 7(1-2), 25-29

Mayes, P. 1970. 'The Port Royal Project'. *Caribbean Conservation Association Environmental Newsletter* 1(1), 37-38

Mayes, P. 1972. *Port Royal, Jamaica: Excavations 1969-1970*. Kingston: National Trust Commission.

McKeown, A. 1997. *Human Skeletal Remains from Excavations at Brimstone Hill Fortress National Park, St Kitts, West Indies, July 1996*. Brimstone Hill Archaeological Project Report No. 5

McKeown, A. 1998. *Human Skeletal Remains from the 1997 Excavations at Site BSH 2, Brimstone Hill Fortress National Park, St Kitts, West Indies*. Brimstone Hill Archaeological Project Report No. 8

McKeown, A. 1999. *Human Skeletal Remains from the 1998 Excavations at Site BSH 2, Brimstone Hill Fortress National Park, St Kitts, West Indies*. Brimstone Hill Archaeological Project Report No. 13

Merrill, G. C. 1958. *The Historical Geography of St Kitts and Nevis, the West Indies*. Mexico: Instituto Panamericano de Geografia e Historia Publication 232

Miller, N.F. And K.L. Gleason. 1994. *The Archaeology of Garden and Field*. Philadelphia: University of Pennsylvania Press.

Mims, S.L. 1912. *Colbert's West India Policy*. New Haven: Yale University Press

Mintz, S.W. 1966. 'The Caribbean as a Socio-Cultural Area'. *Cahiers d'Histoire Mondiale* 9, 912-937

Mintz, S.W. 1985. *Sweetness and Power*. New York: Penguin

Mintz, S.W. and R. Price 1976. *An Anthropological Approach to the Afro-American Past: A Caribbean Perspective*. Philadelphia, PA: Institute for the Study of Human Issues

Moll, H. 1708. *The British Empire in America: containing the history of the discovery, settlement, progress and present state of all the British colonies on the continent and islands of America...with curious maps...* (reprinted and revised 1729)

Morris, E.L., R.Read, S.E. James and T.Machling 1999. '"...the old stone fortt at Newcastle..." The Redoubt, Nevis, eastern Caribbean'. *Post-Medieval Archaeology* 33, 194-221

Mouer, L.D. 1993. 'Chesapeake Creoles'. In T. R. Reinhart and D. J. Pogue (eds) *The Archaeology of Seventeenth Century Virginia*. Courtland, Virginia: Archaeological Society of Virginia (Special Publication 30), pp. 107-123

Mukerji, C. 1997. *Territorial Ambitions and the Gardens of Versailles*. Cambridge: Cambridge University Press

Nagelkerken, W.I.L. 1985. 'Preliminary Report on the Determination of the Location of the Historical Anchorage at Oranje Bay, St Eustatius, Netherlands Antilles'. *Report of the Institute of Archaeology and Anthropology of the Netherlands Antilles, No. 1*. Curaçao

Newton, A.P. 1914. *The Colonizing Activities of English Puritans*. New Haven: Yale University Press

Newton, A.P. 1933. *The European Nations in the West Indies, 1493-1688*. London: A. & C. Black

Nicholl, J. 1966 [1607]. 'An Houre Glasse of Indian Newes'. *Caribbean Quarterly* 12(1), 46-67 [An abridged version is reproduced in Puchas (ed.) 1906, Volume 16, pp. 324-337]

Nicholson, D.V. 1976. 'The importance of sea level changes in Caribbean archaeology'. *Journal of the Virgin Islands Archaeological Society* 3, 19-23

Nicholson, D.V. 1979. 'The Dating of West Indian Historical Sites by the Analysis of Ceramic Sherds'. *Journal of the Virgin Islands Archaeological Society* 7: 52-74

Nicholson, D.V. 1994. 'Slave Pottery found in a Crevice'. *Historical and Archaeological Society of Antigua and Barbuda Newsletter* 45, 5

Nicholson, D.V. 1995. 'Blood and Mud: The naval hospital and underwater artifacts, English Harbour, Antigua'. In Alegria and Rodriquez (eds) *Proceedings of the fifteenth International Congress for Caribbean Archaeology*, San Juan, pp. 45-63

Niddrie, D. L. 1966. 'An Attempt at planned settlement in St Kitts in the early 18th century'. *Caribbean Studies* 5(4), 3-11

Noël Hume, I. 1968. 'A Collection of Glass from Port Royal, Jamaica, with some Observations on the Site, Its History and Archaeology'. *Historical Archaeology* 2, 5-34.

Noël Hume, I. 1979. *Martin's Hundred*. Charlottesville: University of Virginia Press

Noël Hume, I. 1994. *The Virginia Adventure. Roanoke to James Towne. An Archaeological and Historical Odyssey*. Charlottesville: University of Virginia Press

Nuttall, G.F. (ed.). 1939. *Letters of John Pinney: 1679-1699*

Oldmixon, J. 1969 [1741] *The British Empire in America, containing the history of the discovery, settlement, progress and present state of all the British colonies, on the Continent and islands of America (two volumes)*. London: Nicholson

Oliver, W.V. (ed.) *1908 – 1919. Caribbeana*. Six Volumes. London

Olwig, K.F. 1993. *Global Culture: island identity – continuity and change in the Afro-Caribbean community of Nevis*. Amsterdam: Harwood

Orser, C.E. 1988a. 'Toward a theory of power for historical archaeology: plantations and space'. In M.P. Leone and P.B. Potter (eds) *The recovery of meaning: historical archaeology in the eastern United States*. Washington, DC: Smithsonian Institution Press, pp. 313-343

Orser, C.E. 1988b. 'The Archaeological Analysis of Plantation Society: Replacing Status and Class with Economics and Power'. *American Antiquity* 53(4), 735-751

Orser, C.E. 1994. 'Toward a global historical archaeology: an example from Brazil'. *Historical Archaeology* 28 (1), 5-22

Orser, C.E. 1996. *A Historical Archaeology of the Modern World*. London: Plenum Press

Orser, C.E. 1998. 'The Archaeology of the African Diaspora'. *Annual Review of Anthropology* 27, 63-82

Osborne, Francis J. 1974. 'Spanish Church, St Ann's Bay'. *Jamaica Journal* 8 (2-3), 33-35

Palmer, M. (ed.) 1988. *The Mapping of Bermuda. A Bibliography of printed maps and charts*. Paget, Bermuda: Nicholas Lusher, Dealer in Antique Maps and Prints.

Pantel, G.A. 2002. 'The First Caribbean People: Part 2, The Archaics'. In J. Sued-Badillo (ed.) *General History of the Caribbean, Volume 1 – Autochthonous Societies*. Paris: UNESCO, pp. 118-33.

Paonessa, L. 1990. *The Cemeteries of St Eustatius, Netherlands Antilles: Status in A Caribbean Community*. Unpublished MA Thesis, Department of Anthropology, College of William and Mary

Pares, R. 1950. *A West India Fortune*. London: Longmans, Green and Co.

Pares, R. 1960. *Merchants and Planters*. Cambridge: Cambridge University Press: (Economic review supplements 4)

Parry, J.H. and P.M. Sherlock. 1956. *A Short History of the West Indies*. London

Patterson, J.A. and W.E. Klippel. 1999. *African Slave Subsistence: The Faunal Remains from Brimstone Hill, St Kitts*. Brimstone Hill Archaeological Project Report No. 14

Paynter, R. 1982. *Models of Spatial Inequality: Settlement Patterns in Historical Archaeology*. New York: Academic Press

Perry, W. and R. Paynter. 1999. 'Artifacts, Ethnicity and the Archaeology of African Americans'. In T.A. Singleton (ed.) *I Too Am America: Archaeological Studies of African-American Life*. Charlottesville: University Press of Virginia, pp. 299-310

Petersen, J.B. and D.R. Watters. 1988. 'Afro-Montserratian Ceramics from the Harney Site Cemetery, Montserrat, West Indies'. *Annals of Carnegie Museum* 57, 167-187

Petersen, J.B., Watters, D.R. and Nicholson, D.V. 1999. 'Continuity and Syncretism in Afro-Caribbean Ceramics from the Northern Lesser Antilles'. In J. Haviser (ed.), pp. 157-195

Phillips, W. D. 1984. *Slavery from Roman Times to the Early Transatlantic Trade*. Manchester: Manchester University Press

Pinchon, R. 1952. 'Introduction à l'archéologie martiniquaise'. *Journal de la Société des Amériquanistes de Paris* 41(2), 305-352

Pitman, F.W. 1917. *The Development of the British West Indies 1700-1763*. New Haven: Yale University Press

Porter, A. 1995. 'Review Article: Birmingham, Westminster and the City of London: visions of empire compared'. *Journal of Historical Geography* 21(1), 83-87

Posnansky, M. 1984. 'Towards an archaeology of the Black Diaspora'. *Journal of Black Studies* 15(2), 195-205

Priddy, A. 1975. 'The 17th and 18th-century Settlement Pattern of Port Royal'. *Jamaica Journal* 9(2-3), 8-10.

Proudfoot, L.J. (1997) 'Landownership and improvement *c.* 1700 to 1845'. In L. Proudfoot (ed.) *Down: history and society: interdisciplinary essays on the history of an Irish county*. Dublin: Geography Publications

Pulsipher, L.M. 1977. *The Cultural Landscape of Montserrat, West Indies, in the 17th Century: Early Environmental Consequences of British Colonial Development*. Unpublished Ph. D. dissertation, Southern Illinois University, Carbondale

Pulsipher, L.M. 1986. 'Seventeenth-Century Montserrat'. *Historical Geography Research* 17. Norwich: Ego Books

Pulsipher, L.M. 1991. 'Galways Plantation, Montserrat'. In H.J. Viola and C. Margolis (eds) *Seeds of Change*. Washington, DC: Smithsonian Institution Press, pp. 139-159

Pulsipher, L.M. 1994. 'The Landscapes and Ideational Roles of Caribbean Slave Gardens'. In N. Miller and K. Gleason (eds) *The Archaeology of Garden and Field*. Philadelphia: University of Pennsylvania Press, pp. 202-221

Pulsipher, L.M. and C.M. Goodwin. 1982. 'A Sugar Boiling House at Galways: An Irish sugar plantation in Montserrat, West Indies'. *Post-Medieval Archaeology* 16, 21-27

Pulsipher, L.M. and C.M. Goodwin. 1988. *Betty's Hope Conservation Project, Betty's Hope Estate, Antigua, West Indies*. Department of Geography, University of Tennessee: Pilot Study Draft Report.

Pulsipher, L.M. and C.M. Goodwin. 1999. '"Here Where the Old Time People Be": Reconstructing the landscapes of the Slavery and post-Slavery Era in Montserrat, West Indies'. In J.B. Haviser (ed.), pp. 9-37

Pulsipher, L.M. and C.M. Goodwin 2001. '"Getting the Essence of It": Galways Plantation, Montserrat, West Indies'. In P. Farnsworth (ed.), pp. 165-203

Ragatz, L. J. 1928. *The Fall of the Planter Class in the British Caribbean, 1763-1833*. New York: Century Co

Ramsay, J. 1784. *An Essay on the Treatment and Conversion of African Slaves in the British Sugar Colonies*. London

Ravell, A. 1780 [1775]. *St Christophers or St Kitts, surveyed by Anthony Ravell, Surveyor General of St Christophers, Nevis and Montserrat. Engraved by Thomas Jeffreys, Geographer to the King*. Reproduced in Jeffreys (1780).

Rennard, R. nd. *The Vieux Fort Sugar Industry*. Unpublished Ms.

Richardson, B.C. 1983. *Caribbean Migrants – environment and human survival on St Kitts and Nevis*. Knoxville: University of Tennessee.

Richardson, B.C. 1992. *The Caribbean in the Wider World, 1492-1992: A regional geography*. Cambridge: Cambridge University Press.

Richardson, D. 1987. 'The Slave Trade, Sugar and British Economic Growth 1748-1776'. In B.L. Solow and S.L. Engerman (eds), pp. 103-133

Richeson, A.W. 1966. *English Land Measuring to 1800: Instruments and Practices*. London: Society for the History of Technology and Massachusetts Institute of Technology

Righter, E. 1990. 'Land use history: environmental management at Plantation Zufriedenheit between A. D. 1683 and A. D. 1817'. *Proceedings of the 11th International Congress for Caribbean Archaeology*, San Juan, pp. 472-485

Righter, E. 1997. 'The ceramics, art, and material culture of the early ceramic period in the Caribbean islands'. In S. Wilson (ed.) *The Indigenous People of the Caribbean*. Gainesville: University Press of Florida, pp. 70-79

Roberts, G. W. and Byrne, J. 1966. 'Summary Statistics on Indenture and Associated Migration Affecting the West Indies, 1834-1918'. *Population Studies* 20, 125-134

Robertson, Reverend R. 1732. *A Detection of the State and Situation of the Present Sugar Planters of Barbadoes and the Leeward Islands*. London

Roughley, T. 1823. *The Jamaica Planter's Guide*. London: Longman, Hurst, Rees, Orme and Brown

Rouse, I. 1953. 'The Circum-Caribbean Theory, an archaeological test'. *American Anthropologist* 55(2): 188-200.

Rouse, I. 1964. 'Prehistory of the West Indies'. *Science* 144 (3618): 499-513.

Rouse, I. 1992. *The Tainos: Rise and Decline of the People who Greeted Columbus*. New Haven: Yale University Press

Rowlands, M. 1998. 'The Archaeology of Colonialism'. In K. Kristiansen and M. Rowlands. *Social Transformations in Archaeology: Global and Local Perspectives*. London: Routledge, pp. 327-333

Rowlands, M. 1999. 'Black Identity and Sense of Past in Brazilian National Culture'. In Funari *et al.* (eds), pp. 228-245

Said, E. 1978. *Orientalism*. New York: Vintage Books

Said, E. 1993. *Culture and Imperialism*. London: Vintage Books.

Sanders, S. 1988. *Architectural Style on St Eustatius*. MA Thesis, Department of Anthropology, College of William and Mary

Sandiford, K.A. 2000. *The Cultural Politics of Sugar. Caribbean Slavery and Narratives of Colonialism*. Cambridge: Cambridge University Press

Saunders, K. (ed.) 1984. *Indentured Labour in the British Empire 1834-1920*. London: Croom Helm.

Savage, A. and G.F. Schroedl 1999. *Metal Buttons and Miscellaneous Personal Items from the 1998 Excavations at Sites BSH 2 and BSH 3, Brimstone Hill Fortress National Park, St Kitts, West Indies*. Brimstone Hill Archaeological Project Report No. 11

Schroedl, G.F. 1997. *A Report on the July 1996 Archaeological Investigations at the Brimstone Hill National Park, St Kitts, West Indies*. Brimstone Hill Archaeological Project Report No. 1

Schroedl, G.F. 1998. *A Report on the July 1997 Archaeological Investigations at the Brimstone Hill Fortress National Park, St Kitts, West Indies*. Brimstone Hill Archaeological Project Report No. 7

Schroedl, G.F. 1999a. *A Report on the 1998 Archaeological Investigations at the Brimstone Hill Fortress National Park, St Kitts, West Indies*. Brimstone Hill Archaeological Project Report No. 12

Schroedl, G.F. 1999b. *Archaeological Survey at the Western Base of Brimstone Hill, St Kitts, West Indies*. Brimstone Hill Archaeological Project Report No. 15

Schroedl, G.F. 2000a. *A Report on the 1999 Archaeological Investigations at the Brimstone Hill Fortress National Park, St Kitts, West Indies*. Brimstone Hill Archaeological Project Report No. 17.

Schroedl, G.F. 2000b. *Metal Buttons and Miscellaneous Ornaments and Personal Items from the 1999 Excavations at Site BSH 2, Brimstone Hill Fortress National Park, St Kitts, West Indies*. Brimstone Hill Archaeological Project Report No. 18

Schroedl, G.F. 2000c. *Archaeological and Architectural Assessment of Charles Fort, St Kitts, West Indies*. Charles Fort Archaeological and Historical Project Report No. 1

Schroedl, G.F. 2000d. *A Photographic Catalog of Structures and Architectural Features at Charles Fort, St Kitts, West Indies*. Charles Fort Archaeological and Historical Project Report No. 2

Schroedl, G.F. 2000e. *Addendum to: Archaeological and Architectural Assessment of Charles Fort, St Kitts, West Indies*. Charles Fort Archaeological and Historical Project Report No. 3

Schroedl, G.F. and T. Ahlman. 1998. *Metal Buttons and Miscellaneous Personal Items from the 1997 Excavations at Site BSH 2, Brimstone Hill Fortress National Park, St Kitts, West Indies*. Brimstone Hill Archaeological Project Report No. 9

Schroedl, G.F., W.E. Klippel, and T.M. Ahlman. 2000. *Slavery in the Context of British Fortifications: The Archaeological Evidence*. Brimstone Hill Archaeological Project Report No. 19

Scoffern, J. 1849. *On the Manufacture of Sugar in the Colonies and at Home*. London: Brown, Green and Longmans

Scott, D. 2004. 'Modernity that predated the modern'. *History Workshop Journal* 58(1), 191-210

Seymour, S. 2000. 'Historical geographies of landscape'. In B. Graham and C. Nash (eds) *Modern historical geographies*. Harlow: Longman, pp. 193-217

Seymour, S., S. Daniels, S. and S. Watkins 1998. 'Estate and empire: Sir George Cornewall's management of Moccas, Herefordshire and La Taste, Grenada, 1771-1819'. *Journal of Historical Geography* 24, 313-51

Shammas, C. 1978. 'English Commercial Development and American Colonization, 1560-1620'. In K.R. Andrews *et al.* (eds), pp. 151-174

Shammas, C. 1990. *The Pre-Industrial Consumer in England and America*. Oxford: Clarendon Press

Sheller, M. 2003. *Consuming the Caribbean: From Arawaks to Zombies*. London: Routledge.

Shelton, R.S. 1995. 'A Modified Crime: The Apprenticeship System in St Kitts'. *Slavery and Abolition* 16, 331-345

Shepherd, N. 2002. 'The Politics of Archaeology in Africa'. *Annual Review of Anthropology* 31, 189-209

Sheridan, R. B. 1951. *The Sugar Trade of the West Indies from 1660 to 1756 with special reference to the island of Antigua*. University of London unpublished Ph. D. Thesis

Sheridan, R.B. 1957. 'Letters from a Sugar Plantation in Antigua, 1739-1758'. *Agricultural History* 31, 3-23

Sheridan, R.B. 1960. 'Samuel Martin, Innovating Sugar Planter of Antigua 1750-1776'. *Agricultural History* 34, 126-139

Sheridan, R.B. 1961. 'The Rise of a Colonial Gentry: A Case Study from Antigua, 1730-1775'. *Economic History Review* 13, 342-357

Sheridan, R.B. 1964. 'Planter and historian: The career of William Beckford of Jamaica and England, 1744-1799'. *The Jamaican Historical Review* 4, 37-45

Sheridan, R.B. 1965. 'The Wealth of Jamaica in the Eighteenth Century'. *Economic History Review* 18, 292-311

Sheridan, R.B. 1968. 'A Rejoinder'. *Economic History Review* 21, 46-61

Sheridan, R.B. 1974. *Sugar and Slavery: An Economic History of the British West Indies 1623-1776*. Eagle Hall, Barbados: Caribbean Universities Press

Sheridan, R.B. 1985. *Doctors and Slaves: A medical and demographic history of slavery in the British West Indies, 1680-1834*. Cambridge: Cambridge University Press

Silliman, S. 2005. 'Culture Contact or Colonialism? Challenges in the Archaeology of Native North America'. *American Antiquity* 70(1), 55-74

Singleton, TA (ed.) 1985. *The Archaeology of Slavery and Plantation Life*. New York: Academic Press

Singleton, T.A. (ed.) 1999. *"I Too am America": Archaeological Studies of African-American Life*. Charlottesville, VA: University Press of Virginia

Sitwell, G.R. 1888. 'A picture of the iron trade in the seventeenth century'. *Journal of the Derbyshire Archaeological and Natural History Society* 10, 28-46

Slayman, A. 1996. 'Letter from Nevis: where the past serves the present'. *Archaeology* 49 (1), 79-84

Sloane, H. 1707. *A Voyage to the Islands of Madeira, Barbados, Nieves, St Christopher and Jamaica, with the natural history of the herbs and trees, four-footed beasts, fishes, birds, insects, reptiles, etc (two volumes)*. London

Smith, A. 1776. *An Enquiry into the Nature and Causes of the Wealth of Nations (two volumes)*. London: W. Strahan and T. Cadell

Smith, F.H. 2005. *Caribbean Rum: A Social and Economic History*. Gainesville: University of Florida Press

Smith, J. 1908 [1629]. 'The beginning and proceedings of the new plantation of St Christopher by Captain Warner'. In J. Smith *The true travels, adventures and observations of Captain John Smith in England, Asia, Africke and America, beginning about the year 1593 and continued to this present 1629*. London. Reprinted in W.V. Oliver (1908)

Smith, R., Lakey, D., Oerthing, T., Thompson, B. & Woodward, R.. 1982. *Sevilla la Nueva: A Site Survey and Historical Assessment of Jamaica's First European Town*. Project Report, Institute of Nautical Archaeology, Texas A & M University, College Station

Smith, V.T.C. 1987. *Fort Charles, Nevis*. Northfleet, Kent: Fortress Study Group

Smith, V.T.C. 1989. *Newcastle Tower, Nevis*. Northfleet, Kent: Fortress Study Group

Smith, V.T.C. 1992. *Fire and Brimstone. The Story of Brimstone Hill Fortress, St Kitts, West Indies, 1690-1853*. St Kitts: Creole Publishing Company/Brimstone Hill Fortress National Park Society

Smith, V.T.C. 1994. 'Brimstone Hill Fortress, St Kitts, West Indies. Part one: History'. *Post-Medieval Archaeology* 28, 73-109

Smith, V.T.C. 1995. 'Brimstone Hill Fortress, St Kitts, West Indies. Part two: Description'. *Post-Medieval Archaeology* 29, 77-106

Smith, W. 1745. *A natural history of Nevis, and the rest of the English Leeward Charibbee Islands in America*. Cambridge: W. Thurlbourn

Solow, B. L. 1987. 'Capitalism and Slavery in the Extremely Long Run'. *Journal of Interdisciplinary History* 17, 711-737. Reprinted in B.L. Solow and S.L. Engerman (eds) 1987, pp. 51-78

Solow, B.L. and S.L. Engerman (eds) 1987. *British Capitalism and Caribbean Slavery: The Legacy of Eric Williams*. Cambridge: Cambridge University Press

Stern, M. 1971. 'A Successful Caribbean Restoration: the Nevis Story'. *American Jewish Historical Quarterly* 61 (supp. 1), 18-32

Steward, J.H. (ed.) *Handbook of South American Indians, Volume 4. The Circum-Caribbean Tribes*. Washington, DC: Bureau of American Ethnology (Bulletin 143)

Stewart, T.D. 1939. 'Negro Skeletal Remains from Indian Sites in the West Indies'. *Man* 39, 49-51

Stoler, A.L. 2001. 'Tense and Tender Ties: The politics of comparison in North American History and (Post) Colonial Studies'. *Journal of American History* 88(3). http://www.historycooperative.org/journals/jah/88.3/stoler.html (consulted 15 June 2006)

Stoneman, J. 1906 [1607] 'The Voyage of M. Henry Challons intended for the North Plantation of Virginia, 1606, taken by the way and ill used by the Spaniards. Written by John Stoneman Pilot'. Reprinted in S. Purchas (ed.) *Hakluytus Posthumus, or Purchas his Pilgrimes, Contayning a History of the World in Sea Voyages and Lande Travells by Englishmen and Others*, Volume 19. Glasgow, pp. 284-297

Sturge, J. and T. Harvey 1838. *The West Indies in 1837 – being the journal of a visit to Antigua, Montserrat,*

Dominica, St Lucia, Barbadooes and Jamaica... London, Hamilton Adams and Co.

Sued-Badillo, J. 1986. *The Caribs, a proper perspective. San Juan: Foundation of Archaeology, Anthropology and History of Puerto Rico* (Occasional Papers in English 1)

Sued-Badillo, J. 1992. 'Facing Up to Caribbean History'. *American Antiquity* 57(4), 599-607

Sued-Badillo, J. 2003a. 'The Indigenous Societies at the Time of Conquest'. In J. Sued-Badillo (ed.) *General History of the Caribbean, Volume 1 – Autochthonous Societies*. Paris: UNESCO, pp. 259-291

Sued-Badillo, J. 2003b. 'Introduction'. In J. Sued-Badillo (ed.) *General History of the Caribbean, Volume 1 – Autochthonous Societies*. Paris: UNESCO, pp. 1-7

Symonds, J. 1999. 'Toiling in the Vale of Tears: Everyday life and resistance in South Uist, Outer Hebrides, 1760-1860'. *International Journal of Historical Archaeology* 3(2), 101-122

Tarlow, S. 2003. 'Act Globally, Think Locally: Colonialism and British Historical Archaeology'. Paper presented at Contemporary and Historical Archaeology in Theory (CHAT) 2003 Conference, University of Bristol (21 November 2003)

Tarlow, S. 2007. *The Archaeology of Improvement in Britain, 1750-1850*. Cambridge: Cambridge Univeristy Press

Taylor, D. 1949. 'The Interpretation of Some Evidence of Carib Culture'. *Southwestern Journal of Anthropology* 5: 379-392

Taylor, E.G.R. 1930. *Tudor Geography 1485-1583*. London: Methuen & Company

Taylor, E.G.R. 1934. *Late Tudor and Early Stuart Geography 1583-1650*. London: Methuen & Company

Taylor, S.A.G. 1965 *The Western Design: An Account of Cromwell's Expedition to the Caribbean*. Kingston: Institute of Jamaica and Jamaica Historical Society

Terrell, M.M. 2004. *The Jewish Community of early colonial Nevis: A Historical Archaeological Study*. Gainesville: University Press of Florida

Thomas, D. 1690. *An historical account of the rise and growth of the West India colonies, and of the great advantages they are to England, with respect to trade*. London: Hindmarsh

Thomas, J. 1993. 'The politics of vision and the archaeologies of landscape'. In B. Bender (ed.) *Landscape: Politics and Perspectives*. Oxford: Berg, pp. 1-17

Thomas, N. 1991. *Entangled Objects: Exchange, Material Culture and Colonialism in the Pacific*. Cambridge: Cambridge University Press

Thoms, D.W. 1969. 'The Mills Family: London Sugar Merchants in the Eighteenth Century'. *Business History* 11: 3-10

Tinker, H. 1974. *A New System of Slavery: The Export of Indian Labour Overseas 1830-1920*. Oxford: Oxford University Press for the Institute of Race Relations

Triplett, D. 1995. Town Planning and Architecture on Eighteenth-Century St Eustatius. Unpublished MA Thesis, Department of Anthropology, College of William and Mary

Trouillot, M-R. 1992. 'The Caribbean Region: An open frontier in anthropological theory'. *Annual Review of Anthropology* 21, 19-42.

Trouillot, M-R. 1993. 'Coffee Planters and Coffee Slaves in the Antilles: The Impact of a Secondary Crop'. In I. Berlin and P.D. Morgan (eds) *Cultivation and Culture. Labor and the Shaping of Slave Life in the Americas.* Charlottesville: University Press of Virginia, pp. 124-137

Trouillot, M-R. 1995. *Silencing the Past: Power and the Production of History*. Boston: Beacon Press

Tudway Quilter, D. 1985. *A History of Wells Cathedral School. Volume 2: the Cedars and the Tudways*. Wells: Wells Cathedral School

Turner, G. 1993. 'An Archaeological Record of Plantation Life in the Bahamas'. In G. Lafleur, S. Branson and G. Turner (eds) *Amerindians, Africans and Americans: Three Papers in Caribbean History*. Department of History, University of the West Indies, Mona, Jamaica. pp. 107-125

Turner, W. 1906 [1606] 'Part of a Treatise written by Master William Turner, Sonne to Doctor Turner of London a Phisitian, touching the former voyage'. In Puchas (ed.) Volume 16, pp. 352-257

Tyson, G.F. and C. Tyson 1974. *An Inventory of the historical landmarks of St Kitts-Nevis*. St Thomas US VI: Island Resources Foundation.

Tyson, G.F, T.S. Mistovich and T. Lolley 1993. *Report of Findings and Recommendations, Cultural Resource Assessment. Old Road, St Kitts, West Indies*. Prepared for Organization of American States, Washington. Basseterre: private printing.

Upton, D. 1985. 'White and black landscapes in 18th-century Virginia'. Places, a quarterly journal of environmental design. 2, 59-72. Reprinted in D. Upton and J.M. Vlach (eds) 1988 *Material Life in America 1600-1860*. Boston: Northeastern University Press, pp. 357-369

Van Der Hoeven, F. 1994. *Protected Historical Sites and Buildings on Sint Maarten – First Group*. Department of Public Housing, Physical Planning and Environment, Island Government of Sint Maarten, Phillipsburg.

Vescelius, G. 1977a. 'A Bibliography of Virgin Islands Archaeology'. *Journal of the Virgin Islands Archaeological Society* 4, 1-16.

Vescelius, G. 1977b. 'Historic Archaeology in the Virgin Islands: Some Recent Discoveries'. *Information* 2(3):1-3. Bureau of Libraries, Museums, and Archaeological Services, Charlotte Amalie, V.I.

Ward, J.R. 1998. 'The British West Indies in the Age of Abolition, 1748-1815'. In Marshall (ed.) *The Oxford History of the British Empire. Volume 2: The Eighteenth Century*. Oxford: Oxford University Press, pp. 415-439

Warner, A. 1933. *Sir Thomas Warner, Pioneer of the West Indies: a chronicle of his family*. London: West India Committee

Waterman, T.T. 1949. 'Some early buildings in Barbados'. *Barbados Museum and Historical Society Journal* 13, 140-8

Watkins, H. 1924. *Handbook of the Leeward Islands*. London: West India Committee

Watters, D.R. 1981. 'A Turlington Balsam Phial from Montserrat, West Indies: Genuine of Counterfeit?' *Historical Archaeology* 15, 105-108

Watters, D.R. 1987. 'Excavations at the Harney Site Slave Cemetery, Montserrat, West Indies'. *Annals of the Carnegie Museum* 56(18), 289-318

Watters, D.R. 1994. 'Mortuary Patterns at the Harney Site Slave Cemetery, Montserrat, in Caribbean Perspective'. *Historical Archaeology* 28(3), 56-73.

Watters, D.R. 1997. 'Historical Documentation and Archaeological Investigation of Codrington Castle, Barbuda, West Indies'. *Annals of the Carnegie Museum* 66(3), 229-288

Watters, D.R. 2001. 'Historical Archaeology in the British Caribbean'. In P. Farnsworth (ed.), 82-99

Watters, D.R. and D.V. Nicholson 1982. 'Highland House, Barbuda. An 18th-century retreat'. *Florida Anthropologist* 35(4), 223-242

Watters, D.R. and J. Petersen 1991. 'The Harney site slave cemetery, Montserrat: Archaeological summary'. In E. Ayubi and J. Haviser (eds) *Proceedings of the 13th International Congress for Caribbean Archaeology*, Curaçao, pp. 317-325

Watts, A.P. (ed.) 1927. *Nevis and St Christopher's 1782-1784: unpublished documents*. Paris: Presses universitaires de France

Watts, D. 1963. *Plant introduction and landscape change in Barbados, West Indies, 1627-1830*. Unpublished Ph. D. thesis, McGill University, Montreal

Watts, D. 1966. 'Man's influence upon the vegetation of Barbados, 1627-1800'. *University of Hull Occasional Papers in Geography* 4, 1-96

Watts, D. 1987. *The West Indies: Patterns of Development, Culture and Environmental Change since 1492*. Cambridge: Cambridge University Press

Webb, S.S. 1979. *The Governors-General. The English Army and the Definition of the Empire, 1569-1681*. Chapel Hill: University of North Carolina Press (for the Institute of Early American History and Culture, Williamsburg, Virginia)

Whitehead, N.L. 1988. *Lords of the Tiger Spirit: a history of the Caribs in Colonial Venezuela and Guyana, 1498-1820*. Providence: Foris Publications

Wilkie, L. 1998. 'Evidence for African Continuities in the material culture of the Clifton Plantation'. In J. Winter (ed.) *Proceedings of the 17th International Congress for Caribbean Archaeology*. Nassau, Bahamas, pp. 326-339

Wilkie, L. 1999. 'Evidence of African Continuities in the Material Culture of Clifton Plantation, Bahamas'. In J. Haviser (ed.), pp. 264-275

Wilkie, L. 2000. 'Culture Bought: Evidence of Creolization in the consumer goods of an enslaved Bahamian family'. *Historical Archaeology* 34(3), 10-26

Wilkie, L. 2001. 'Methodist Intentions and African Sensibilities: The Victory of African Consumerism over Planter Paternalism at a Bahamian Plantation'. In P. Farnsworth (ed.), pp. 272-300

Wilkie, L. and P. Farnsworth, 1996. 'Preliminary Results of the 1996 Archaeological Excavations at Clifton Plantation'. *Journal of the Bahamas Historical Society* 18, 50

Wilkie, L. and P. Farnsworth 1996. 'Daily Life on a Loyalist Plantation: Results of the 1996 Excavations at Clifton Plantation'. *Journal of the Bahamas Historical Society* 19, 2-18

Wilkie, L. and P. Farnsworth 1999. 'Trade and the Construction of Bahamian Identity: A Multiscalar Approach'. *International Journal of Historical Archaeology* 3(4), 283-320.

Wilkie, L. and P. Farnsworth 2005. *Sampling Many Pots: An Archaeology of Memory and Tradition at a Bahamian Plantation*. Boca Raton: University Press of Florida.

Wilkinson, H.C. 1933. *The Adventurers of Bermuda. A History of the island from its discovery until the dissolution of the Somers Island Company in 1684*. Oxford: Oxford University Press

Williams, E. 1944. *Capitalism and Slavery*. Chapel Hill: University of North Carolina Press

Williams, E. 1970. *From Columbus to Castro: The History of the Caribbean 1492-1969*. London: Deutsch

Williams, R. 1973. *The City and the Country*. London: Chatto and Windus

Williams, R. 1976. *Keywords: A vocabulary of culture and society*. London: Fontana

Williamson, J.A. 1926. *The Caribbee Islands under the Proprietary Patents*. London: Milford

Williamson, T. 1995. *Polite Landscapes. Gardens and Society in eighteenth-century England*. Stroud: Sutton Publishing

Wilson, S.M. 1989. 'The Prehistoric Settlement Pattern of Nevis, West Indies'. *Journal of Field Archaeology* 16, 427-450

Wilson, S.M. 1993. 'The Cultural Mosaic of the Prehistoric Caribbean'. In W. Bray (ed.) *The Meeting of Two Worlds. Europe and the Americas 1492-650*. Oxford: Oxford University Press (Proceedings of the British Academy 81), pp. 37-66

Wolf, E. 1982. *Europe and the People Without History*. Berkeley: University of California Press

Womack, Peter 1989. *Improvement and Romance: Constructing the Myth of the Highlands*. London: Macmillan

Wray, L. 1848. *The practical sugar planter*. London

Wright, I.A. (ed.) 1929. *Spanish Documents concerning English Voyages to the Caribbean 1527-1568*. London: Hakluyt Society

Wright, N. & A. Wright 1991. 'Hamilton's Sugar Mill, Nevis, Leeward islands, Eastern Caribbean'. *Industrial Archaeology Review* 13, 114-141

Wylie, A. 1995. 'Alternative Histories: epistemic disunity and political integrity'. In P.R. Schmidt and T.C.

Patterson (eds) *Making Alternative Histories: The practice of archaeology and history in non-western settings*. Santa Fe: School of American Research Press, pp. 255-272

Wylie, A. 2002. '"Heavily Decomposing Red Herrings": middle ground in the anti-/postprocessualism wars'. In A. Wylie, *Thinking Through Things: Essays in the Philosophy of Archaeology*. Berkeley: University of California Press, pp. 171-178

Yamin, R. And K.B. Metheny (eds) 1996. *Landscape Archaeology: Reading and Interpreting the American Historical Landscape*. Knoxville: University of Tennessee Press

Yentsch, A. 1994. *A Chesapeake Family and its Slaves: A study in historical archaeology*. Cambridge: Cambridge University Press

Yorke, P. C. 1931. *The Diary of John Baker (1712-1779)... solicitor-general of the Leeward Islands*. London

Young, Sir W. 1793. *A Tour through the Several Islands of Barbados, St Vincent, Antigua, Tobago and Grenada in the years 1791-1792*. Reprinted in B. Edwards 1819, volume 4, 258 ff.

www.ingramcontent.com/pod-product-compliance
Lightning Source LLC
Chambersburg PA
CBHW061000030426
42334CB00033B/3306